D1070935

Systems Analysis in Organizational Behavior

THE IRWIN-DORSEY SERIES IN BEHAVIORAL SCIENCE

EDITOR JOHN F. MEE *Indiana University*

ARGYRIS *Interpersonal Competence and Organizational Effectiveness*

ARGYRIS *Organization and Innovation*

CARZO & YANOUZAS *Formal Organization: A Systems Approach*

CUMMINGS & SCOTT *Readings in Organizational Behavior and Human Performance*

DALTON & LAWRENCE (eds.) *Organizational Change and Development*

DALTON & LAWRENCE (eds.) *Organizational Structure and Design*

GUEST *Organizational Change: The Effect of Successful Leadership*

KELLY *Organizational Behaviour*

KUHN *The Study of Society: A Unified Approach*

LAWRENCE & SEILER, WITH BAILEY, KATZ, ORTH, CLARK, BARNES, & TURNER *Organizational Behavior and Administration: Cases, Concepts, and Research Findings* rev. ed.

LORSCH & LAWRENCE (eds.) *Studies in Organization Design*

LYNTON & PAREEK *Training for Development*

MASLOW *Eupsychian Management: A Journal*

MASSARIK & RATOOSH *Mathematical Explorations in Behavioral Science*

O'CONNELL *Managing Organizational Innovation*

ORTH, BAILEY, & WOLEK *Administering Research and Development: The Behavior of Scientists and Engineers in Organizations*

PORTER & LAWLER *Managerial Attitudes and Performance*

PRICE *Organizational Effectiveness: An Inventory of Propositions*

RUBENSTEIN & HABERSTROH (eds.) *Some Theories of Organization* rev. ed.

SCOTT *The Management of Conflict*

SEILER *Systems Analysis in Organizational Behavior*

WHYTE *Organizational Behavior: Theory and Application*

WHYTE & HAMILTON *Action Research for Management*

Systems Analysis in Organizational Behavior

BY

JOHN A. SEILER, D.B.A.
Associate Professor
Graduate School of Business Administration
Harvard University

WITH SIGNAL CONTRIBUTIONS BY THE FOLLOWING MEMBERS OF THE HARVARD BUSINESS SCHOOL FACULTY:

DOUGLAS R. BUNKER, PH.D.
Assistant Professor

JAY W. LORSCH, D.B.A.
Assistant Professor

RALPH M. HOWER, D.C.S.
Professor

PAUL R. LAWRENCE, D.C.S.
Professor

1967

RICHARD D. IRWIN, Inc. and THE DORSEY PRESS

HOMEWOOD, ILLINOIS

Third Edition

First Printing, January, 1967

Second Printing, September, 1967

Third Printing, February, 1968

Fourth Printing, September, 1968

Fifth Printing, June, 1969

Sixth Printing, February, 1970

Seventh Printing, July, 1970

Case material of the Harvard Graduate School of Business Administration is made possible by the cooperation of business firms who may wish to remain anonymous by having names, quantities and other identifying details disguised while maintaining basic relationships. Cases are prepared as the basis for class discussion rather than to illustrate either effective or ineffective handling of administrative situations.

Library of Congress Catalog No. 66–29978

PRINTED IN THE UNITED STATES OF AMERICA

To Katy

Foreword

THIS IS a book about concepts selected to be useful in practice. As the title indicates, the field of practice is that of administration, especially in business organizations, but with reference to other kinds of formal organizations as well.

Some hold that conceptual study provides answers or solutions for the problems which practitioners encounter. But questions must be asked before they can be answered, and asking meaningful questions is often more difficult than answering them.

I believe that this is especially true for administrators, who live and work among the phenomena of organizations. They are so much in and of the stream of happenings, so close to the events, that it is difficult for them to achieve a perspective on the patterns underlying the events. Without this perspective they may find that time and again they have addressed symptoms rather than causes, or have incorrectly evaluated as *personal* successes or failures events whose outcomes have had deep roots in the intersections of the economic, technological, social and human dimensions of the organizational settings in which they work. The problems they encounter are nonpersonal in the sense that they do not go away when an administrator changes. On the contrary, the sources of the problems remain in the interconnections among those who work in the organization. These are pervasive problems in organizations, to be encountered at the highest and lowest levels of a hierarchy as well as in between.

Ideas can help to clarify these patterns and the problems that result from their interplay. They can help to sort out the happenings to which it is important that an administrator attend. Thus, there is a role for concepts in ordering and giving coherent meaning to the phenomena a practitioner encounters as he goes about his work. Ideas can guide his attention to aspects of events he might otherwise overlook, expanding, enriching and structuring the meanings he assigns to experiences beyond those provided by the limits of his personal life.

A person does not acquire through reading alone the skill of interrelating ideas and practice. This is as true in the field of organizational behavior as in any other field. This is a book, therefore, to be studied, not just read, in connection with the happenings or reports of happenings of life and work in formal organizations. The concepts presented in it were not selected to be admired. Rather they are meant to be used in connection with the stubborn phenomena of human behavior in organizations. They will throw some, but not complete light, on the way these events happen. They provide schemas for investigating, diagnosing and acting on the human-social aspects of problems arising in organizational settings. They provide some answers, but more guidance as to what questions it might be well to ask next to gain the understanding that is necessary for the effective resolution of particular situations.

When they do not provide such understanding, the serious student of phenomena in organizations will do well not to cast these concepts aside quickly. Rather he may still find them useful to throw into relief the aspects of the situation he fails to understand. Then new questions for inquiry may suggest themselves to him. For chance still favors the prepared mind, and he who has conducted his study in this fashion will have prepared his mind to create new and fruitful ideas.

Professor Seiler and his colleagues have chosen with care from among the ideas and concepts that have been broadly fruitful for the practice and study of the human aspects of administration. They do not claim finality or completeness for the selection they have made. I believe the book is a timely step in an important direction, and I am glad to write the foreword for it. The book should serve well the needs of the rapidly increasing number of participants in industrial and university programs for general administration at many levels of experience and in many lands.

GEORGE F. F. LOMBARD
Louis E. Kirstein Professor of Human Relations
Associate Dean for Educational Programs

Introduction

THIS BOOK might be called "a thinking man's guide to human behavior in organizations." It is written for those who want to strengthen the intellectual frameworks they use for making sense of the way people behave in formal institutions of one kind or another. The experience of reading and studying the chapters which follow will be like any other attempt you have made to develop your interpretive skills. Our subject matter is the behavior of human beings involved in organized work, but the process of analysis is the same as if our focus were upon economics, politics or English literature. The goal is to wrest meaning out of symptomatic evidence.

"Organizational Behavior" is the current phrase denoting a subject matter, an area of research, and a slice of life which have been characterized by a number of different titles. The last, "Human Relations," fell into disuse because it became so heavily associated with what was perceived as a "keep 'em happy" attitude. In most cases this perception did an injustice to the work of academic and practicing professionals concerned with the subject. It arose from an understandable haste on the part of administrators of one kind or another to find more effective ways of doing their jobs. Almost any half-formed and yet-to-be-researched idea which came from the "Human Relations School," as it was called, swept like wildfire into some segments of industry and government. Many of these ideas were founded on evidence indicating that there were vast reserves of human resource locked up by some age-old and either fallacious or half-true assumptions about human motivation and the nature of organized work. This evidence was, and still is, provocative. But the excitement which it aroused far outstripped the extremely tentative conclusions which legitimately could be drawn from it, producing some disasters, albeit a few triumphs.

Fortunately, there were those who were determined not to throw the evidence out with the faulty conclusions. They learned a great deal from these disasters and triumphs and from the considerable and increasing amount of new knowledge which has been, and is being, generated about how and why people carry on as they do. This book is a result of that learning.

One thing we learned was that being well-intentioned and working hard to improve the productivity, satisfaction and development of people at work is not enough. Working "smart" is important too. A prescription, no matter how attractive it might sound, is worth no more than luck if it is administered in the absence of an adequate way of thinking about and analyzing specific, live situations. Time and again, managers who are outstandingly successful in one situation perform abysmally in another. Administrators, guided by the good results of, say, sharing responsibility with a group of subordinates, are frustrated by their failure to replicate those results with another group of associates. What is lacking is a way of making the specifics of each situation reveal the clues upon which appropriate management action can be based. It is not enough to deduce from "currently useful generalizations" what will work. An inductive search for the meaning behind existing behavior is a prerequisite. But the inductive process needs a methodology, some kind of structure which is relevant to any type of organizational setting, yet practical and tangible enough to be put into everyday use.

We all have some kind of structure for ordering our experience into manageable form. An interesting way of demonstrating this fact is by asking you to think of two acquaintances who are much alike and a third who is different from each of them. List the qualities which represent their similarities and differences. You will find that the items on your list can be divided into several categories—physical, intellectual, emotional, and so on. These represent your characteristic coding scheme for describing people, or some part of that scheme, at least. If you add to each quality you have listed, other qualities which either go with the first or are opposite from it, (e.g., red hair is often associated with a fiery temper, bright and aggressive are a match, but young and cautious or athletic and studious don't usually mix), you will find yourself describing some theories of personality which you commonly employ to explain behavior. This exercise for revealing your categories and theories about individual personality can usually be complicated by characterizing groups or organizations by the same method you have applied to individuals.

It is precisely this type of categorizing and theory building which we shall be exploring here. The only difference is that the categories and categorical relationships with which this book deals have, on the whole, been somewhat less subjectively developed, being based on empirical research and the subsequent conceptualization and reconceptualization which relatively objective research makes possible. The differences, however, are significant.

Our idiosyncratic analytical methods, categories, and theories stay with us because they are satisfying, at least in the absence of clearly perceived alternatives. Some of their satisfying qualities arise out of the fact that they help us behave effectively. Our only interest in exploring new analytic schemes, if this were all there were to our ways of thinking, would be to increase the probability that our acts would be more effective. Such an exploration, though arduous, would otherwise be rather straightforward. But some of our ways of thinking derive their satisfying qualities from their capacity to bolster our self-esteem or to settle issues which make us uncomfortable. Exploring new concepts which contest with our more familiar and personally satisfying ones will not only be an arduous process but also a discomforting one. Although several sections of the book will deal explicitly with this kind of discomfiture, all an author can do about the problem in any real sense is to extend his sympathy, and plead that the reader try, where he can, to explore the motives behind the way he presently thinks about human behavior in organizational situations.

The human condition not only has implications for our exploration of new ways of thinking about human behavior; it obviously has a telling effect on what we do in relation to that behavior, no matter how valid our analyses might be. While effective action is improbable without adequate understanding, achievement of understanding is no guarantee of effectiveness, either. We know people who are incisive analysts of the human scene but who are no better and perhaps worse than the rest of us in turning in a good interpersonal performance. It would be misleading to imply that study and mastery of the contents of this book will have any appreciable effect on interpersonal skills. There *are* experiences which can increase one's interpersonal skills but studying this book is not one of them. This is true even though the last chapter will comment briefly on some of the attributes of the process which is involved in moving from analysis, through decision making, to action.

The development and forebears of the Harvard Business School course called Human Behavior in Organizations I, for which much of the present volume's content was originally prepared, are ample evidence of the difficulty which is associated with trying to combine intellectual comprehension with what might be called social skill. Shortly after World War II, when the first organizational behavior course to be required of all master's degree candidates was introduced, the course design was strongly slanted toward the social skill focus. Class discussions of cases involving human problems in business were purposefully freed of most instructor-initiated conceptual structure and substantive knowledge. This type of design was conceived as a way of focusing student attention on the relation between case problems and the real-life working relations which naturally emerge in the classroom. As assumptions about the motivation of case characters were being challenged in the discussion, those same assumptions were being displayed among students and between them and the instructor. The goal was to keep intellectual achievements closely linked to experience and, by so doing, to make internalization of intellectual discoveries more likely.[1]

Through a decade of this kind of pedagogical experimentation, in which the pendulum swung back and forth between intellectual and social skill emphases, more became known about organizational behavior and some of its sources. It became more tempting to work on intellectual comprehension of human behavior issues than had seemed practical previously. So, a new curriculum was developed, involving a course broken down into subtopics such as group behavior, individual development, and supervisory relationships. Each section included not only relevant case problems but abstracts of appropriate research findings and descriptions of concepts apropos of each topic.[2] The focus moved substantially away from social to intellectual skill training. Soon, however, course instructors became impatient with the disparity between their students' intellectual command of organizational issues and their capacity to use that command effectively in real life. While the course content grew in intellectual substance and structure, class foci reverted increasingly to attending to the social skills involved in dealing with organizational behavior. In consequence, neither the intellectual nor the social skill aspects of learning were optimized by a compatible relation and emphasis. Either one or the other, but not both, seemed a viable focus at any one point in time.

It became convenient to separate these two foci when, in 1962, the School year was first divided into three roughly equal periods. Three courses were developed. The first was designed as an intellectual skill

---

[1]See J. D. Glover and R. M. Hower, *The Administrator: Cases on Human Relations in Business* (4th ed.; Homewood, Ill.: Richard D. Irwin, Inc., 1963) for the kinds of discussion that were dealt with in classes of this period.

[2]The course design during this era is reflected in the book by Paul R. Lawrence and John A. Seiler, *Organizational Behavior and Administration: Cases, Concepts, and Research Findings* (rev. ed.; Homewood Ill.: Richard D. Irwin, Inc. and The Dorsey Press, 1965).

course in which the contents of this book were studied. Its goal was to help students learn how to analyze organized human behavior and how to use the results of organizational behavior research. Students were encouraged to prepare solutions to the several case problems that they were assigned in conjunction with each of the conceptual readings, which parallel this book's chapters.[3] But no real effort was made to combine the development of intellectual with social skill. As a result, students perceived the role of the course and the subject under study more clearly and, in a shorter time, reached or surpassed previous levels of analytical ability.

In the second course, students were assigned membership in their own task-oriented organization and, with the aid of observation and communication tools, practiced not only an intellectual command of their own organizational behavior but methods for taking action on the basis of that intellectual command. The goal of the course was to help students internalize the intellectual achievement of the first course through the development of their social skills.

The third course then brought students back to study cases of organizational problems, to design solutions for those problems, and to develop implementary plans for those designed solutions, in the context of now internalized intellectual abilities and with the appreciation of the social skills required to bring about the change effectively. Naturally, the second and third courses employed concepts and readings distinctly relevant to their own area of study, but as clearly related to each other and to this book's chapters as possible.

All three of these courses are and will indefinitely continue to undergo development. Three years of experience with them, however, seem to substantiate the conviction that learning to think and learning to act comprise largely a sequential rather than a simultaneous process. The whole job cannot be achieved effectively without consciousness of the other or without nearly immediate reinforcement of analytic training by real-life practice. But, clarifying what the major focus of learning is—first on analytical skill, then on social skill—seem essential.

This book, then, represents the first stage in an ongoing process. It is the "talking *about* ideas" stage, not the "*using* ideas" stage. Although it includes some cases upon which to try out the analytic ideas which it contains, its fruitfulness really depends on self-conscious practice with its concepts and knowledge, in either a real-life or simulated setting.

---

[3]Cases used in this first course were taken primarily from *Organizational Behavior and Administration (op. cit.).*

The practicing businessman has automatic recourse to such settings, while the student must, if his other coursework does not adequately provide it, seek involvement in organizational situations where his new skills may be tempered. As either practitioner or student, however, one way to begin to relate the book's conceptual scheme to life is to write your own case from a situation in which you have been or are involved and, as a first step, to analyze that situation using the model whose description is contained in succeeding chapters.

The book is organized around a central idea, that organizational behavior can most adequately be thought of as occurring in a system of interdependent forces, each of which can be analyzed and set in the perspective of other forces. The basic analytic framework which has evolved from this idea is appropriate for the analysis of behavior occurring in any kind of organizational setting, be it superior-subordinate, staff-line, interdivisional or small work group. After Chapter 1's exploration of the general character of systems and Chapter 2's outline of the categories to be used in the scheme, succeeding chapters examine the specific character of each of four forces which determine behavior, as well as the dynamic nature of behavior, itself. The final chapter reviews important elements of the framework and draws some relationships between analysis and action.

Since the basic idea in the book is how to comprehend forces in dynamic interplay with one another in a never-beginning, never-ending systemic relationship, it is somewhat arbitrary to choose where to begin and where to end. Ideally, one might suppose, the proper way to address the book is to read it through once, quickly, without paying too much attention to details. A second, more painstaking reading would then make possible a sense of the totality which is being presented. However, if this course of action is not convenient, the reader may content himself with the fact that each chapter makes reference to all other chapters as the book progresses. It is advisable, however, to review the first two chapters from time to time, to keep in touch with where one is in the overall scheme.

In the second chapter, which outlines the analytical scheme, a relatively simple case of a business situation has been analyzed in detail, using the specific elements of the scheme. While the case problem being analyzed is somewhat rudimentary, the reader is encouraged to follow it through from beginning to end as a check on his understanding of how the analytical framework can be used most effectively. Five of the succeeding chapters conclude with several simple cases upon which to try out the analytic ideas of Chapter 2 and of the chapter which the cases follow. Once again, it will be worth the reader's time to analyze these cases in detail and, in four of the five chapters, to answer the questions relating to each case. He may check his answers by referring to subsequent information about the case situation.

A great many instructors have participated in the course from which the contents of this book have sprung. Each has contributed to the ideas in the book in untold ways. Several have made signal contributions which I wish to acknowledge more specifically here, as well as at points in the book, itself. The following men have taught the course at one time or another since its inception: Professor Joseph C. Bailey, Associate Professor Louis B. Barnes, Assistant Professor Douglas R. Bunker, Assistant Professor Gene W. Dalton, Assistant Professor Dexter C. Dunphy, Assistant Professor Larry E. Greiner, Professor Ralph M. Hower, Professor Paul R. Lawrence, and Assistant Professor George H. Litwin. George Litwin helped pull together some of Chapter 1's ideas on functional analysis. Douglas Bunker did the work on Chapter 3. Paul Lawrence developed Chapter 6, with the aid of Gene Dalton on an earlier version. Ralph Hower, assisted by Jay Lorsch, prepared Chapter 7. Jay Lorsch also helped prepare an early version of Chapter 5. Jay Lorsch and Larry Greiner worked together on a paper whose ideas are reflected in Chapter 8.

Before the present course came into being, a number of the men referred to above, and others, contributed in significant ways to the development of ideas which now find their way into this book. In the most immediate past, the men in addition to those listed above, are: Associate Professors David Moment and Arthur N. Turner of Harvard; Associate Professor James Clark of U.C.L.A.; and Robert L. Katz, Lecturer, Stanford University. Previously, Professors George F. F. Lombard, John D. Glover, Edmund P. Learned and Fritz J. Roethlisberger of Harvard and James R. Surface of the University of Kansas, and others, set the direction which we now follow. The following, serving as research assistants or associates, helped prepare the cases used throughout the book: Mrs. Sally Hyde Jurgeleit, Mrs. Candace Kennedy Gottschall and Mr. J. B. M. Kassarjian.

Mrs. Bernard R. Redgate, Miss Marylin Mastronardi and Miss Anne Rangell have helped prepare the manuscript for print.

The cases used in this book are individually copyrighted by the President and Fellows of Harvard College, except for the Gordon Foundry Company case which is copyrighted by the University of Alberta. The

Although I am deeply indebted to all those who have in direct and indirect ways contributed to this book, I, of course, take full responsibility for its errors of commission and omission.

Boston, Massachusetts
January, 1967

JOHN A. SEILER

Table of Contents

CHAPTER 1

Systems and the Analysis of Functions

OUR EXPERIENCES indicate that while some actions we take produce the effects we want, others do not. Furthermore, when we are dealing with situations in which human beings play a large part, the proportion of undesirable or surprising effects seems to rise. This unfortunate comparison appears to depend on two conditions: (1) our knowledge of human behavior is more limited than what we now know about the physical world; and, (2) the student of human behavior is, himself, human. These two conditions are related in interesting ways. Particularly important for our purposes in this book is the fact that some of our peculiarly human qualities make it more difficult for us to use what *is* known about human behavior, as relatively limited and tentative as that body of knowledge may be. It is our purpose in this first chapter to examine one of those peculiar human qualities—let's call it a habit of thinking—to see if we can discern what its sources and consequences are and then to explore an alternate way of thinking which, if we can successfully adopt it, may decrease the probability that our actions will produce unexpected consequences.

The Single-Cause Habit

The habit of thinking which seems so important in determining how objectively valid our understanding of human behavior is has to do with common ideas about causation. Stated simply, we humans have a tendency to think that the effects we observe are rather simply caused; in fact, that effects often have single causes. The automobile accident was "caused" by the carelessness of one of the drivers—or by "criminal" automobile engineering—or by dangerous road conditions—or by any *one* of a number of *single* factors which can and are cited in particular instances of automobile collision. We could draw up a virtually infinite list of these "single causes" of automobile accidents, and if we did so, we might be struck by the fact that many, if not all, of the items on our list play some causative role in any *single* accident which we might choose to examine.

Strange, is it not, that when we stop to think about the complexity of causation the idea does not seem particularly bizarre. We would consider it idiotic, for example, to think that an accident could have happened as it did, or could have happened at all, if there were no road, no other cars, no driver, or no engine. In fact, when you put your mind to it, any one of millions of possible alterations in the situation could have caused a nonaccident. Yet, we customarily think about accidents and other events as having single causes. "How did it happen?" we say. "Asleep at the wheel"; "Blew a tire"; "Must have had a heart attack"; "Must have been nuts"; come back the answers. Usually, we are quite satisfied by these simple answers. If we have no particular interest in or responsibility for the event, our satisfaction probably has little negative consequence. If our involvement is less casual, however, our habit of being satisfied with simple causes may be serious, indeed, for we may subsequently take action on an extremely superficial or even erroneous understanding of what has, in fact, taken place.

Habits do not spring from oblivion. They, too, are multiply caused. Let's look at some of the underlying reasons for our assumption of simple causes. First, let's try an analogy. Imagine the world before Copernicus. What would your senses tell you about the relation between sun and earth? Precisely the same thing which, as children, we had to unlearn—that the sun revolves about the earth. Now two important factors operate in this analogous situation. First, our eyes tell us the sun "comes up" and "sets." (Note that we still use the old, pre-Copernican way of talking about this phenomenon.) To be asked to disbelieve our senses is to threaten us, for if we cannot rely on our senses, what can we rely on? How can we hope to cope? Second, to be asked to believe that the earth is not at the center of the universe is similarily threatening, since such a conception seems to relegate man to some subordinate position, subordinate to who-knows-what other worlds and uncontrollable conditions. It is scarcely surprising that Copernicus' revelation was not joyously acclaimed at the time he announced it.

Essentially, the same two factors underly our single-causation habit. First, our senses tell us that when we press on the accelerator, the car speeds forward. When we turn the steering wheel, the car follows suit. When our reflexes are dulled, we have accidents. Second, it is important for us as human beings to consider ourselves at the center of things, controlling conditions, making things happen, not just playing a role, perhaps even a rather subordinate role, in how things come out. So, our immediate perceptions of events and our need to feel potent and in command lead us to our habit of seeing simple cause and effect where, on relaxed reflection, we can easily see multiple causation at work.

One other related element in the situation tends to reinforce this habit, and it works most effectively where human behavior is involved. Life is, after all, extremely complicated. Our difficulty in understanding our own motivation and behavior is constant reminder of that fact. Yet, to avoid a feeling of helplessness, we must be conscious of some sense of understanding. One way to achieve that sense is to assume that explanations are simple and simply found. These are human qualities, these bases for our conception of causation, and, like the rest of our being, are to be understood rather than condemned. But, if we can find another set of assumptions, another habit of thinking which does not destroy our trust in our senses, does not dehumanize us, and does not destroy our confidence in our ability to understand, *and* one which, at the same time, improves the chance that our behavior will have the effect we desire, then we might be willing to complicate our notion of causation. Let's examine this possibility.

Multiple Causation and the Idea of "System"

If the single-cause assumption is inadequate, an obvious substitute is the assumption that events are caused by many forces working in complex relation to each other. If we are interested in establishing the conditions within which the frequency of automobile accidents is reduced, then we would be well advised to comprehend the primary factors associated with such events and the relationships of those factors to one another. If, for example, the 1966 flare-up of congressional attention on safety devices and design-manufacture practices in the automobile industry is to achieve its goal of making automobile fatality statistics less appalling, it must comprehend the relationships among road conditions, social mores, dominant psychological states of drivers, and a host of other factors, in addition to the adequacy of the machine. It would be ironic, indeed, if, as a result of governmental investigation, auto companies significantly improved auto safety features, thereby creating an even greater confidence in the automobile than now exists—an increased confidence which, in turn, reinforced a false sense of security in the automobile, which, when combined with inadequate roads, desires for speed and thrill, and so forth, produced even greater carnage than is now the case.

One assumption containing in its essence the notions of multiple causation and complex interrelation of forces is denoted by the word "system." A system, in the simplest sense of the word, is a "set of objects together with the relationships between the objects and between their attributes."[1] In this basic, abstract sense, everything is related to everything else. All physical objects, for example, are "systemically related" to each other by the fact that they have distance from one another, can be related by their comparative size, and so on. The mathematicians and pure logicians find this all-encompassing relativity useful, but we, as people interested in human organization, need a more limited and, for our purposes, a more operable idea of systems. It is useful for us to think more narrowly of "natural systems," units whose parts depend on each other for the continuance of significant aspects of their present state of being. The distinction being drawn between the notions of a "natural system" and a "set" is a matter of degree, of course. If a physical object is moved, this technically has an effect or effects on all other physical objects in the universe. By some immeasurable degree, moving this particular object shifts the weight relationship among all objects. Without any observable change taking place in other objects, a movement of one still creates a change in the property of other objects insofar at they may be described as being at a certain distance from the moved object. But, these effects simply are not of sufficiently great magnitude in any particular case for our interest to be aroused by such a conception. But natural systems, such as the human body or even a unit so large as the solar systems, are composed of objects and relationships in which changes produce effects of the kind we are interested in understanding and, perhaps, influencing. The interdependence between the parts of a natural system, for example, the sensitive relationship between the condition of the heart and the state of the lungs, is the primary characteristic we wish to focus on first in becoming intimately familiar with the system idea. "The interdependence of the variables in

[1]A. D. Hall and R. E. Fagen, "Definition of System," *General Systems,* Vol. I (1956), pp. 18–28.

a system is one of the widest inductions from experience that we possess; or we may alternatively regard it as the definition of a system."[2]

So, our first observation on the way toward building a conception of the world adequate for understanding and dealing with human behavior is that *everything* is related to *everything else* in such a way that a change in any one thing produces a change in everything else. Our next step, however, arises from the realization that such an observation is rather overwhelming. All one can do in the face of an ultimate relativity is to marvel at it and go on to something more limited and more manageable. But we do not want to go to the other extreme, following the human tendency to think in terms of simple or single causal relationships. Rather, we can turn to the notion of natural systems, subunits of the total relativity we observe, subunits described by the fact that the relationships among the parts of those subunits are rather intimate. By this we mean that a change in one of those parts has an effect on the other parts of the subunit which is of vastly greater magnitude in terms of intensity and pervasiveness than the effects of a change in the same part of the subunit on things outside the subunit.

Let's take some examples of what we mean from the realm of natural systems occurring in organizations. Consider what happens when you eat something at lunch which is difficult for your stomach to digest. Glands become more active, blood circulates more rapidly and converges on the troubled area, muscles contract in an effort to reject the disagreeable food, and so on. There is a general mobilization of the organs in your body to deal with the change which has taken place in your stomach. All of this activity has occurred as yet with no observable impact on elements outside of you. In fact, we can think of your stomach as having no direct effect upon things outside of your body. That is not to say, however, that the changed state of your physiological system does not, in turn, have effects on your nervous system, which effects, combined with a leaden feeling in the pit of your stomach, have subsequent effects on your psychological disposition toward the outside world. It is likely, in fact, that when you return from lunch to a meeting with members of your work group, that you assume the role of a changed element in the system of relationships among the men and women with whom you work most closely. These working relationships define the next larger level of system, a social system in this case, in a

[2]L. J. Henderson, *Pareto's General Sociology* (Cambridge, Mass.: Harvard University Press, 1935), p. 86.

hierarchy of ever larger systems whose boundaries encompass the smaller systems of which they are composed. Your short temper arising out of physical discomfort may unbalance social relationships achieved before lunch in such a way that old points are rehashed and no new progress is achieved. Your colleagues mobilize to deal with your irascibility, some trying to placate you, perhaps, while others take the opportunity they find in your apparent irrationality to punish you and thus play out with you some long-standing emotional conflict.

One result of your group's postlunch problems is that the deadline for your group's report to the next level of management is missed. However, your state of mind cannot be related directly to the effects of the missed deadline in the next higher organizational system—let's say, in the division of which your boss is general manager. Rather your state of mind (and body) helped create a new condition or exacerbated an old set of circumstances in your work-group system. It was the mobilization of that whole work-group system which had effects on other parts of the larger system of which your group is one element.

We could go on with this detailing of subsystem effects on larger systems indefinitely, much as in the timeworn adage, "For want of a nail the shoe was lost; for want of a shoe the horse was lost; for want of a horse the general was lost; for want of the general the battle was lost; for want of the battle the war was lost"; and so on, *ad nauseam.* As in this old saw, we can move to ever smaller subsystems and to ever larger systems. At every level, however, there is a system boundary within which interdependent forces are at play in intimate interrelationship, producing a total effect on the whole system. That combined effect then becomes a change in the relationships between the system and other such systems which are bounded by the intimacy of their higher level interdependence. Using our example of the unhappy lunch, it might look somewhat as shown in Exhibit 1.

Now, how can we use these rudimentary ideas to help us understand human behavior in organizations? The answer to this question is in two parts. Since we seek a way of thinking about human behavior which permits us to account for multiple causes without being overwhelmed by infinite complexity, the idea of a hierarchy of subsystems first permits us to look at the relatively limited number of events taking place within a particular system and between the relatively limited parts of that system. We can understand what is happening between the members of a work group, for example, before we go on to try to comprehend what is happening at the division level of complexity. We can understand what is going on within a person before we go on to try to fathom what is going on between him and others in his social system. When we focus on the individual as a system to be understood, we do not have to focus on the internal states of all the other individuals with whom he has important relations. All we have to know about those other individuals is how they affect him or, to put it another way, set limits within which the person we want to understand is operating. We take the *results* of their internal systems' complexities into account as they impinge on him. In other words, we deal with one set of complexity at a time.

Exhibit 1

COMPANY DIVISION SYSTEM

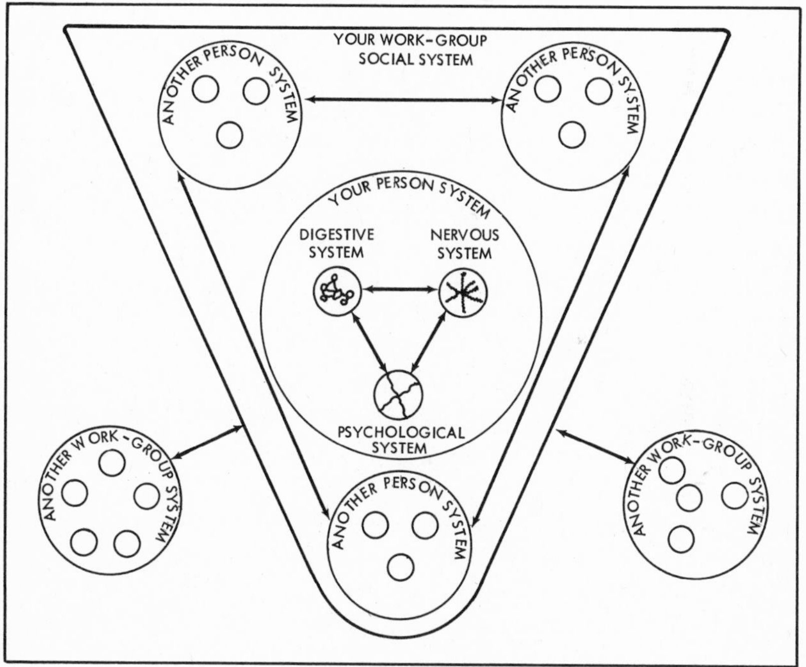

Second, in order to act effectively in response to what is going on, we do not have to know all that *can* be known about every potentially relevant system, all about everything which has a conceivably important effect on what we are interested in. If such were not the case, we would never get through analyzing the first problem we encountered, since everything is related to everything else in an infinitely complex chain of interdependence. Instead, we establish who we are, what our role is, what our competence is, and what our goals are. Then we choose to analyze the internal workings of those systems whose internal condition is something we can and want to do something about. Other systems whose internal condition is beyond our competence or role or desire to influence are taken into account only insofar as their effects impinge on the internal workings of systems we *are* trying to influence.

For example, think of the difference between the role and competences of a psychiatrist on the one hand and a production manager on the other, both concerned with a single event: A worker in the production department is unable to continue his work, complaining of headaches which he attributes to mistreatment by his fellow workers. Which systems are relevant to the roles and competences of the psychiatrist and of the manager? Ideally, at least, the production manager is responsible for the social system of workers who work in his department. When a cue such as a disturbed worker comes to his attention, he wonders whether something is going wrong in the social system's internal workings which could have effects even more far-reaching than that evidenced by the case of a headache. He sets about to gather facts about the relationships among his workers, perhaps delving into physical conditions in the factory, supervisory practices, incentive systems, the backgrounds and expectations of relevant workers, and so on. He does not focus on the internal workings of the psychological system of the disturbed worker except as that condition is an effect of (and an element in) the internal workings of his production workers' social system.

On the other hand, the psychiatrist who may be sought out by the disturbed worker takes the internal workings of the psychological system of the worker as his focal point of analysis, making himself aware of the effects of the social system from which the worker has come only as those effects impinge on the internal workings of his patient's system. The psychiatrist is bent on helping his patient to understand his own internal state so that the patient may better deal with social systems in which he is implicated. The production manager is bent on helping his production system so to constitute itself that it can productively use the resources available to it. The manager seeks actions—be they in personnel selection, reward systems, work procedures, and so on—which will optimize the use of the production system's resources. The psychiatrist seeks actions—be they in self-clarification of past experiences on the part of the worker, in clearer self-recognition of the worker's identity as a person, in more realistic self-appraisal of skills, and so on—which will optimize the worker's use of his internal system's resources. Ideally, the manager and the psychiatrist do not confuse their separate roles and competences, although they may seek each other's counsel in order to understand better how the internal systems appropriate to each of their roles affect, and are affected by, the focal system of the other's role.

The hierachy-of-systems idea, then, allows us to concentrate on understanding one internal system at a time without becoming immobilized by infinite complexity; it allows us to treat some systems as external environment, some as the producers of internal effects and some in the full complexity necessitated by the nature of our goals, responsibilities, and skills. The idea of system, in a sense, frees us from the compulsion to oversimplify by making the complexity that is characteristic of human behavior in organizations conceptually manageable. It also urges us, by insisting that we define the focus of our study before we begin analysis, to clarify our role and to admit to the limits and strengths of our abilities to act.

Equilibrium—A Property of Systems

But we know something about the characteristics of systems other than that their parts are interdependently related and that each system is composed of subsystems and, together with other related systems, is a subsystem of a larger system. Another characteristic of systems is that the relations between their parts tend toward a steady state—toward a balance of forces which is stable and enduring. In its simplest form this tendency toward stability or equilibrium is a conservative striving for the status quo. The sleeping human body is a good example of this most primitive form of equilibrium. How often does one experience, and later regret translating an alarm clock's ring into a benign signal requiring no bodily change—perhaps by dreaming of answering the telephone and permitting sleep to resume undisturbed? Similarly familiar is the cold night's experience of dreaming of rising to fetch another blanket, until, finally, the cold becomes unbearable and we awake. This tendency toward nonchange, toward continuing the sometimes hard-won balance among internal systems is by no means the only or even the dominant striving among human beings—there are equally strong drives for change and growth, as well. But we can see in the human organism an unusually fine self-regulatory system operating to keep various facets of the body in balance, increasing the flow of adrenalin, quickening the pulsations of the heart, speeding breathing in response to some external or internal stimulus. So fine is the body's achievement of equilibrium under normal conditions that a special term, *homeostasis,* is applied to the body's steady state, implying not just a statistical probability of equilibrium but rather a regulatory mechanism whose function it is, in fact, to maintain internal balance.

Maintenance of the status quo in organizational systems is less frequent than in the case of biological systems, but it can be observed. A few primitive societies such as that of the Eskimo or the African Bushman can be conceived as maintaining an unchanging balance among internal social forces. This is possible because of the remarkable stability of their environments, albeit at a very low level of abundance. In a few cases, industrialized societies still evidence organizations hewing to a status quo of some generations' duration, particularly where extended family systems are coincident with corporate systems. These examples are increasing rarities, because few environments are now so static as to permit an effective maintenance of former internal conditions.

The type of equilibrium that we are more likely to find might be called a dynamic or moving equilibrium, like that of the developing human body. Just as human organs mature, mental processes sharpen, and glands become more or less active, causing constant changes among the relations of the body parts, so the organization incorporates new equipment, develops new special competences, expands physically, and adds new products, throwing old relations into imbalance, out of which new relations, at least equal in viability to the old, must be discovered. The adolescent is a good example of this type of striving for stability in the midst of growth. Some of his members grow faster than others, he has to pick up his feet or fall over them, his hands seem all thumbs. Slowly and seemingly at command, compensatory faculties develop apace so that muscles respond more quickly to long legs and ham hands.

But the human body ceases to be a satisfying analogue to social and organizational systems at this point because, while death is certain for the human body, infinite growth seems to be possible for social organization. It is as though organizations go through continual phases of stability and balance, then awkward adolescent changes, then new levels of stable equilibrium. During periods of change, two tendencies are at war—one striving to keep the stability already won—the other striving toward a renewed and strengthened relation between the organization and its environment, presumably toward a longer-term and broader stability in the future than past internal balance would have allowed.

When an equilibrium moves in pace with (perhaps somewhat ahead of or slightly behind) the organization's environment, the strength of the organization, if not its short-run internal peace, seems assured. When a company bolsters its research staff, throwing greater power toward the technologists and less toward others, how can balance be restored? Perhaps it is only possible through a reselection of men in other departments. Perhaps it comes through mutual reexamination of complementarities. Perhaps it comes from building research laboratories far from the main body of the company. If increased research is responsive to market changes, then some new balance will tend to be found among internal units. The only stable element in a moving equilibrium, then, is the tendency toward balance, each successive balance being that between subunits which have quite different characteristics from what they had before. To borrow from the human body once more, when a man loses his eyesight, he begins to develop remarkable senses of hearing, smell, and touch. If one imagines that the body requires a certain level of sensory stimuli to help guide it in relation to its environment and if all five senses are available, then no one sense need be at a sharp pitch. If one sense is lost, then compensatory strengths tend to develop, striking a new balance among the remaining organs to offset the fact that one has been removed. (Of course, there are cases where homeostatic tendencies thwart medical attempts to help the body survive, as when the body rejects a foreign kidney, even though its own kidneys no longer function. Humans and organizations both can seek equilibrium to the detriment of their survival.)

So, while equilibrium is constantly tended toward, disequilibrium may also occur. Despite strivings to the contrary or, as in the case of the kidney transplant, where two tendencies are, or appear to be, mutually destructive, parts of the organism or organization can work at cross-purposes in the direction of partition. Sometimes partition is a kind of resumption of balance, as when partners divide the business and go their separate ways, or, as when a neurosis, the condition of so-called split personality, permits withdrawal of the individual from internally disequilibrating forces coming at him from his environment. But disequilibrium can, in the case of a completely unexpected or uncontrollable catastrophe, bring a system to complete destruction—to suicide or complete withdrawal—to the dying out of companies unable to emerge from dying industries. This is particularly likely when organizations or individuals have enjoyed a considerable period of internal stability previous to sudden change.

Feedback—The Mechanism Underlying Dynamic Equilibrium

One way to conceive of a system is to think of it as an entity into which elements are introduced, transferred, and emitted. The idea of a system as an input-output mechanism is relatively simple when it is exemplified by a production system into which raw materials are transmitted, are combined and shaped into salable products, which are then shipped out and sold. The input-output idea becomes somewhat more complex when one conceives of technological ideas, for example, as being introduced into the system, modified for the system's purposes, and finding their way into the environment in the form of products, sales ideas, and so forth.

The input-output idea is further complicated by the consideration that what comes out of the system influences what subsequently goes in. If products sell, this confirms management's ideas about the wisdom of making more of what has been sold, and management modifies its raw materials orders to maximize salable output. If a technological idea improves productivity, management tends to reward the technologists in the system. The operation of this information loop which alerts the system to the effects of its behavior and permits modification of system behavior is called feedback.

Some of the simplest examples of feedback mechanisms are electromechanical in nature. Servomechanisms such as automatic pilots and inertial guidance systems are examples of feedback control mechanisms. They measure deviation from preset goals and correct for that amount of deviation. Human beings are organic feedback systems. Threading a needle—trial, error, correction, retrial—is a good example of the human feedback process. So is driving a car or almost any athletic activity. Social systems provide good examples, as well. Work groups often test their superiors to see what behavior will be tolerated. Newcomers and the groups they join get their bearings on each other by trying out small amounts of behavior—telling a joke or turning out a certain amount of production—to see what effects will be produced.

The feedback process is the means by which equilibrium is achieved. The work group tests management to see what level of productivity is expected. Management's response through various rewards and punishments helps the group create a viable balance between its demands and those of management. The sales group tests its customers—and the production department—to see what the optimum order lead time is, finding a viable balance between two of its most important related systems. As a type of behavior is confirmed in the creation of a viable balance of relationships, that behavior is reinforced, and less and less testing is necessary. Consequently, when someone or something attempts to change the balance of relations—if customers begin to put more pressure on salesmen—production managers tend to discount salesmen's complaints. If patterns are undisturbed for years, then systems find it extremely difficult to adapt to change, because they have cut themselves off from a feedback which has had so few new messages in it for so long that no one pays much attention to it anymore. Furthermore, old internal relationships often are so satisfying to the members of a social system that they psychologically ignore or translate into more acceptable terms the available feedback information.

So, the natural systems which the business manager is trying to understand and influence can be expected to tend toward a stable balance of internal relationships. Since these systems are, themselves, parts of larger systems which also tend toward internal stability, and since change is characteristic of our industrial society, the tendency toward internal stability is constantly in conflict with forces of change from the environment. The manager can alert himself to the manifestations of dynamic equilibrium by looking at the way in which feedback from current behavior does or does not influence future behavior.

"What Is and What Could Be"—Optimal Equilibrium

The tendency of organizations to seek equilibrium, no matter how dynamic and frequently changing the levels of stability may be, seems to paint a picture of inexorably conservative forces at work. It is a matter of common observation, in fact, that organizational systems do have strong conservative tendencies. The appearance and the fact of conservatism in system operation contain some potentially fortunate and some potentially unfortunate connotations for those who aspire to responsibility for management of those systems.

Political observers are quick to compare the two-party system in the United States with multiparty or single-party systems in other countries. They point out that in the strong, unified representation of political viewpoints from both ends of a conservative-liberal spectrum comes a remarkably stable political development. Where a single party rules, the swings in direction are so extreme that the achievements of opponents tend to cancel each other out and even regression is likely. Where a multiparty system is in operation, although the swings in direction are not so great, the canceling-out process still operates, the only difference being that cancellation takes place before action occurs rather than after. A balanced conservatism, then, seems to promote gradual development without either violent regression or precipitate change. Equilibrating tendencies, therefore, can be conceived as promoting stable growth.

Another favorable side to the tendency toward stability is more personally relevant to the individual charged with responsibility. Imagine an organization which was not, by some fluke, subject to the rule of equilibrium. How could anyone trust himself enough to take that action which, in the absence of subsequent testing by system forces, could be counted on not to be totally destructive? Were the manager to be so alone in his potency, and realize how potent he was, he might well become immobilized. Instead, he can relax somewhat in the realization that no matter how wrong he might be, there are forces which will help the organization to survive his blunders. The same conservatism is as true of individuals as it is of organizations, of course. Despite the varying influences which play upon each one of us, we generally maintain a remarkably steady progress in a particular direction. While I may not turn out to be very effective in trying to influence another person if I don't understand what is going on inside his system (or inside me), at least I rarely have to become obsessed by the fear that my behavior could be devastating.

On the unfortunate side of the equilibrium ledger is the chance that once the potency of equilibrium forces are fully comprehended, we may come to feel powerless. Even after we have overcome the diagnostic problems which this book addresses, and feel confident of our basic understanding of the forces which are producing human behavior in an organization, we could become frozen by the apparent strength of conservative tendencies to constrain behavior in past patterns.

Perhaps there is some help for us in contrasting two ways of thinking about action. One, the more traditional, is that we act on problems and make them go away. When productivity is declining we tell our subordinates to increase productivity, or we go out on the work floor and speak to the workers about their obligation to the company, or we institute a pay raise, or we redesign the product to make it simpler to produce. These "actions on problems" may have some effect, but the chances are that we will be disappointed by the fact that so great an effort has produced so little result, perhaps an unexpected result, at that. We tend to come to problems with an expectation that change springs from our personal intervention. This expectation is bound by its oversimplicity to be frustrated.

Another way of thinking about taking action concerning a drop in productivity is to try to put our organization "in the way of" conditions which favor greater production. We analyze those elements of the system which are obstacles to natural tendencies on the part of our individual and social organizations to produce, and then we try to remove those obstacles. We are not turning unproductive systems into productive ones—we are removing obstacles to a more optimal equilibrium.

There is no more basic reason for presenting the ideas in this book than that those ideas be useful for the achievement of more fruitful equilibriums in organizations. The tendency toward equilibrium is a fact. The tendency toward optimal balance is not. The administrator's challenge is to find ways, through his understanding and imagination, to uncork more effective balances between systems. It is not humanistic values but a considerable body of clinical observation and methodical research which leads us to the conclusion that the work group hostile to management is not experiencing the *only* viable balance between itself and other systems. While conflict between systems is inevitable by the definitional differences between systems, there is no evidence to support the idea that that conflict is inevitably nonproductive.

Normative Judgment and the Process of Analysis

Our goal is to make sound decisions and take effective action in regard to organizational behavior issues. But, it is necessary to make a distinction between the requisites for analysis and the requisites for taking action. We discussed earlier the necessity of establishing one's role, goals, and competence in order to choose one's focus of analysis—to determine which systems one would choose to analyze in depth and which systems to take into account only because they have effects on the focal system. In so establishing one's point of view, we run the risk of then carrying on our analysis of the focal system or systems without realizing that our point of view is distorting our perceptions and limiting our ability to render a valid diagnosis, i.e., a diagnosis upon which effective action may be based. If we succumb to letting our goals and our values color what we are observing, the chances are that our diagnosis will stop short at the level of "good" and "bad" types of evaluation instead of at the level of understanding how interdependent forces relate to each other. The chances are, too, that this hasty evaluation will lead to precipitate action, since what is "good," by definition, is to be supported, and what is "bad" has to be stamped out.

We fall prey to allowing our role to determine what we see in the world because we fail to state, even to ourselves, what the frame of reference is from which the pronouncement of good or bad is made. If we could analyze the point of view of the evaluator—and keep constantly in mind the effect that that point of view has on our analysis—then we could save ourselves from shallow diagnosis and purely symptomatic action.

Let's examine a few ways in which these unhappy results occur. Say we observe some politicians committing larceny. Particularly if our own taxes are involved, we are likely to become angry, to condemn the thieves, and to join in setting up a hue and cry for their punishment. Without regard to the immediate effectiveness of our action, what may we learn from it? We can learn that we get seriously upset when someone takes something not legally theirs, particularly when we have a personal interest in what has been taken. But what have we learned about the complex conditions which led to these crimes and to the probability that these crimes are not unique in our community? Are we in a better position, knowing what we now know, to bring about conditions which will prevent a recurrence of such crimes? The most likely outcomes are that the thieves will be punished or that investigations will drag out until everyone has forgotten the incident and that we can shortly expect to hear of more evidence about malfeasance in public office. The quick assumption of a normative position prohibited analysis of significant causes.

Take a somewhat simpler example. It is difficult these days to avoid reading reports of the destructive effects of insecticides. The story usually goes that a group of property owners complains of insect infestation. Insecticide spray is applied to nearby swamp areas. Soon thereafter bird watchers and soil conservationists complain that contamination of food sources and destruction of fish and bird eggs have cost swamp areas their wildlife and that subsequent plant and algae formations have destroyed much of the swamp's utility as a water storage area. The original evaluation of insects as "bad" led to an experiment (though it was called a solution) whose results were not only mixed in effect but entirely foreseeable. All the necessary knowledge for prediction of the actual outcome was available. The interdependent factors which prohibited the use of that knowledge were: the intrusion of a personally involved point of view in the process of collecting and analyzing the facts, simple cause-effect thinking, and a disposition to act on symptomatic evidence.

The problem of hasty evaluation is not an easy one to deal with. If our diagnoses are not to remain idle theorizing, then some value orientation is required from which action takes its direction. If a firm is to grow, someone must take a position about the direction in which he, personally, wants it to grow. Personal involvement, then, is essential.

However, the diagnosis of the firm and its environment, which is essential to narrowing the choices within which the personal choice is made, must be unbound by a "good-bad" evaluation. Thus, both objectivity and subjectivity are required of the administrator.

It may help simply to realize that one's role requires different mental and psychological moods at different points in time. At one time, one must be open to all the facts, as free as possible of one's own disposition to "like" some things, not others, and as aware as possible of the inevitability that one will like some things and not others, no matter how hard one tries to be objective. At another time, one must gird oneself and choose that direction among all those possible, the one with which one feels he can most profitably live, then embark on it.

Another way to put it is to ask when those observing an administrative situation should agree with each other and when they should not. The answer must be something as follows: They must seek agreement on what is happening and why it is happening. Within the practical limits of their ability to interpret and of the knowledge which is available to them, there is, ideally, only one right diagnosis of what is going on. But it is statistically unlikely, if not impossible, to find any two men who are so much alike in background and personality that they would choose to, or could, act identically in any particular situation. So they should not necessarily expect to agree upon their choices of action. Their only commitment regarding action should be that they agree on what the nature of the consequences of their actions will be upon the world around them.

We find, then, that despite the help we may get from thinking systemically about organizational behavior, we still have to deal with the fact that we who are trying to understand other humans in action are, ourselves, human, with a lot of feelings about what we observe. We cannot escape this humanness, even if we wanted to. All we can do is try to be aware of it, take its likelihood into account as we review what we think we understand about events around us, be somewhat suspicious of ourselves, and try being as systematic as we can in the process of carrying on our diagnoses.

Systems Analysis as an Analysis of Functions[3]

There is one idea which has remained implicit in our discussion of the properties of systems so far. Making it explicit and examining it

---

[3]This section of Chapter 1 was influenced by ideas expressed in a paper by Raymond A. Bauer, titled, "Problem Solving Behavior in Organizations: A Functional Point of View," which appeared in M. M. Hargrove, I. H. Harrison, and E. L. Swearingen (eds.), *Business*

(Continued on next page)

carefully, before we go on in the next chapter to the detailed methodology of analyzing systems in organizations, should help us in our goal of being systematic. That idea is the concept of "function." Very simply, one variable is a function of another if its magnitude varies with the magnitude of the other. It is quickly apparent that, by definition, systems are composed of units whose properties are in functional relationship to each other. So, the "functional point of view" and "functional analysis" are intrinsic to the idea of systems. But let's see what is not so immediately apparent about the concept of function.

We take for granted that some things can only be described in terms of the functions they perform. How could we effectively describe a spark plug without describing the part it plays in the operation of an internal combustion engine? This point of view which is so natural in the case of spark plug behavior is not so common a point of view in the case of individual and organizational behavior. For example, we are not so likely to ask what functions the thieving behavior of the aforementioned politicians played in the various systems in which the politicians were engaged. At least, we tend to restrict ourselves to a limited number of systems (probably having to do primarily with the personal fortunes of the politicians) out of all of those in which the thievery had some effect. Quite likely, for example, the larceny was functional for the maintenance of a patronage system which was functional, in turn, for the strengthening of a political party which, in turn, was functional for the powerful representation of minority groups, and so on and on. Equally likely, the larceny, or the pattern of behavior which it exemplified, was dysfunctional[4] for the maintenance of confidence in government among people in majority group social systems, was dysfunctional for the viability of financial systems, and so forth, both of these dysfunctions producing reactions functional for arousing support among the members of the opposing political party, and on and on. While it would be unusual for us to evaluate a spark plug as good or bad except in reference to its function for the system in which it operates, we tend not to be so thorough in spelling out the functions of more complex behavior which is implicated in many systems.

First of all, then, we note that behavior is functional or dysfunctional

---

Policy Cases: With Behavioral Science Implications (Homewood, Ill.: Richard D. Irwin, Inc., 1963). Assistant Professor George Litwin was instrumental in bringing focus to bear on these ideas.

[4]The "dys" prefix is a convention denoting "impairment," one which has been borrowed from medical language and has become customary in conjunction with "function," in preference to the looser "dis."

for some behavior in the system or systems in which the behaviors take place. There is no such thing as behavior being "functional," period. It must be functional *for* something else. Guard against the temptation to say that some behavior is "functional" without stating for what. To use the word functional without specifying "functional for what," is just another way of saying "good," and there is no benefit in replacing a short word with a long one when it contributes no additional meaning.

Second, human and organizational behavior, unlike that of the spark plug, is inevitably engaged in a number of different systems. Managers deal with personality systems (many of them), social systems (many of which overlap), and formal systems of various sizes and interrelationship, such as departments, divisions, subsidiaries, and the firm. Any particular behavior is likely to have functions and/or dysfunctions for other behavior in any or all of these systems, and we need to be scrupulous in detailing the functions and dysfunctions for all the systems so implicated.

Third, a statement describing a behavior's function for some explicitly stated system does not necessarily imply an evaluation of the performance of the system given this particular behavior. All we can say, for example, when we examine the role of a permissive supervisor is that his permissive behavior has certain functions for the work-group systems involved and for other groups with whom the supervisor has contact. His behavior likely has dysfunctions for some or all of those systems, too. So, while "functional for" does imply a supportive relationship—a consistency between the behavior we are trying to understand and the direction in which the effected system is going—it does not specify the significance of that support, nor, by itself, does it describe the possible dysfunctions which the behavior may have for the same system.

Fourth, there is a tendency to confuse a function with a consequence or a visible change. The visibility of effects has no necessary relation to the significance of the functionality. An informal lunching pattern among executives, for example, may produce no visible change in behavior, while a staff Christmas party may produce all manner of visible changes. It would be unfortunate, however, to assume that the party was more functional for, say, worker cohesion, than the pattern of lunches. In fact, the lunch pattern may be an important element in facilitating intergroup relations which, in turn, supports staff cohesion, while the effects of the party may quickly disappear. The fact is that such behavior may simply be functional for the *maintenance* of systems in their present state and, as such, its effects are difficult to measure and compare. We need to understand the conditions under which there are differences in the functions which two behaviors have for a system and explore the qualities which lead us to observe visible consequences in one case and not in another.

There are two classic pitfalls into which users of functional analysis have fallen. One is to assume that because a given piece of behavior has a function for the behavior of a system, that that function was intended. Behavior has both intended *and* unintended consequences. Seldom do we find a work group taking a coffee break for the purpose of communicating technical information across formal organization boundary lines, but so doing may have this consequence, in fact. If management is aware of the multifunctionality of this coffee-break practice, it may be reluctant to oppose it on other grounds. So, we need to be sensitive to the unintended as well as intended consequences of the behavior we are observing.

The second fallacy Bauer[5] calls the "Pangloss fallacy" from Dr. Pangloss of Voltaire's *Candide.* Dr. Pangloss was disposed to find some functionality in the most disastrous of events, "pontificating that after all, 'everything is for the best in this best of all possible worlds.' " We need to guard against the tendency to think that because a particular pattern of behavior is functional for the maintenance or development of some system that that is sufficient justification of the pattern. If a work group is restricting productivity, a behavior pattern functional, perhaps, for the group's sense of dignity and for its internal cohesion, that does not necessarily lead us to the conclusion that productivity restriction is either desirable or immutable. There is no reason why we should not seek to find conditions under which the group can maintain its dignity and internal integrity through other behaviors than minimizing output. Identifying a relationship between variables is vastly different from evaluating that relationship as optimal, as we have already noted.

The ideas behind functional analysis fall into that class of concept which, while deceptively simple at the outset, has tremendous power and universal application when internalized into one's customary way of approaching problems. Some glimmer of the potency of these ideas may be generated if you think about some formal or informal responsibility you may now or in the past have had for some kind of organized

[5]*Op. cit.*

behavior. How differently might you have acted had you naturally come to that situation trying to discover the multifunctionality of any particular piece of behavior you can remember for the various people in that situation? None of us can claim to be fully aware of the various functions of any piece of behavior, but if we have a sense that there are many functions and dysfunctions to any behavior we observe, we start from a position of curiosity which produces a greater chance for effective action than do simpler assumptions. The rest of this book's exposition will depend heavily upon the reader's continual exploration of the use of the ideas underlying the functional point of view.

Summary

Two customs of thought have been contrasted—the habit of thinking in single-cause terms and the habit of conceiving of behavior as multiply caused. The idea that interdependent forces underlie behavior has been used to define the word "system." Thinking systemically frees us from oversimplification by making understanding of complexity manageable. Equilibrium, or the tendency toward a balance of forces, is one property of systems. Equilibrium is more often dynamic than static, representing a constant seeking of balance rather than a status quo. Each system's internal balance is in conflict with pressures from other systems to adapt to the effects of their striving for internal balance. The feedback process or flow of information back to the system about its performance is the process by which equilibrium is approximated. Equilibrium is not necessarily, or likely to be, optimal. We can help free the system from constraints to its finding a more productive balance of relationships. In the process, we need to be aware of our tendency to bias our understanding by our normative positions. But our normative positions must come into play at the point of decision and action. An effective way to avoid premature position taking is to think of behavior as multifunctionally related to a number of systems. The idea of "functional for" is inherent in the concept of system, but the effective use of functional analysis requires a rigorous understanding of the implications of functional relationships.

These ideas are basic to the diagnostic framework which will be presented in the next and following chapters. It is highly recommended that the reader satisfy himself that the ideas are clear and that their applications are evident before he goes on to Chapter 2. It is further recommended that Chapter 1 be thought of as a basic orientation for the entire book. Should the reader feel lost at any time as he studies further chapters, he may well rediscover his way through reviewing what he has just read.

Some Basic References on System Theory

ASHBY, W. R. "General Systems Theory as a New Discipline," *General Systems,* Vol. III (1958), pp. 1–6.

BAUER, R. A. "Problem Solving Behavior in Organizations: A Functional Point of View," in HARGROVE, M. M.; HARRISON, I. H.; and SWEARINGEN, E. L. (eds.), *Business Policy Cases: With Behavioral Sicence Implications,* Homewood, Ill.: Richard D. Irwin, Inc., 1963.

BERTALANFFY, L. VON. "General System Theory," *General Systems,* Vol. I (1956), pp. 1–10. (Also see articles by this author in various issues of *Biology* and *Science.*)

BOULDING, K. "General System Theory–The Skeleton of Science," *Management Science,* Vol. II (1956), pp. 1–10.

HAGEN, E. E. *On The Theory of Social Change.* Homewood, Ill.: Dorsey Press, 1962.

HALL, A. D., and FAGEN, R. E. "Definition of System," *General Systems,* Vol. I (1956), pp. 18–28.

HENDERSON, L. J. *Pareto's General Sociology.* Cambridge, Mass.: Harvard University Press, 1935.

LEIGHTON, A. H. *Human Relations in a Changing World.* New York: E. P. Dutton & Co., Inc., 1949. (Also included in PAUL R. LAWRENCE, and JOHN A. SEILER, *Organizational Behavior and Administration: Cases, Concepts, and Research Findings,* Rev. ed., pp. 26–29. Homewood, Ill.: Richard D. Irwin, Inc., and Dorsey Press, 1965.

RADCLIFFE-BROWN, A. R. *A Natural Science of Society.* Glencoe, Ill.: Free Press, 1957.

ROETHLISBERGER, F. J., and DICKSON, W. J. *Management and the Worker.* Cambridge, Mass.: Harvard University Press, 1946.

TRIST, E. L. "Socio-Technical Systems." Tavistock Institute of Human Relations, Doc. No. 572, November, 1959.

CHAPTER 2

Sociotechnical Systems

IN THE previous chapter our goal was to outline the basic properties of systems in general and to develop ideas pertinent to the analysis of any type of system. While the examples we used were often of social systems, this choice was a matter of convenience. Now let's turn our undivided attention to the analysis of a particular type of social system, that in which formal organization plays a significant role. We shall be talking henceforth mostly about business organizations, although our comments will usually be just as apropos of other kinds of formally organized institutions.

Our goal in this chapter is to begin reducing to comprehensibility the complex interdependence of forces which culminate in organizational behavior, most particularly that behavior whose results can be measured by more or less objective levels of productivity, subjective senses of satisfaction, and the sometimes ineffable signs of human, group, and organization development. We shall begin the process of bringing these forces within manageable bounds by dividing them into basic types, since we want to be able to summarize subclusters of information before we are called on to summarize our understanding of the operation of the system as a whole.

First of all, there is a major division of forces between those operating within the system and those operating in the environment. While the system and its environment are interdependently related, we have already defined a system as a set of forces *more intimately* related to each other than they are to forces outside the system. An assimilated member of a cohesive production work group behaves in more direct and closer relation to the expectations of other members of his group than in relation to the expectations of members of an associated engineering group, for example. Where we find members of formal groups, salesmen are often good examples, responding more directly to people or events outside their formal group than to people and events within, to customers instead of to fellow salesmen, for example, then we have found a case of a salesman-customer system which more dominantly influences the behavior of salesmen than do the forces arising from the weaker system connecting salesmen to each other.

In thinking of the external-internal system distinction, it is necessary to realize that we are dealing in a business organization with a multitude of systems of varying sizes, complexity, and types of relation to their external environment. The individual person, himself, forms a psychobiological system. He and a close friend or working partner will form a two-person system. They together or separately may be members of small working and/or social groups. These groups, in turn, will comprise departmental or subcultural systems, and so on, up the ladder of system size and complexity.

We should make explicit, also, the implied suggestion that one person or group may be an element in several systems at once. This is true not only in the sense that a man is a member of a subgroup, and by that membership also belongs to the group of which the subgroup is a part, but also it applies to simultaneous memberships in entirely different groups—for example, a foreman is usually part of his work group's system, and he is also a member of the group of foremen who meet with their department manager each morning to plan the day's work. Understanding these dual or multimemberships is important, since we inevitably encounter behavior which is not explicable simply in terms of the information we have about the particular system in which the behavior is occurring. For example, the foreman's behavior in relation to his subordinates may be heavily influenced by the expectations of his superior and by those of his fellow foremen. If the foreman becomes unresponsive to attempted influences on the part of his subordinates, he may be rejected by them and cease to be a member of the work-group system for which he is formally responsible.

These complexities of system overlap, or what might be thought of as "environmental penetration" of systems, demonstrate that in varying degrees systems are open rather than closed to their environment. When we discussed equilibrium in Chapter 1, we noted that the degree of openness of a system is critical to its survival and stable growth. If a business organization is so open to the events occurring around it that it responds to every shifting wind, it cannot develop any internal stability and momentum. Conversely, if a system is not responsive to external events, the results of its internal stability eventually become marketless. So, no matter how open or closed a system's relation to its environment, our analysis of that system's behavior must account for significant forces external to the system.

A system may be thought of as having two kinds of relations with its environment. First, the environment imposes certain constraints within which the system must more or less live. The business firm is constrained by raw material sources, governmental regulation, customer demand, and so on. The small work group has its assigned task, place of work, wage level, work rules, and attitudes of associated groups as some of its constraints. But systems not only respond to their environments, they also act upon them. The firm chooses among available raw materials, selects its employees, stimulates consumer demand, and so on. The work group may have union representation which wins it higher wages, it may find ways to dominate associated groups, and it may set its own pace of work within the constraints set by management.

The constraints imposed on a system and the selections which its members make from among those elements which are available to it in the environment may, for the purposes of understanding human behavior in organizations, be thought of as involving three types of variables: *human, technological,* and *organizational.* That is, the environment may be conceived as forcing its way or being invited into the system in these three guises and, once inside the system, these three variables interrelate and produce behavior. We can only understand that behavior by understanding how these three forces operate with each other.

Human Inputs

The founder of an organization, his executives and successors, and their subordinates bring with them to the organization certain skills, knowledge, physiological conditions, social status, accustomed ways of behaving, motives, needs, expectations, values, and ways of thinking about themselves and the world. The particular people and, thus, the particular assortment of these personal qualities in an organization depends to some extent on the kinds of jobs which are open, the kinds of technical skills required, the levels of pay offered, the system's working conditions, the type of people already in the system, and so on. Thus, the human input is a function of the technological and organizational inputs of the system. The particular mixtures of personal qualities is a strong influence on the social mores of the system, although once the system is functioning and has developed some history, the mores are a strong influence on who enters or stays in the system and on how he behaves while he is there. We will have more to say later about the influence of social relationships on system behavior.

Technological Inputs

The type of industry a company is in and the type of technology with which a work group is engaged highly influence the stability of the system's environment and, thus, its internal balance. Electronic and space technology, for example, tend to be associated with rapid obsolescence, frequent change in volume of work, continual transfer of personnel, constant retraining, and so on. This dimension of technology, then, helps explain why people in these industries often form weak social relationships, develop only slight commitment to any particular organization, and conduct themselves in such a way as to establish their individual reputations in forms which are easily communicated to strangers.

Technological variables influence system behavior in other ways, too—by the limits they place on how the total job may be divided up among people and groups, by the status relations among people and groups as these are reflected in educational requirements, positions of primacy in the flow of work, etc., and by such mundane but critical factors as the physical positioning of people in relation to each other (close enough to talk, for example) and by the tangible conditions of work such as noise level, temperature, or whether flammability of the product or process prohibits smoking. Apparent in these examples is the interrelation of technical, human, and organizational inputs. Technical skill requirements place a constraint on the kind of personal backgrounds which we will find in the system. What latitude there is in the nature of the technology for dividing the work of the firm into subunits will largely determine divisional and departmental structure and the number and kind of supervisory positions.

Organizational Inputs

Once an organization establishes its goals, determines its product strategy and otherwise decides what kind of business it is in, many subsequent choices have been made for it by those prior decisions. As we have seen, the selection of people and the broad structure of the organization are considerably restricted by these even more basic predeterminations. But many aspects of its choice of organizational input are still open. The particular procedures it uses to schedule orders, or gather information about performance, its salary levels, incentive systems, and the particular styles of leadership it rewards can be chosen from a wide spectrum. Of course, technology and the particular selection of people will affect these choices, as will such things as popular ideas about what is effective practice in these various areas. All of these organizational elements will affect the behavior of people in the organization. These variables are specifically intended to influence behavior in ways favorable to the organization, based on such presumptions as how an incentive system will affect productivity levels. Of course, these organizational designs often have unintended consequences, too.

A Fourth Input—Social Structure and Norms

As the reader may have suspected, organizational behavior is not so simply explained as the three classes of input described above might indicate. What complicates matters is the fact that human beings are social animals. They do not operate as discrete individuals responding only to their own internal makeup, to the nature of the tasks they are assigned, and to the financial rewards and punishments provided by the organization in which they work. Their behavior is also guided by whether it will be approved or disapproved by their fellows, whether it will help them gain or keep the acceptance of others, and whether it will increase or diminish the amount of influence they have among those whose affection and respect they value.

When people come into an organization, they are, by the nature of the technology and organization of that system, thrown together with certain other people. Over time, a set of shared ideas about what is permissible and what is forbidden emerges from the separate sets of values which each person brought with him to the group. These shared ideas are expressed in normative precepts about what one should and should not do, and they are usually accompanied by a set of rewards and punishments designed to encourage and reinforce adherance to these norms. Furthermore, those who work together begin to be stratified socially, partly by the degree to which they conform to the norms, partly due to the social status and skill level which they bring with them from outside the system or develop within it. These norms and positions within the group bear directly upon the behavior which occurs in the system. Of course, the social group's rules and the positions of its members have no necessary congruence with the formal rules and positions stipulated by the formal organization, although they undoubtedly will have been influenced by formal elements in the system.

Social structure and norms, then, are products of the human, technical, and organizational inputs of the system, but out of this convergence emerges a force which operates in its own right as an important input and determinant of behavior in the system. When, for example, a group of men is selected to work on a special project, the personalities and skills of these men, the nature of the tasks, and the position of the group in the organization have much to do with how that group will perform. But so will the degree of cohesion among members of the group, whether the group's norms support or deviate from the expectations which management has of group behavior, whether the group develops a clear informal leadership or finds itself torn by peer competition and so on.

Describing Organizational Life by Its Four Inputs

One way of reviewing our categories of the forces which determine organizational behavior is to picture how a man might describe his job in terms of each of these four inputs. *Human inputs:* "My job is an exacting one. It requires a good technical education, a lot of patience, a good sense of humor, and not caring if you get your hands dirty." *Technological inputs:* "My job involves keeping the various production units informed of schedule changes, material availability, and things like that. I'm running around all the time between my office and the factory. I hardly ever have a chance to sit down." *Organizational inputs:* "I'm a foreman at Jones Manufacturing. My boss is a good guy, keeps us involved on decisions. The pay is good—we have a profit-sharing plan. The way the system works, I'm due for a promotion pretty soon. My big problem is that part of the work my group should be doing is controlled by another department, and it frustrates me and my guys not to be able to finish up the whole job." *Social inputs:* "There's a nice bunch of guys where I work. They stick by each other. They really give the business to anybody who doesn't pull his weight. One of the boys is a joker—keeps us laughing all the time. Bill tries to keep him out of trouble, but it's hard. Bill's our spokesman pretty much, whenever we need one."

These everyday descriptions of work demonstrate the direct influence which our four categories of input have over behavior. But behavior, itself, is a seeming mass of undifferentiated "stuff," as yet. Let's see if we can break behavior down into some categories that will give us more confidence in our ability to explain just how our inputs operate.

The Categories of Actual Behavior

We can usefully think of three aspects of behavior, remembering always that, just as our inputs influenced each other in the process of influencing behavior, our three aspects of behavior will be interdependent.

Activities. Perhaps the most obvious aspect of behavior is that people do things—they act. They walk, talk, work with their hands, and sit and think. These acts are each influenced by human, technological, organizational, and social factors. One's acts tend to reflect how tired he is, in what mood his wife left him in the morning, and how great his preoccupation with keeping things under control is. He acts in response to the technical demands which his job places on him—perhaps he is paced by a machine, seeks to escape the heat of his workroom as often as possible, or finds it necessary to leave his isolated office frequently to go talk with friends or associates. Activities are often closely associated with organizational factors, such as the way the organization is subdivided, perhaps making a great many meetings necessary or causing special integrative jobs to be performed; the way supervisors behave, causing enthusiastic carrying out of plans or recalcitrance and resistance; the way procedures for checking on performance and rewarding behavior have been established, tending to tempt people to fudge reports, keep double sets of accounting records, or perform tasks which, though little related to getting the real job done, make the actor look good. Finally, social norms influence such things as how hard a man works or where he goes to eat lunch. Social status may affect whether a man speaks for his group or holds his tongue.

Interactions. People not only act; more often than not, they act in relation to other people. Different personalities, technologies, organizational positions, and social situations are functions of varying degrees and patterns of aloneness or groupness. The gregarious individual may seek opportunities to talk beyond the communication which is required by the job or allowed by formal rules. A job design which puts people in close physical proximity and an organizational division of labor which forces them to rely on each other to get the job done tend to increase the incidence of interaction between people. A social system which demands a high degree of loyalty and support of group members will tend to make those members keep in close touch with each other.

Sentiments. As people act and are acted upon, they develop feelings about what they are doing, about what is being done to them, and about the people with whom they are associated. These feelings are, of course, intimately related to their own personalities. If their prior experience has, for example, led them to feel inconfident of themselves, they tend to see in the behavior of others evidence of a devaluation of their own capacities which, in turn, may elicit feelings of depression or anger. Various aspects of the technological, organizational, and social situation tend to stimulate feelings of this kind, and others, depending on the predispositions of the individual person.

It becomes immediately apparent that each of the three categories of behavior—activities, interactions, and sentiments—has a great deal of influence on the other, just as the four inputs do. What a person does, for example, by virtue of the particular technical and organizational forces which are in operation, tends to influence whether he works with other people and, if so, with whom and, to some degree, how. People thus thrown together tend to form fairly definite feelings about one another, positive and negative. These sentiments, in turn, influence how the person acts in regard to those with whom he works, perhaps stimulating helping and sharing activities and interactions, but just as likely producing some kind of punishing activity or even complete rejection and avoidance of those for whom negative sentiments are felt. Thus, the interdependence of our categories is not reduced by our having identified and separated them, but the chance that we can carry through a piece-by-piece accounting of their interdependence is somewhat increased.

Functions and Feedback

We have nearly completed our description of the categories of elements in organizational systems. All that is left is to breath a little life into what by now may seem a rather static picture of inputs and behavioral effects. One may get the feeling from the discussion so far that he has been watching a film which suddenly stops with the actors caught permanently frozen in midmotion. People come into the organization with their unique backgrounds, technologies are chosen and put to work, organizational decisions are made and implemented, and a social system springs up. Out of all this come people acting, interacting, and feeling. But how does change take place? Certainly, once begun, organizations do not go on forever in an unending pattern of repetitive behavior.

We spent considerable time in Chapter 1 examining the qualities of the idea of functional analysis and how that idea might usefully be put to work to help us relate things to each other without either falling prey to simple, good-bad evaluations or to oversimplification of cause and effect. As we set out to discover where important interdependence between elements of the system existed, we said we would talk and think in a particular way about that interdependence. We would say that a particular behavior or pattern of behavior or characteristics of our inputs was *functional or dysfunctional for* the development or continued existence of some other behavior, behavior pattern, input characteristic or output, the last stated in terms of such things as productivity, satisfaction, or development. We said that we could expect any one element of our system to be functional for some things, dysfunctional for others and, sometimes, even, functional *and* dysfunctional for the same thing at different times or even at the same time.

We also said that systems contained feedback mechanisms, a special case of functional relationship. It is feedback which gives life to our system. If we say that spacing people closely together at work is functional for the maintenance of a feeling of cohesion among the members of the work group, we are talking about the reactions of people to specific conditions. The functionality statement implies a human-social process. Someone perceives the condition and responds to it. If we go on to observe that a feeling of group cohesion actually exists, i.e., that factors other than spacing, such as noise or interpersonal conflict, are not dysfunctional for cohesiveness in such degree as to nullify the functionality of spacing for developing and sustaining cohesion, we may also observe signs of satisfaction on the part of our workers, a function of their sense of belonging to a common social unit and of their pleasure in being able to talk about their problems and pass the time of day. This satisfaction has feedback effects on the system, tending to keep people from moving on to other jobs, to stimulate efforts to bring friends into the organization, and so on. Satisfaction, then, feeds back into the system and is functional for the stability of the system. However, cohesion may at the same time be functional for the development of group norms restricting levels of productivity. These norms may emerge because they are functional for helping less capable workers feel they will escape management censure. They may also be functional for strengthening the attractiveness of the group in that they give group members something interesting to do and offer them a way of controlling their work situation to some degree. Whatever its other functions, however, work restriction is dysfunctional for productivity. Information about the restricted level of productivity is fed back to management through the company's reporting system. As a result, management may decide to space the workers farther apart to make it more difficult for them to check productivity rates and peg production. Thus, one of the inputs to the system, i.e., job layout, is altered as a result of previous system outputs, and the feedback loop is complete. But the loop is never closed. All we need do to convince ourselves of that fact is to speculate on the chain of functions which management's respacing will have started, and we'll see that another output will emerge to feed back into the system, stimulating an effort on the part of some individual or group to alter inputs in such a way as to produce outputs more desirable to them than those that now exist.

Applying System Categories to the Analysis of Actual Organizational Behavior

The first step in making our system idea directly applicable to any organizational situation which we may be called on to study and to do something about is to pull all of our categories and their relationships together and set them down in a diagram so we can get a mental picture of how we might arrange the sorting out of facts and the drawing together of significant meanings. Such an elementary framework for diagnosing human behavior in organizations appears in Figure 1. With this mental picture in mind—a way, in fact, of diagramming the facts of an organizational situation on a piece of paper—let's look at a specific case of organizational behavior and see what we can do with it. What follows is a four-part case from the files of the Harvard Business School. Between Parts 1, 2, and 3 we shall analyze the situation using our diagnostic scheme. After Part 3, the reader will have a chance to try his hand at analyzing and predicting subsequent behavior on the basis of his analysis. Part 4 will serve as a check on his predictions.

UTILITY POWER COMPANY

Part 1

Members of engineering management at the Utility Power Company were, in 1959, searching for a method to increase the work capacity of the distribution section. Pressures for expansion of the company's electri-

Figure 1

AN ELEMENTARY FRAMEWORK FOR DIAGNOSING HUMAN BEHAVIOR IN ORGANIZATIONS

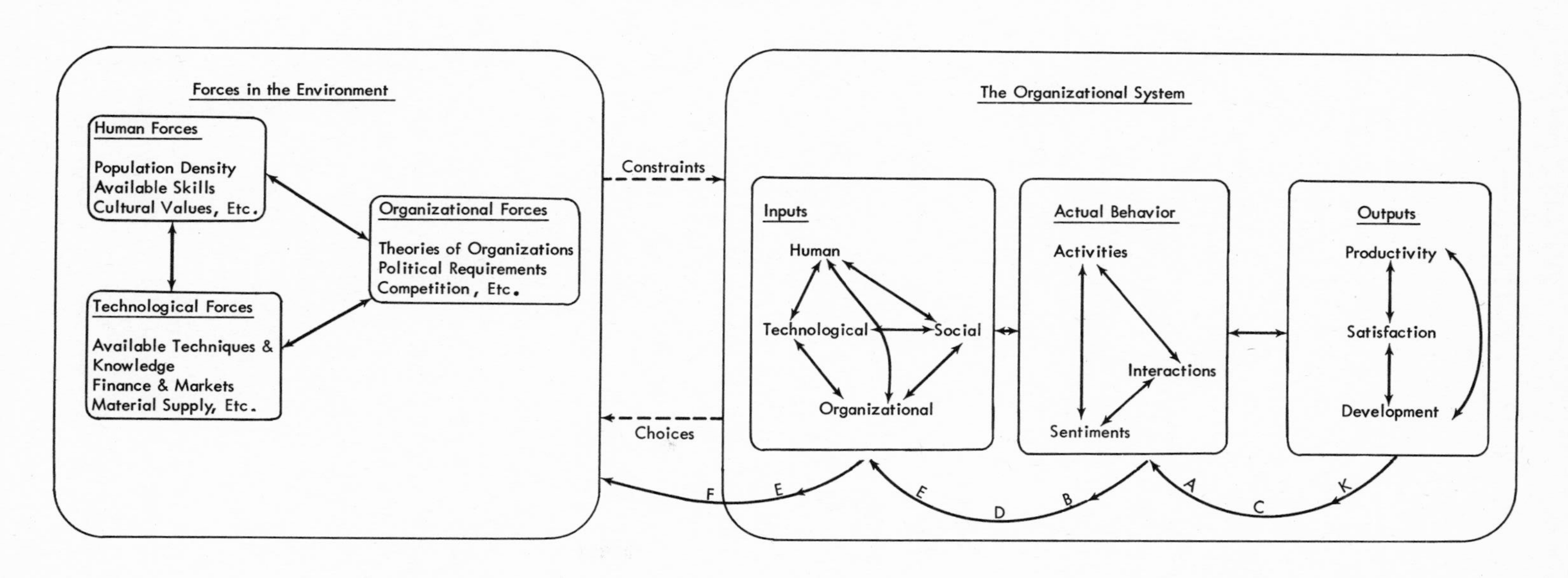

cal distribution system were increasing rapidly, calling for a marked improvement in the speed with which construction and renovation designs were made available to field construction crews.

The Utility Power Company held a franchise covering a large area of the midwestern part of the United States. Its distribution territory was divided into four regions, each responsible for the construction, maintenance, and operation of power substations, transmission lines, and auxiliary equipment, as well as for commercial activities related to customer service. The regional offices relied upon a central engineering group, the distribution section, for the design and cost information required in expanding their service facilities.

The distribution section was housed at company headquarters, located approximately 150 miles from any one of the regional offices (see Exhibit 1). Two teams, in each an engineer and a draftsman, reported to the

Exhibit 1

THE UTILITY POWER COMPANY

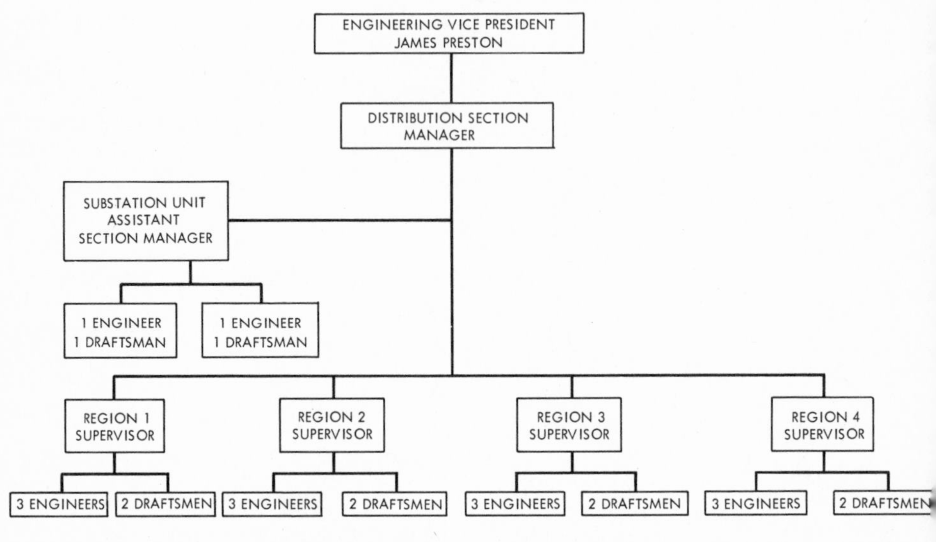

assistant section manager. Their exclusive assignment was to design and estimate costs for power substations throughout the company's franchise area. The section manager directly supervised four teams, each composed of an engineering supervisor, three engineers, and two draftsmen. Each of these four teams was responsible for designs and cost estimates for all other equipment requested by a particular distribution region. Regional work loads and priorities varied from time to time. There was a certain amount of transfer of personnel between teams as a result, although, because all regions were exerting pressure to have their work completed, team supervisors usually found reasons to hold onto their team members.

The distribution engineering teams had each developed close, friendly working relationships over the years. Engineers and draftsmen were salaried and nonunion. The men of each team had considerable opportunity to work closely together. It was the custom for all members of a team working on a particular engineering problem to travel together for several days at a time surveying some portion of a region's extensive territory. On their survey trips and at the home office, each draftsman felt himself to be as closely integrated into his team as were the engineers. Although there were obvious distinctions of technical status (for example, each supervisor had his own office, the engineers of each team were located together, and the draftsmen of all teams worked in one large room), there appeared to be little formal barrier between team members as they worked together. Even across team lines, there appeared to be a great deal of informal, friendly interchange of information.

The draftsmen of each team, in addition to routine drafting duties, were frequently assigned those elementary design and estimating problems of which their engineering colleagues found them capable. The availability of such work made technical and salary advancement for the draftsmen a readily attainable goal. Furthermore, some of the engineers showed considerable interest in helping draftsmen, particularly those who were enrolled in correspondence schools or night courses, to improve their technical skills.

The distribution section had operated in the foregoing manner for many years. Since World War II, a number of engineers and a few draftsmen had been hired as replacements and as increases to the overall engineering capacity of the section. In spite of these additions, however, a backlog of essential projects from the field had steadily mounted. Repeated efforts to obtain qualified new men, particularly draftsmen, had met with little success.

Now, let's try diagramming this information, selecting from all of the information what seem to be the factors and relationships which we need to take into account in order to figure out what to do about the backlog problem. We'll start at the right-hand side of the diagram, at the "outputs," and work our way back. In other words, we start where problems show their symptoms, since problem solving is the manager's goal. By focussing on the elements within the system which are closely associated with problem outputs, we automatically limit the amount of information about the total system which we have to deal with.

The Outputs

High productivity but falling behind demand.

Satisfaction at a high level with low apparent turnover.

Development of draftsmen high but in insufficient numbers.

Development of work groups but an insufficient capacity of the organization to keep pace with needs for its services.

Now what are these outputs functionally related to among our categories of behavior?

What is related to productivity level?

Dysfunctional:

a) Unsuccessful attempts to obtain qualified new men.

b) Team travel (this activity and interaction may also be functional for productivity).

c) Resistance to transfer of draftsmen between teams.

Functional:

a) Close, friendly working relations.

b) Interchange of information within and between teams.

c) Assigning engineering work to draftsmen.

d) Development of draftsmen's technical skills.

What is related to satisfaction level?

Dysfunctional: (no evidence of dysfunctions, unless constantly being behind creates some dissatisfaction).

Functional:

a) Friendly working relations.

b) Team feeling.

c) Challenging work for draftsmen.

d) Teaching and learning.

e) Chance to win advancement.

f) Draftsmen feeling "like an engineer."

What is related to development?

Dysfunctional: Lack of growth in number of qualified men in the section.

Functional: Training activities and relationships.

As we look at behavior in its functional relationship to outputs, then, it looks like we have a real problem with the scarcity of qualified new men. Equally or more important, team activities and interactions appear to be both functional and dysfunctional for productivity. On the one hand, there may be some time and manpower lost when the whole team travels, though the evidence is somewhat thin on this score. Furthermore, inflexibility in cross-team transfers seems to be creating an undetermined lack of efficiency. But team organization seems functional for productivity in that it associates teams with responsibility for a region's needs. Team operation is also functional for productivity through the medium of derived satisfactions in team membership and in the development of draftsman skills. If it turns out we cannot acquire new men at a faster rate, then can productivity be increased by some change in the organization of work? Or would a reorganization cost more than it gained?

Looking at the problem of attracting new qualified men, we quickly find that we have no data to go on. We can only speculate. Do the present human inputs, by their homogeneity, unduly restrict the population from which we can reasonably attract new people? Or do our highly satisfied people indicate that, if anything, we could expect them to have created a favorable reputation in the community for work at Utility Power? Are the technical inputs such that we are presently prohibited from finding any but a few new people or are the technical aspects of the distribution section's jobs so competitively attractive as to lead us to expect many applicants, other things being equal? Are organizational inputs like salary level, fringe benefits, and other formal aspects of work competitively attractive? Apparently, leadership styles are well accepted, so this aspect of organizational input seems to be in our favor. So far as social inputs go, all we can see seems to be functional for attracting new people, although it is conceivable that the distribution section has an image of "groupiness" which repels men more accustomed to individual work.

No matter how perceptive our speculation might be, analysis of the system gives us no real clue to ways to increase qualified staff. We have done all we can with the information we have. For now we must assume that whatever solution may be found for the backlog of work, it will not involve the addition of significant numbers of new draftsmen and engineers.

Our attention turns, then, to an analysis of team organization as a possible source of relief for the backlog problem. We have already speculated that productivity may be adversely affected by team travel and by some degree of inflexibility in temporary cross-team personnel transfer. On the other hand, productivity level is apparently functionally related to a number of aspects of team organization: close and friendly relations, members feeling a part of the team, challenge to junior men, helping in the development of junior men within a team. We even find that interteam communication operates freely, despite team organization. We need to find out what inputs are functionally related to these aspects of distribution section behavior in order to find out what latitude we might have in reducing whatever nonproductive elements there may be in team and other aspects of the way work is performed.

Human inputs and team behavior:
Dysfunctional: No evidence.
Functional:
a) We might assume that engineers and draftsmen enjoy group work.
b) Both engineers and draftsmen appear to enjoy the teaching-learning process.

Technical inputs and team behavior:
Dysfunctional:
a) All draftsmen housed in a common room. (But this appears to be functional for cross-team communication.)
b) Pressure from short-run imbalance in regional loads to transfer draftsmen between teams.
c) Teams in closer proximity to each other than to client regions. (Also functional for cross-team communication.)

Functional:
a) Team's identification with a region through responsibility for the region.
b) Close team living relation in the field.
c) Need for several skills to complete a project prompts a team of complementary members.
d) Team engineers located in their own office.

Organizational inputs and team behavior:
Dysfunctional: Interteam transfer procedure.
Functional:
a) Regional organization.
b) Separate supervisor for each team.
c) Internal promotion possibilities (encouraging intrateam training).
d) Equality and participative supervisory styles.
e) Engineers and draftsmen all salaried, nonunion; few distinctions which might be divisive.
f) Permissive rules in assigning engineering work to draftsmen.
g) Travel allowances making team travel possible.

Social inputs and team behavior:
Dysfunctional: Close personal relations among draftsmen of various teams.
Functional:
a) Long-standing relationships with well-established expectations of stability.
b) Intrateam helping and cohesion norms.

We are led by the human, technical, and organizational reinforcements of team cohesion to expect that team social systems would be highly resistant to any change which would weaken the association of a man with his team. Probably a crucial factor in keeping the team focus from being dysfunctional for interteam communication and transfer is the common room arrangement for draftsmen. Another element which may be limiting the dysfunctional potential in a rigid team system is an apparent norm of competence which probably stimulates cross-team communication around common technical problems.

We have laboriously detailed our functional analysis of this elementary description of a work-unit system for several reasons. First, we want to be clear about what the analytic elements of our framework mean and about how they can be linked together to help us understand what is going on. Second, being laborious with simple sets of data should help us become more expert when we get to more complex systems. Third, we shall soon turn to a description of what the Utility Power managers did in response to their mounting backlog of work, and we want to be prepared to trace the impact of those actions throughout a system whose previous internal relations we well understand. Normally, though, we could speed through this type of analysis much more quickly by the use of shorthand devices. Let's look at how such shorthand might look on a diagram of this first part of the case (see Figure 2). We normally would want to draw arrows between the functionally related items in each category, noting by a + or — whether these relations were functional or dysfunctional for each other. We have not done so on this sample diagram because, as one might expect, the cross-hatching of arrows is confusing unless the reader, himself, developed the diagram. Instead, let's reorganize our diagram by the major forces which seem to be at work, namely, the inputs and outputs of teamwork, the inputs and outputs of cross-team work and the inputs and outputs of individual development behavior (see Figure 3).

Having sorted and resorted the small amount of information in Utility Power, Part 1, in an effort to be entirely clear about how our analytical scheme can be used, let's turn to a description of what management proposed to do to remedy the backlog problem and see if we can put our analysis to fruitful use.

UTILITY POWER COMPANY

Part 2

In 1959, Philip Hawkins, the distribution section manager, proposed to his superior, James Preston, that the distribution section be reorganized along more efficient and more highly productive lines.

Hawkins' plan entailed the establishment of a draftsmen's "pool."

Figure 2

UTILITY POWER COMPANY

SHORTHAND DIAGRAMMATIC ANALYSIS OF PART 1

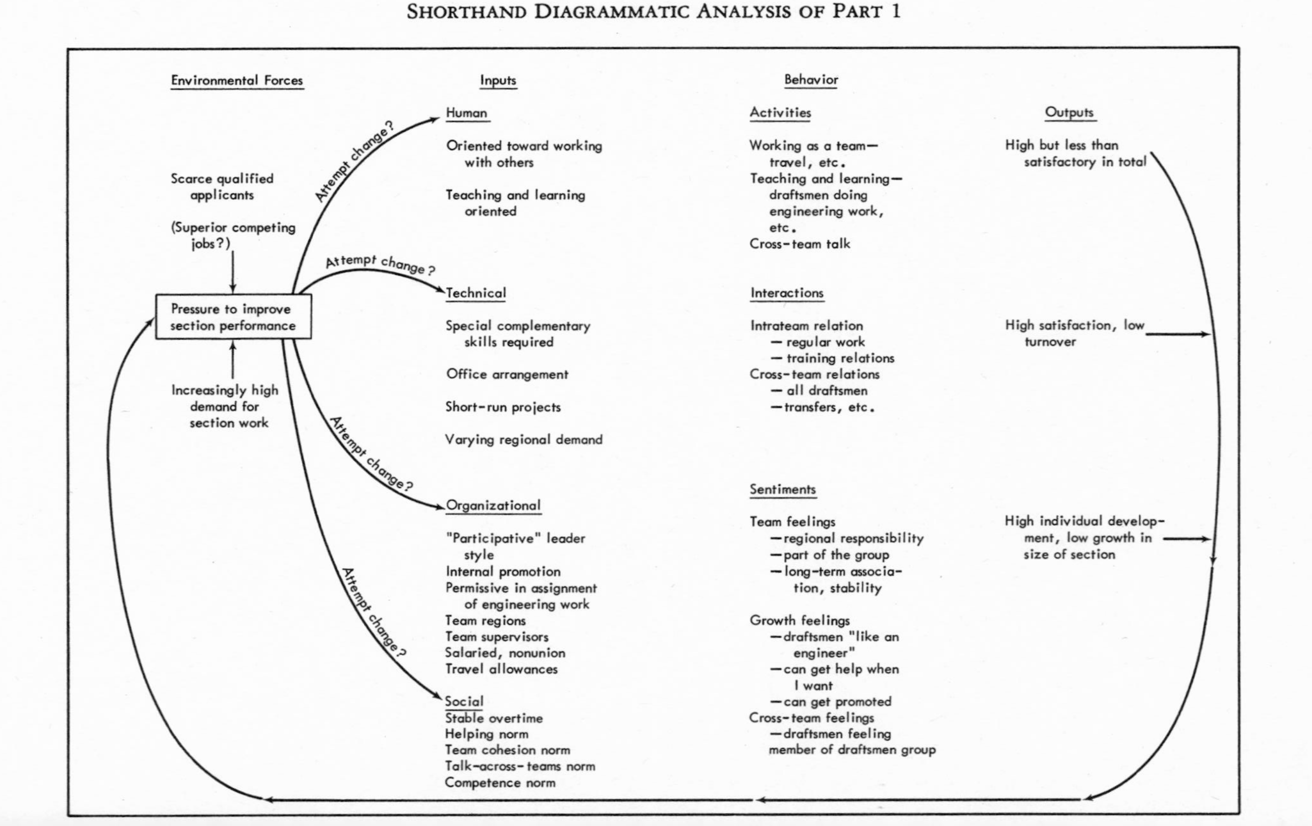

Figure 3

UTILITY POWER COMPANY

Rediagramming Part 1, Focusing on Team, Cross-Team, and Individual Development Behavior

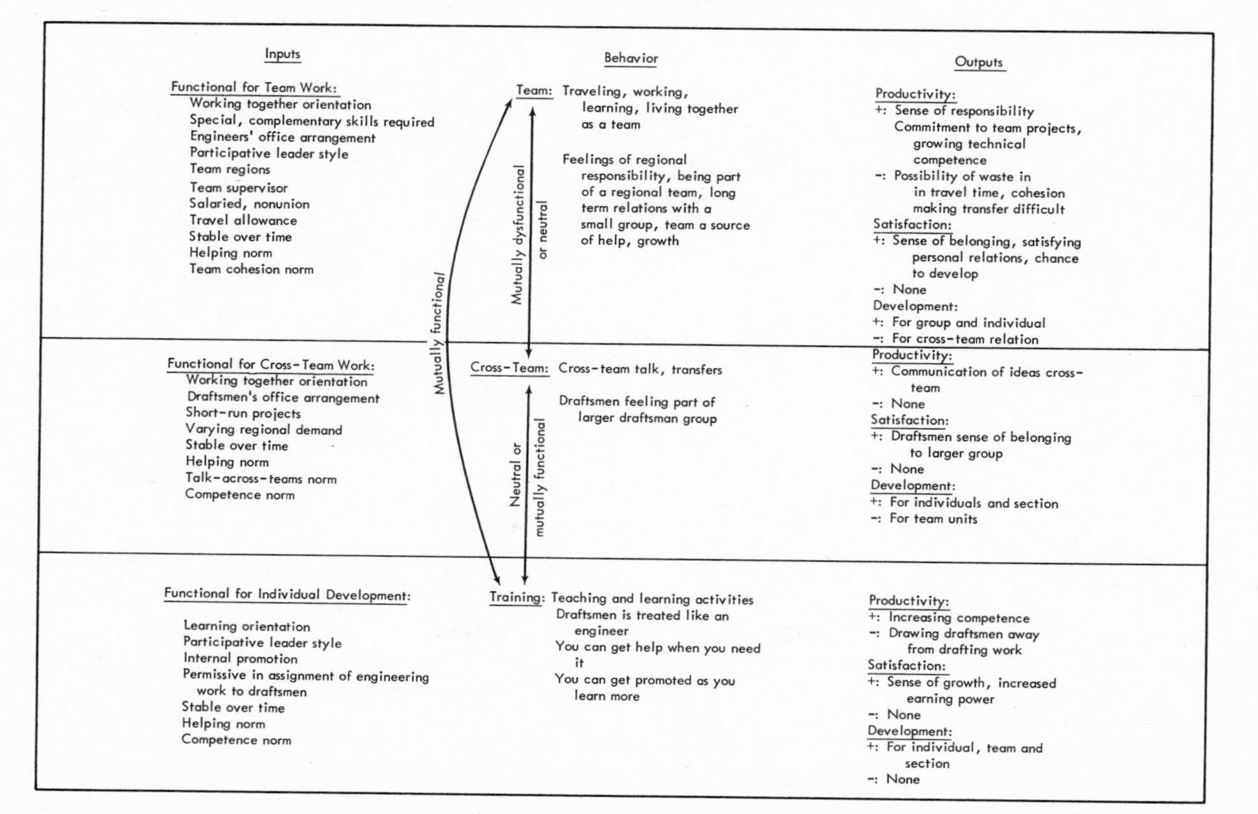

Under this proposal, all draftsmen would be removed from team affiliation, to be placed under the supervision of a chief draftsman. Exhibit 2 shows the proposed section organization. The new supervisor would assign

Exhibit 2

UTILITY POWER COMPANY

PROPOSED ORGANIZATION OF THE DISTRIBUTION SECTION

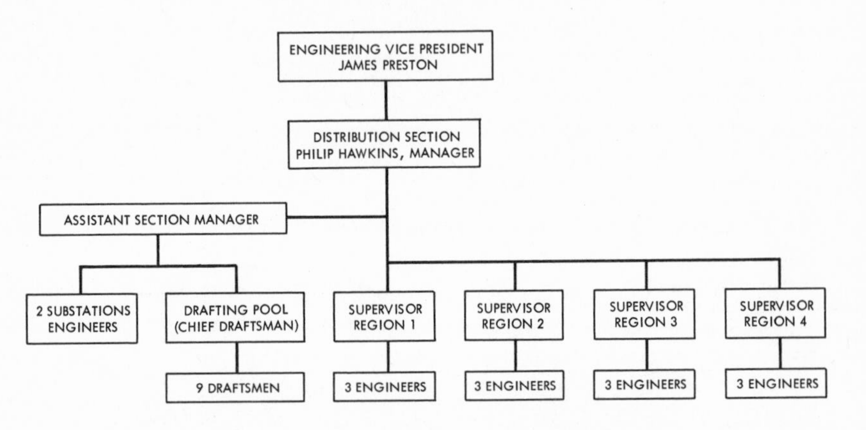

to draftsmen the work received from engineers according to his estimate of the individual capacities of his men and by reference to a predetermined priority schedule. Hawkins predicted that the new system would increase available drafting time and, through greater specialization, would enhance the productivity of engineers and draftsmen alike.

The proposed system was to have several additional benefits. It would remove the causes for the "sloppy setup" in controlling supplies and in operating printing and duplicating machinery. Stocks of drafting supplies had traditionally been haphazardly maintained, with occasional depletions of materials occurring unnoticed. Similarly, reproducing machinery had not been giving good service because, it was believed, each draftsman was operating the equipment to secure his own print requirements. The pool arrangement would make it possible to assign to the chief draftsman a girl who would be in charge of the stock room and the duplicating and printing equipment.

Preston agreed to study Hawkins' ideas in preparation for further discussions a few days hence.

After several discussions of the plan to reorganize the distribution section, the engineering vice president agreed with the section manager that the institution of a drafting pool would improve the section's capacity to meet its work schedule. The following implementary plan was considered by both men to be essential.

Key to the success of the pool would be the choice of a chief draftsman. It was agreed that the job would require a man with obviously superior technical ability. Since the new supervisor would have to be chosen from the ranks of the present drafting group (no outsider being available for consideration), he would have to have won the respect of all the men who were to report to him. One of the draftsmen, Roger Manson, was believed to be "head and shoulders" above the rest. Hawkins reported that Manson was working hard to increase his drafting skill, that he was more objective and aggressive in his work than the others, and that he had been given more advanced engineering work than any other draftsman. Manson had been with the distribution section for six years, somewhat less than had the majority of the draftsmen. Previously, he had spent five years as a Utility Power Company substation maintenance man. He was 33 years old, about average for the drafting group. While supervisory experience would have been desirable, none of the draftsmen possessed that qualification.

It was decided, first, to advise Manson in confidence of the new plan in order to ascertain his willingness to accept the supervisory position. Manson would be warned that he would have to rely upon the leadership which the respect for his ability would generate, rather than upon his formal position. In no case would heavy-handedness be advisable.

Assuming that Manson would accept the new job, Hawkins was to call a meeting of the entire section, including clerks and stenographers as well as engineers and draftsmen. At this meeting, he would carefully explain the nature of the change and the reasons for it. The new chief draftsman would be introduced and his duties outlined. Questions would be solicited and discussed until it appeared that the change was well understood. On the presumption that this meeting would proceed successfully, the new organization would be put into effect the next day.

Early in October, 1959, Hawkins, in a confidential meeting, proposed to Manson that the latter assume the duties of the new section post, that of chief draftsman. After listening to Hawkins' description of the job and the authority limits within which he would be expected to function, Manson eagerly accepted the position. Over the next week, the two men met several times to plan for the organization of a drafting pool. Both men were enthusiastic about the potentialities of the new plan.

Very simply, then, there were to be several modifications to organization inputs. Instead of working with a small group of engineers all the time, on a limited set of projects, a draftsman would take jobs from engineers of any team, depending on the draftsman's qualifications to do the work, his availability for new work, and the priority assigned to the work. Apparently, draftsmen were to become more specialized in their work, i.e., to perform a more limited type of work, as a result of the new organization. No change was contemplated in work location, from what we can tell. We do not know if draftsmen were to continue to travel with engineers, but let's assume that there would be no change in that practice, at least insofar as management prescription was concerned. The draftsmen would now report to a chief draftsman, a former peer, instead of an engineering supervisor. We may assume that the supervisor would, to some degree, be involved in and even reduce the technical necessity of some direct draftsman-engineer work relations. Lastly, draftsmen would no longer operate common equipment or secure their own supplies, having a girl to handle those tasks for them.

If we diagram these new inputs to the distribution section system, we might then be able to predict what behavior and what outputs would result. In all likelihood the reader can make a number of predictions from his command of the prior set of system relationships, without careful analysis, but let's continue to be systematic, both to understand the analytic process better and to be sure we do not overlook anything. A new diagram of the system, showing only changes in the system, actual and predicted, appears in Figure 4.

We find from our diagramming that the old team cohesion and training activities will, of necessity, be reduced or abolished, and that relationships will be aggravated by the imposition of the chief draftsman intermediary. (We might have noted, by the way, that the enthusiasm of the new chief and of management for this plan could be predicted to have prevented them from making as objective an analysis as we who are not involved have done.) We can predict from knowing how satisfying prior relationships were that both engineers and draftsmen will seek to approximate those former conditions within the new framework, that where that is not possible they will complain and that, as a net result, whatever theoretical time and skill savings which might technically have been contained in the plan will be more than nullified by these dysfunctionalities. The only possible exception will be the positive effects of the centralized operation of the supply room, duplicating machinery, etc., unless this change becomes associated with the negative feelings surrounding other aspects of the change. We could go on to make more specific predictions concerning the probems the new chief draftsman would face by virtue of his particular background in relation to the men he is to supervise and to the engineers but the major outlines of our predictive analysis are sufficiently clear for us to move on and see how the changes, in fact, fared.

Figure 4

UTILITY POWER COMPANY

CHANGE IN INPUTS AND PREDICTED BEHAVIOR AND OUTPUTS, PART 2

Environmental Forces

Scarce Applicants ↔ Increased Demand → Backlog

Changed Inputs

Organizational
- Teams restricted to engineers
- Draftsmen's pool
- Work assigned on basis of:
  - — specializations
  - — priority
  - — availability of draftsman
- Promotion and training now responsibility of chief draftsman
- Chief draftsman to perform some liaison between engineers and draftsmen
- Draftsmen relieved of service functions
- Management enthusiasm for the plan
- New chief draftsman warned to win respect, not exercise formal authority
- Plan to present reorganization at a meeting of all personnel
- Plan to be put in effect immediately

Human
- Chief draftsman a former peer
  - —considered technically superior
  - —respected as a competent
  - —less seniority than average
  - —average age for draftsman
  - —no supervisory experience
  - —eagerly accepts the job
- New girl
  - —unknown background

Technical
- No change in overall task, work locations, etc.

Activities

- Narrower range of activities for each draftsman
- Reduced opportunity for training
- Greater opportunity for draftsmen to do board work
  - —less engineering type work
  - —less drafting services work
- More time spent trying to circumvent restrictions on old team activities

Interactions

- More interaction between draftsmen and chief draftsman
- Less contact with previous team engineers
- Less contact with a specific group of regional people
- More attempts to work with old team, in spite of barriers to doing so

Sentiments

- Frustration on part of draftsmen:
  - —more restricted work
  - —less sense of growth, chance for advancement
  - —less direct contact with engineers
  - —lost feeling of being part of a team and responsible for a region, a whole job
- Frustration on part of engineers:
  - —uncontrolled relation with draftsmen
  - —having to work through an intermediary
  - —less chance to act in a teaching capacity
- Satisfaction on part of draftsman:
  - —better drafting services

Outputs

Productivity
- Lower than previously
  - — old patterns would be sought when possible
  - — much energy consumed in finding ways to circumvent new organization and in complaining
- High productivity in supplies and central services function

Satisfaction
- Lower for all concerned, including the chief draftsman who will be the focus of blame for changed conditions

Development
- Lower than formerly

UTILITY POWER COMPANY

Part 3

On October 12, a meeting of the full section was called, the plan was explained in detail, and the chief draftsman's appointment was announced. A number of questions arose and were discussed. By the end of the meeting, everyone involved appeared to understand the change and its implications for each individual. On October 13, the plan was put into effect.

During the remainder of October and through November, the pool system seemed to be shaking down well. There were minor grumblings now and again from engineers who believed a job of theirs had not been given sufficient priority by the chief draftsman. But in the drafting room, cooperation seemed high, and the production of drawings was much improved. The chief draftsman had introduced several new techniques for correcting and reproducing drawings which had significantly reduced the need for tedious corrections and redrawing. The supply situation was brought under control, files were straightened out, and the appearance of the drafting room, in general, was radically improved.

The persistence of one custom, a holdover from the team system, seemed to be reducing the potential for further increases in the production of drawings, however. Engineers continued to take former teammate draftsmen on field survey trips. On these trips, which lasted several days, draftsmen took notes, and even carried some of the less complex jobs through the cost-estimating stage of design upon their return to the section office. In consequence, these men were out of Manson's control for a week or more at a time. Despite the problems which this custom posed for the chief draftsman's effective scheduling of work, production of the pool was more than satisfactory.

Then, through December and the early months of 1960, Hawkins began to observe signs of increasing discontent. He heard from some of the engineers that their draftsmen friends had confided in them their growing impatience with the chief draftsman. They reported such comments as: "I used to like that guy; but now that he's got his new job, he thinks he can push any kind of petty job on me and expect me to thank him for it." Others remarked: "The work just isn't interesting like it used to be. You never know what's going on with a job. You draw a piece of it, and it gets whipped away from you before the ink is dry."

Hawkins also observed a mounting friction between the engineers and the chief draftsman. Manson and Hawkins had agreed that the chief draftsman would have to know a good deal about each job in order to schedule drafting work properly. Particularly, Manson felt that this knowledge was critical for his ability to check drawings, as he always did, before returning them to the engineer for final authorization. However, several of the engineers referred to Manson's efforts as "interference." They remarked, in Hawkins' presence, that they could not help being impatient with having to "go through the whole story again" for Manson's benefit. They talked as though Manson stood between them and the draftsman, with whom they were "anxious to get down to cases."

In February, 1960, Hawkins began to notice that production of designs for field construction crews was falling off. The engineering supervisors reported to Hawkins that their engineers and a number of draftsmen were highly discontented. The supervisors warned that something had to be done before a full-fledged explosion occurred. One of them even suggested that the pool idea be abandoned and that the section revert to the team system of operation.

By the middle of March, 1960, Hawkins was convinced that some immediate action would have to be taken to reverse the productivity trend of his section. The situation had been alleviated for a time by a change in the policy for capital plant additions. Formerly, every addition in excess of $1,500 net estimated cost was the responsibility of his section. That amount had been raised to $2,500, thus eliminating about three fourths of that minor estimating work which draftsmen were capable of handling on their own. However, Hawkins felt sure that with increasing labor and materials costs, many of these small jobs would soon be back under his jurisdiction.

Hawkins discussed the worsening situation with the chief draftsman. Manson, however, was convinced that the new capital-additions policy would provide the relief needed to make the pool system operable. Nevertheless, Hawkins felt that the pool idea had proved unsuccessful, and he determined to abandon it in favor of a modified team system.

After consultation with the engineering supervisors, Hawkins decided to retain the centralized supply and reproduction facilities in charge of a girl who would report to one of the substation design engineers. Otherwise, the pool idea was to disappear altogether. The teams were to be reconstituted, with the express provision that each supervisor was to arrange for the loan of draftsmen between teams whenever the need arose. Whenever these mutual arrangements failed, the matter was to be brought to the attention of the assistant manager.

Manson was to be reincorporated, at his present salary level, into one of the teams. Hawkins, in discussion with Manson, stressed that this action was not to be construed as a reprimand of the chief draftsman. In fact, it was simply a response to an unworkable organization which had been initiated by the section manager. Hawkins told Manson that he realized the ex-chief draftsman would probably feel awkward at first about his new status but that he should do his best to adjust to it. Simultaneously, Hawkins met alone with the engineering supervisor in whose group Manson would work. He received assurances from the supervisor that the pool system and Manson's position in it were closed issues.

Shortly thereafter, a general meeting of the section was called. Hawkins explained that the pool idea had not succeeded, as everyone knew; that its failure was no one's fault, except possibly his own; and that a modified team arrangement, as previously described, would go into effect immediately. The assignment of draftsmen to the teams was also announced at this time.

Were it not for the fact that each of our predictions of what would turn up in Part 3, based on the information contained in Parts 1 and 2, stemmed very logically from a step-by-step analysis of how aspects of the organization were functionally related, we might be accused of having read ahead before making our predictions. While much of the richness of detail of Part 3 was lacking in our predictions, we were close enough to the actual outcomes to be confident that we would not have chosen the particular modifications that the distribution section manager did in trying to solve the backlog problem.

At the end of Part 3 another set of changes is set in motion. What might we predict from:

1. Retention of the centralized supply and reproduction facilities.
2. Reconstituted teams.
3. Clear provision for cross-team transfers, including negotiations through the assistant manager, if necessary.
4. Return of Manson to membership in one of the regional teams (with assurances of cooperation from his new supervisor and acceptance of responsibility for the pool failure on the part of the distribution section manager).

Try diagramming these changes in the context of what you know about the operation of the system to date, predict behavior and outputs and then check Part 4, below, to see how well you did.

UTILITY POWER COMPANY

Part 4

In December, 1960, Hawkins reported that the revised team system of operation in his section had proved successful. By means of several follow-up efforts on Hawkins' part, excellent cooperation between teams had been achieved, and draftsmen were often sent on temporary loan to other teams whenever drafting commitments warranted. There had been some anxiety at first about the adjustment of Manson; but after several months, he appeared to be reasonably well integrated into his team. The productivity of the section seemed to Hawkins to be at an all-time high.

Summary

In this chapter we have sought to put systems analysis to work on the specifics of formal organization systems. We began by seeking to break information about an organizational system down into convenient categories whose characteristics we could sum up and functionally relate to the characteristics of other information categories. We began by separating information internal and external to the system. We compared two types of relations between a system and its environment—constraints and choices. Within the system we distinguished broadly between inputs, behavior, outputs, and feedback. Within inputs we distinguished human, technical, organizational, and social categories. In examining behavior, we referred to activities, interactions, and sentiments. We divided outputs into levels of productivity, satisfaction, and development. Feedback we characterized as the dynamic process of information flow within the system which stimulated system reinforcement or change.

We examined a rather simple description of an organizational problem, using our categories, starting out with the evidences of a problem in the system, and organizing our analysis of behavior and inputs in relation to those problem symptoms. After we had analyzed the system by our diagnostic framework, we took the description of management's attempted solution to the problem and, through analysis, predicted the behavior and outputs which would result. Since outputs were not satisfactory to management, we had another chance in Part 3 of the case to try our hand at predicting how management's second attempt at problem solving would fare.

With this exposition and exemplification of the basic analytic framework proposed by this book, we are ready to turn to the enrichment and complication of some of the major categories of the framework. We will begin in the next chapter by examining more fully some aspects of the human inputs to behavior.

CHAPTER 3

Human Inputs

by Douglas R. Bunker

A SET of conceptual tools for thinking about human personality and motivation is an essential component of a book concerned with organizational behavior. This necessity holds not only because individual predispositions constitute one category of the determinants of behavior in our analytic scheme but also because whatever the topical focus or the nature of the case at hand, our implicit ways of thinking about personality will profoundly influence our understanding of organizational behavior. Our comprehension of all the other inputs in sociotechnical systems will be conditioned by our concepts of man.

The concept of personality minimally implies two basic propositions about people: First, that each person is unique. Second, this uniqueness has continuity through time and across situations. Like most simple assertions, these statements are correct in what they say but incorrect in what they fail to say. They are incorrect in light of what we know about the common characteristics among members of the human species, about the evidences of cultural uniformity, about adherence to group norms, and about the influence of role requirements on human behavior. Nevertheless, the recognition of persistent and individual differences is fundamental in both the behaviorial sciences and in administrative practice. In organizations, the uniqueness of the individual underlies the great attention given to processes of selection, training, and placement. Indeed, the belief in the continuity and systematic integrity of individual character is the underpinning for all administrative decisions which involve the attribution of knowledge or skill to persons.

For the administrator to be optimally effective then, he must have a way of thinking about personality which will enable him to bring order to the mass of observations of individual behavior he continuously accumulates. The first step toward improving our ability to understand individual behavior is to make our present assumptions and ways of categorizing personality patterns explicit. Once they are visible, we can test them for internal consistency and coherence, for their communicability to other people and for their correspondence with other's views, and for their practical utility in predicting and explaining our own and others' behavior across time and situations.

What Personality Constructs Shall We Use?

An organizing set of concepts and categories is required to bring order to our experience of human diversity and complexity. Each of us possesses and automatically employs some framework for organizing our perceptions of people. In their primitive form these category systems are implicit and somewhat idiosyncratic. Although they are usually satisfactory enough to get us by in interpersonal situations, they commonly are not optimal for helping us reduce ambiguity, clarify communication, and find sufficient bases for coordinated activity. Our information processing limitations are amply exemplified by the way we attend closely to some aspects of human behavior and are totally unaware of others. Since we commonly make such selections automatically and unconsciously, it is worth wondering about the characteristics we ignore. Do our observational habits actually yield the information we need to make decisions? Do our categories provide enough of a picture of the person to enable us to claim to "understand" him or to support reality-oriented decisions concerning him? While the answer to these questions must most often be no, it seems likely that recognizing how incomplete and inaccurate our characterizations can be provides a basis for correcting for bias and distortion. This recognition should lead us to collect more information along a broader range of dimensions and from a greater variety of sources.

Ability Constructs

One set of human input concepts frequently used by administrators has to do with ability or aptitude. Performance is often attributed to particular kinds and amounts of coping capacity. This cluster of constructs[1] includes general intelligence, special talents, and such other

---

[1]In this chapter, concept and construct will be used interchangeably to refer to a set of rules for classifying and organizing experience according to a dimension or category system. We shall refer mainly to *personal constructs,* the classification systems people use to organize their perceptions of other people.

aspects of basic human endowment as energy level, reactivity, visual and auditory thresholds, muscular strength, coordination, and temperament. It also includes acquired sensory and motor skills and problem-solving competence based upon knowledge and practice. Ability concepts focus our attention upon the instrumental value of some aspect of personality and help us make sense of performance differences among individuals. Measures of such general abilities as intelligence and verbal aptitude correlate well with performance over a wide range of tasks. Fortunately, certain well-defined sensory-motor skills are reliably associated with successful performances of such special tasks as taking-off and landing jet aircraft.

One of the problems with ability constructs, however, is that their explanatory power is often overestimated. The fact that they account for some of the variability in performances has led managers to ascribe complete causation to them, to the neglect of other predispositional concepts and situational factors. Managers sometimes infer that there is a difference in ability between two operators, even though their observation of performance has been extremely limited and they have not explored a multiplicity of other causal variables. The explanatory value of their inference of ability differences is allowed to go untested. The tendency to use ability constructs preemptively is particularly troublesome when the range of general or relevant special abilities in a group is relatively narrow, as it is in a graduate school classroom, in a group of candidates for top-management positions in a company, in a collection of experienced machinists, or in almost any other group of preselected peers. In instances where simple and convenient ability constructs fail to discriminate, we find we need a more complete model of individual differences to understand the behavior we observe.

Both the scientific and popular literature abound with candidates for enriching our repertory of constructs for understanding people. Concepts of instinct, habit, drive, motive, need, goal, value, cognitive system, self-concept, ego-defense, interest, and many more have been widely used. But understanding people does not proceed by word magic. We don't by naming something comprehend it. What we need are some rules for selecting constructs and for testing their utility. The following criteria should help:

1. Select concepts which have clear and consistent rules for connecting concrete observations with abstract labels. Be certain that there are standard ways by which you or others could reliably discriminate be-

tween people who do or do not possess a particular charatceristic.

2. Choose concepts that encompass the maximum number of observed facts.
3. Keep your selection of concepts simple. Invoke only as many concepts as are necessary to make sense of your observations.[2]
4. Test your selection for its predictive power. To what degree do your concepts permit an understanding which helps you predict future behavior?

Neither these criteria nor candidates to test against them are new. Formal research on personality and performance gives us many conceptual building blocks that both meet the criteria and have some relevance to the kinds of behavioral observations administrators and students of administration have to sort out.

Cognitive Systems as Predispositions

The capacity for the acquisition of a symbolic language is at once unique to man and universal among men. Scientists are not the only ones who use concepts, classification schemes, and theories. While our commonsense "theories" and categories may be implicit and primitive, their possession and use is essential. Human behavior is not determined simply by the stimuli to which man is exposed in his immediate environment. Behavior is also a function of the individual ways in which men selectively perceive aspects of their environment, organize their perceptions into meaningful units, and assign value to these meanings on the basis of past experience.

Cognitive systems have both a structure and a method of operation. Structurally, there are single cognitive elements, concepts, cognitive systems, and expectations. Cognitive elements include perceptions, beliefs, ideas, and evaluations, i.e., any simple unit of information. A concept is a rule for classifying cognitive elements into categories. For example, a concept of size provides us with rules we can use to sort objects into slots labeled small and large;[3] the concept of chair involves definite rules by which we distinguish between chairs and non-

---

[2]Criteria 2 and 3, combined, approximate a statement of the traditional law of parsimony, that economical explanations should be favored over more complicated interpretations if they account for the available facts equally well.

[3]A person may have several special concepts of size, depending upon the class of objects being observed. Also, some category sytsems are not discrete at all but consist of continuous dimensions. More sophisticated concepts are often stated in quantitative scales rather than in terms of nominal (present or absent) or ordinal (more or less) discriminations. Person concepts in common use, however, are ordinarily not highly sophisticated.

chairs; a concept of kindness implies classification rules for the discrimination of those classes of behavior which are viewed by the person possessing that concept as kind. Individuals quite likely differ in the types of behavior they classify into kind and unkind categories and, to the degree that they do so, they possess different concepts of kindness. Cognitive systems are the integrated conceptual and propositional schemes which are employed by people to organize their experience of the world. Such schemes represent all of the concepts and category systems and their interrelations, which a person uses to process information. Expectations are hypotheses about the nature of the world and of future events derived from the concepts one uses to organize experience and from the frequencies of occurrence experienced in the past. They may also be described as the subjective probabilities which we assign to particular future events.

Functionally, a cognitive scheme operates as a selective screening system through which parts of the total environment are brought to awareness, categorized, and assigned meaning. The system mediates the person's transactions with the "real" world. Adaptive behavior is facilitated when our constructions of reality are representative enough of objective probabilities to permit us to anticipate the consequences of one course of action or another. When a person has the capacity to revise his categories in order to accommodate new experience, the long-range effectiveness of his functioning is facilitated.

Cognitive schemes are referred to by general semanticists as personal maps of the world whose adequacy can be tested by how well "maps" fit "territories." But the utility of a map is not only that it can reflect reality and guide its owner's behavior toward desired ends. It can also represent the world in such a way as to minimize the owner's anxiety and uncertainty about where he is in the world.

One general characteristic of cognitive systems has been described by the theory of cognitive dissonance developed by Festinger[4] and his associates. Through a number of clever experiments, they have demonstrated that when incompatible or dissonant cognitive elements are in a person's awareness, a tension arises which prompts activity toward reducing or eliminating the dissonance. Festinger's statement of the basic propositions of this theory is as follows:

1. The existence of dissonance, being psychologically uncomfortable,

---

[4]L. Festinger, *A Theory of Cognitive Dissonance* (rev. ed.; Evanston, Ill.: Row Peterson, Revised Editions, 1965).

will motivate the person to try to reduce the dissonance and achieve consonance.

2. When dissonance is present, in addition to trying to reduce it, the person will actively avoid situations and information which would likely increase the dissonance.[5]

Festinger argues with some evidential support that dissonance reduction is a general motivating factor. Dissonance may be reduced by behavior changes, altering ways of thinking, and by selective exposure to new information. To illustrate the theory, let's assume that a manager has just made a decision in favor of one of two alternate courses of action. Following the decision, his tendency will be to seek evidence which confirms the correctness of his choice. If the results are negative, a dissonance is created between his idea of himself as a competent manager who makes correct decisions and his awareness of having made an incorrect decision. He can reduce his feeling of dissonance in a variety of ways: by discounting the validity of the negative evidence; by asserting that the apparently unfortunate decision was coerced by his superior; by finding intervening factors which he could not have anticipated, but which adversely influenced the outcome; or by retracting and revising his decision. While the latter alternative may be most adaptive for task accomplishment, it may be resisted if it seems to require a revision of the manager's conception of himself as competent.

Because dissonance theory says that people will tend to minimize dissonance among elements of their self-concepts as well as between their self-concepts and their cognitions of their environment, the resolution of dissonance involves finding the best fit among the most central and valued parts of one's view of self and of the world. If the manager in the above example possesses a concept of himself as having basically a good competence batting average, then he can maintain self-esteem and still acknowledge a mistake. If he sees himself as absolutely competent, however, the only way for him to preserve his self-image is to discount the validity of the negative evidence.

While dissonance theory provides a model of how cognitive systems function, it is not very illuminating about individual differences. Harvey, Hunt, and Schroder[6] do provide a basis for discriminating among people with respect to the nature of their cognitive systems, which we

[5] *Ibid.*, p. 3.

[6] O. J. Harvey, D. E. Hunt, and H. M. Schroder, *Conceptual Systems and personality Organization* (New York: John Wiley & Sons, Inc., 1961).

shall describe briefly. These authors array concepts along a concrete-abstract dimension. Those they label concrete are seen as simple, closely related to the stimulus, and absolute. Abstract concepts tend to be more complicated, less bound to the stimulus, and more relative. If concepts are seen as programs for ordering and interpreting sensory experience, concrete concepts are rigid and limited by the input, while abstact concepts permit higher order discriminations and integrative combinations.

Harvey *et al.* suggest that total cognitive schemes may be seen as arrayed along this concrete-abstract dimension also, so that different people may be characterized as being at different positions along a concrete-abstract continuum in cognitive style. This dimension is not to be confused with a general intelligence scale. Rather, it describes tendencies toward abstract or concrete ways of thinking by which people of equal intelligence, as it is conventionally measured, may be discriminated. In general terms, the extremes of the continuum are defined as follows: People with concrete cognitive schemes are unable to take an "as if" attitude, tend to confuse wishes with reality, tend toward absolutism and categorical thinking, tend to be rule oriented and predisposed toward ritualism. The opposite end of the scale is marked by the ability to consciously and willfully take a mental position, to differentiate between outer and inner worlds, to plan ahead, and to shift mentally from one aspect of the situation to another with ease.

Four stages of progressive cognitive development are postulated in this model. Explicit in this conception of stages is the notion that persons not only develop through identifiable plateaus but that their development may be temporarily or permanently arrested at any particular stage of conceptual development by adverse external factors. While space does not permit us to provide more elaborate description of the Harvey, Hunt, and Schroder theory, we present their four stages below as an example of a useful way of sorting out individual differences in cognitive systems:[7]

Stage 1 *Unilateral Dependence*
Acceptance of external control, moral absolutism, preoccupation with authority, lack of differentiation between rules and their purposes, sensitivity to limits imposed externally.

Stage 2 *Negative Independence*
Rebellion toward external constraints, undifferentiated rejec-

[7] *Ibid,* Chapter 4.

tion of rules and authority, resistance, development of internal control, self-assertion.

Stage 3 *Conditional Dependence and Mutuality*
Taking into account other's intentions and wishes, objectification of the social environment, tolerance of ambiguity, experimenting with alternative views of self, others, and events, cooperation and competition as alternatives to submission, dominance, or automatic opposition, provisional connectedness with people.

Stage 4 *Interdependence*
Mutuality and autonomy integrated with one another, informational and objective exchanges with environment, experience intrinsic rewards from work rather than dependent upon rewards from external sources, abstract standards developed through the exploration of alternative solutions against a variety of criteria, strong views held without distorting incoming information, predominantly reality-oriented behavior.

This scheme provides a way of discriminating between cognitive systems in a general way. There are, however, a number of other respects in which the cognitive systems people employ may vary. To begin with, *the category specifications may differ.* To the proper Bostonian matron who, Cleveland Amory reports, described her route to California as "via Dedham," the "West" may include everything beyond the Hudson River. The Cleveland or Cheyenne resident's category specifications for the "West" would be different. A second kind of difference may be in the *degree of differentiation* within a given experiential realm. The four-year-old tends to label as "red" quite a broad band of the color spectrum, while the adult decorator makes a great many discriminations within the same wavelength limits, and assigns different names to each. People also differ with respect to the *relative accessibility* of one set of categories as opposed to another. This difference may be illustrated by describing differences among observers who view a new building upon its formal opening. One person may respond to the aesthetic merits of its form, another to its structural stability, and yet another to its appropriateness in relation to intended function. Each of them might have reacted to the building in the terms of the other, but for each, one set of categories—aesthetic, structural or functional—was more "ready" than others.

Similarly, upon meeting a person for the first time, one person may note how friendly and warm he seems, another may attend to his intelligence and competence, and a third may comment on his relative standing in the social hierarchy, because for each a particular set of categories was "cocked" and more accessible than alternatives. While each of us uses a variety of categories, some tend to be more frequently employed than others. One person can, therefore, be distinguished from another in terms of the differential ordering of his categories with respect to accessibility. Other differences in cognitive systems have to do with their degree of internal integration versus compartmentalization, of rigidity versus susceptibility to change, and the amount of complexity in the relationships among categories. All of these differences constitute relatively enduring predispositions toward certain ways of experiencing and behaving toward the world.

Differences between people in cognitive organization can have direct effects upon performance in the work setting. Certain job specialties require unique conceptual tools and cognitive styles. For example, the manufacturing manager must make a variety of meaningful discriminations among various methods, materials, and product specifications. Whether the person in that role possesses appropriate conceptual tools or not determines both his capacity to comprehend his operations and his success in sending and receiving intelligible technical communications. But equally as important are other aspects of his conceptual apparatus which influence how well he may communicate with subordinates, other department managers, his family, or members of the board. For instance, a manager characterized as being at Harvey *et al.'s* stage 3 or 4 in his cognitive development is able to be significantly more effective interpersonally than is a manager at stage 1 or 2. Similarly a person with a wide repertory of interpersonal constructs will tend to be more effective than one with a limited range of concepts, because he will be able to act on more adequate information about the intentions, views, and activities of others. Successful job performance for the administrator or coordinator depends upon both technical and interpersonal competence, and interpersonal competence requires an ability to process information from other people so as to keep communication channels with them open.

Enduring Motives as Predispositions

The child's first experience with objects, and later with their symbols, are invested with emotion. Objects and events are not merely experienced and classified with cool intellectual detachment; they are responded to as pleasurable or painful. The most primitive discriminations—and those which dominate infancy—are those along the pleasure-pain dimension. The associations of objects and activities with intense feelings are the first kinds of associations made by the child. It is a fact that some of these linkages with pleasure or pain are established early and under conditions that make them resistant to extinction. This fact requires us to give them important recognition as predispositional factors. Recent research findings[8] indicate that these intense affective associations are the basis of specialized motives which may be described as *tendencies to strive* for particular types of goals. Goal orientations of this kind which have been experimentally identified include the *need for achievement,* the motive to compete successfully with an objective standard of excellence; the *need for affiliation,* the motive to establish positive affective relationships with other people; and the *need for power,* the motive to influence others, to exercise control over others, to be in a position of authority.

The strength of these learned needs may vary greatly from one person to another. A particular type of need may be either irrelevant for a person or of moderate to high strength as a factor shaping his response to the world. Furthermore, the needs for achievement, affiliation, and power have been found to be independently distributed in the general population. That is, if a person has a high need for achievement, it is equally probable that he has a high or low need for affiliation or power. An individual may have high levels of need on all three dimensions, low levels on all three, or any number of other possible combinations of strength of need.

The ways in which particular motives develop may be illustrated by describing the processes by which the need for achievement is shaped by early experience. Persons with a strong need for achievement tend to have childhood histories of early and positive independence training, of being rewarded for efforts toward self-reliant mastery of their environment by success and approval. For these people, the association of pleasure with early efforts to achieve and with successful results is

---

[8]John W. Atkinson (ed.), *Motives in Fantasy, Action, and Society* (Princeton, N.J.: D. Van Nostrand Co., Inc., 1958). See especially Atkinson's "Towards Experimental Analysis of Human Motivation in Terms of Motives, Expectancies, and Incentives, pp. 228–305." See also David C. McClelland, *The Achievement Motive* (New York: Appleton-Century-Crofts, 1955).

so intensive and enduring that in situations in later life which present an opportunity to test mastery, the anticipation of the same feelings of gratification experienced in childhood direct the person's efforts toward the achievement goal. Though the process is not necessarily conscious, the adult who anticipates pleasure from achievement directs his strivings toward this attainment.

While the achievement motive provides a model which has been made explicit by experimentation, it is only one of a theoretically infinite number and variety of predispositions to behave which may develop through emotionally laden childhood associations. Differences may be observed between people not only in the strength of a particular kind of motive but also in the variety of motives which influence their behavior. Particular classifications and names for motives are only convenient constructs used by researchers to bring order to their observations.

Values as Predispositions

Values are frames of reference people use to assess the goodness of an object. As such, they constitute a third class of predisposing factors. They differ from motives in that they are internalized, personal versions of social standards about what should be so, rather than primitive, often unconscious tendencies to act. A second way to distinguish values from motives is by their general application. A man's values tend to be applied to others as well as to himself, while his motives are only relevant personally. For example, if one values thrift, he will usually apply thrift as a standard of judgment to the behavior of others as well as to himself. Conversely, a thrift motive will influence only the behavior of the person for whom it is an internal goal. Where a motive and value are congruent, the motive may be important in producing behavior consistent with one's explicit standards, but one's values and motives do not always fit together neatly.

This lack of fit helps to account for the fact that values and behavior do not always match well. Where one's values are out of phase with other types of predispositions, it is not surprising that expressed behavior may deviate from one's own standards. Consciousness does not exercise complete dominion over unconscious forces. This matter is further complicated by the fact that an individual's value system may contain disparate elements. Although values may be hierarchically ordered, there is often enough lack of clarity about the relative priority of certain values so that in some situations, all of the available courses of action must violate some value positions, while conforming to others. According to Scott,[9] "Perhaps the most significant function of moral values for human behavior is the capacity they lend to the individual to sustain his efforts in the face of adversity." Values may enable a person temporarily to withstand immediate situational pressures because they represent accumulated lessons from the past or important ties with reference groups. In situations in which a great deal of uncertainty exists concerning an appropriate course of action, the person can resort to his values as an economical way of reaching a decision.

Values are acquired and modified by the experience of being rewarded and punished for approved or forbidden acts, by observing the experience of others in similar circumstances, and by both formal and informal instruction. While value systems first emerge in childhood, they are susceptible to change in content throughout adult life. Personal value systems, like other cognitive elements, tend toward both internal consistency and congruence with the explicit norms of the social groupings toward which one is attracted.

The Interaction of Predispositions

So far we have described three principal types of predispositions: cognitive systems, motives, and values. Let us now examine some ways in which they may operate together. Although the strength of a particular motive tends to be stable over a long time span, the readiness to act in a particular way with respect to that motive varies with the situation. If a person has a high need for achievement but his present environment does not present any cues which may lead him to define the situation as one in which there is at least a moderate probability of obtaining achievement gratification, the achievement motive will not be aroused or engaged. *A motive is aroused and becomes operative only when a person's cognitive field includes an expectancy that the performance of some act will lead to the attainment of the goal of that motive.* For example, a person's affiliation motive will only be aroused as an influence upon behavior when other persons are either actually or potentially present. Also, achievement motives will only become operative when the person's view of the situation includes awareness of tasks or problems which create the expectancy of success following striving. Atkin-

[9]William A. Scott, *Values and Organizations* (Skokie, Ill.: Rand McNally & Co., 1965).

son[10] adds a third variable, incentive: "the magnitude of the reward or potential satisfaction anticipated, should the expected consequences occur."[11] Summarizing, the strength of a tendency to act in a particular way at any given point in time is a function of three variables: the stable strength of relevant motives, the strength of the expectancy that the act would bring desired results, and the magnitude of the anticipated incentive.

$$\begin{matrix}\text{Motive} \\ \text{Strength}\end{matrix} \times \begin{matrix}\text{Expectancy of} \\ \text{Goal Attainment}\end{matrix} \times \begin{matrix}\text{Magnitude of} \\ \text{Incentive}\end{matrix} = \begin{matrix}\text{Effective Motivation} \\ \text{to Behave}\end{matrix}$$

To illustrate, two students face an objective examination in a required course in which both have only moderate interest in the subject matter. They are members of a class which is homogeneous with respect to academic aptitude. However, one is high in the need for achievement and the other is low. This situation is one in which the expectancy of successful competition with an objective standard is high. Either man could with effort perform very well on the test. In this instance, however, the man with the higher need for achievement performs significantly better than the one with low need for achievement because the former's achievement motive is aroused by the situation to meet the challenge by strenuous and effective preparation. If, in addition, the preservation of a high grade-point average (valued incentive) were at stake, the resultant motivation could be boosted yet higher. In another situation without need-for-achievement arousal properties, the two men may perform at the same level. For instance, if the relevant issue were a matter of relative influence or political success, the motivational difference between the two men might not obtain, since the achievement dimension on which they differ is not involved.

Individual patterns of motivation unconsciously influence the choices of cognitive categories people employ in perceiving and thinking about other persons. Those with high needs for affiliation but low needs for achievement, for example, will tend to use categories which fit this motivational profile: friendly-unfriendly, warm-cold, close-distant. Persons with moderately high needs for power, however, will tend to use power-related categories, such as strong-weak, influential-noninfluential, or high-low, much more frequently than persons who are low on the need for power. If the level of motivation of a particular kind is extremely

[10] Atkinson, *op. cit.*, p. 60.

[11] The power of an incentive is a function of the person's value system.

high, the range of categories one may use may become severely restricted. Under this condition, the perception of other persons may easily be distorted and incomplete. The pattern of motives is usually well enough balanced so that the range of categories available is broad and thus the ability to understand others is not impaired.

The ways in which motives interact with properties of work situations can be illustrated from research. Vroom[12] reported that persons with a strong need for independence develop more positive attitudes toward their jobs and greater motivation for effective performance when they participate in making job decisions. For persons with a low need for independence, the opportunity to participate had no appreciable effect upon job attitudes and motivation for effective performance. In this instance, where there was a stable need for independence, it was engaged only when the expectancy of fulfilling independence goals was provided by the opportunity for participation. Where the participation opportunity was not available, needs for independence were not aroused in the interest of effective performance and positive work attitudes.

A second study of the relationships between motivational measures and work orientations indicates the way in which predispositions (motives, in this case) tend to fit with the types of roles being performed in an organization. When members of a management group were asked to select the idea men and social leaders among them, Moment and Zaleznik[13] found a tendency for those described by their colleagues as idea men in an organization to have a higher average need for achievement than both those who were seen as social specialists and those who were underchosen on both task and social dimensions. High need for achievement subjects appear to select achievement-relevant activities and are perceived by coworkers as playing these roles.

Moment and Zaleznik also report data bearing upon the relationship between need for achievement and the kinds of general functional roles occupied by managers. Among a population of 78 high-level executives, 75 percent of those in marketing were above the median on need for achievement, while the comparable value was 41 percent for those in control and finance, and 36 percent for those in production and engineering. The characteristics of the marketing function provide a greater mean expectancy of achievement[14] than other functional areas.

---

[12]Victor Vroom, *Work and Motivation* (New York: John Wiley & Sons, Inc., 1964).

[13]D. Moment and A. Zaleznik, *Role Development and Interpersonal Competence* Boston: Harvard Graduate School of Business Administration, Division of Research, 1963.

[14]Situations attractive to persons with high need for achievement are characterized by opportunities for behavioral control of outcomes (not chance), moderate risk taking, and immediate knowledge of results.

High-need-achievement men seem to gravitate toward jobs in which the expectancy of achievement gratification and magnitude of incentives are high.

These brief references illustrate two ways in which individual motives are expressed in work behavior. First, in interaction with expectancies and incentives, they determine the amount of effective motivation for job performance. Second, high motive strength leads one to make career and job choices which will maximize the probability of attaining the motive-relevant goal.

The implications of this motivational model for the administrator are several:

1. He must seek to recognize the variety of needs or motives among those with whom he works, and acknowledge that, given their historical roots, they cannot be easily altered by volition or external edict.
2. Given a particular collection of people at any point in time, the principal way for a manager to facilitate the motivation for productive effort among organizational members is to create conditions which optimize the expectancy of goal attainment and to make the incentives which are available in the work situation visible to members.
3. In selecting new members, the administrator should take motivational variables into consideration. Moreover, both the general organizational climate and the motivationally relevant properties of particular jobs should be considered in formulating the particular combination of motives to be selected in each instance.
4. Administrative decisions can be improved when accurate information about the motivational properties of personnel, organization, and technology are taken into account. Managers need to acquire skill in assessing the motivational content of both individual and group behavior and the climate and structure of the organization.

The Person as a Set of Predispositions

In the preceding sections of this chapter, we have presented several types of predispositional constructs separately, describing the ways in which cognitive systems, motives, and values may influence individual behavior. We have indicated also how each of these classes of variables helps us to understand important differences among people. Although we have discussed one way in which motives, cognitions (i.e., expectations), and values interact to determine effective motivation for an act in a particular situation, our analytic approach has largely neglected the person as a unitary whole, with his own unique history and consciousness of self. Indeed, a self-identity, the way in which one defines and feels about oneself, is a pervasive and potent predispositional factor.

Though each infant may be unique in some respects, a self-identity is not given at birth. It develops through time as one experiences his bodily sensations, his personal impact on his environment, and the reactions of others to him. A variety of constitutional, cultural, role, and situational factors interact to give shape to the emerging self. As the child becomes aware of parts of his world, he differentiates himself from the world around him and acquires a rudimentary identity.

One set of determinants of the shape the self will take are hereditarily transmitted constitutional factors such as sex, rate of growth, sensory reactivity, and energy level. They are important not only in setting capacities and limits but also as basic terms in the definition of self. The way a person views himself and the feelings one has about self may be profoundly influenced by the ways in which significant others react to one's relative size, sex, strength, color, general attractiveness, and physical vitality. A clear sense of one's basic physical and mental endowment is a foundation for identity.

In its most general form, a cultural heritage provides the individual with an identification as a member of a continuing group with shared ways of doing things, shared assumptions about the world, and shared values. The individual may reject some aspect of this inheritance, but the culture remains a framework for his activities and his individual development. Even the opportunities for deviation are provided as part of the package. Acquiring a culture and digesting it in some individual form are universal developmental tasks. Identity is shaped as one acquires culturally defined skills, attitudes, and behavior patterns and as one receives messages of approval or disapproval for particular acts. A sense of being different, safely conforming, superior, inferior, valued, or unimportant in specific respects is communicated continuously to the developing person, and all these impressions accumulate to modify, elaborate, or clarify identity.

The number and kind of roles one plays (for example, son, father, student, teacher), and the length of experience and nature of performance in these roles, constitutes a third set of determinants of a self-concept. In one respect, each role becomes a partial identity in which all of the behavior patterns, values, feelings, and views of self associated with that role are organized. The expectations and reactions of other people are often communicated to the person in connection with particular role performances, thus shaping the view of self in a particular role. While a developing identity is more than a composite of various partial identities associated with work, family, and other roles, a person's unique role experience has an important impact upon identity.

Finally, there is a variety of almost accidental events and circumstances which influence conceptions of self. Kluckhohn and Murray[15] label as situational determinants such things as the premature death of a father, a family move from one part of the country to another, the fact of being the first or last born. These are the unique, largely unprogrammed happenings which can expose the changing self to new expectations, relationships, and reactions, thus altering the course of development.

Although the growth of self-identity is a highly individualized process, subject to sudden shifts, spurts, and regressions, it is possible to generalize about the direction of growth when learning is normal, unblocked, and continuous. White[16] has described four major developmental trends:

1. *The stabilizing of ego identity*—increasing independence from external evaluations and an increasing capacity to exert influence outward with the more complete realization of one's potential.
2. *The freeing of personal relationships*—increasing freedom from anxiety and defense so that one's behavior may be increasingly appropriate in relation to immediate realities.
3. *The deepening of interests*—increasing capacity to invest oneself in the exploration and mastery of particular objects in the environment.
4. *The humanizing of values*—increasing appreciation of the social purpose of standards rather than accepting them as absolutes, also growth toward making values more personally meaningful and integrated with an articulated life view.

As one approaches adult life, what he sees himself to be and what he aspires to be constitute images which he strives to clarify and confirm.

The Person in the Work Setting

To understand the operation of predispositions, we need to know about the characteristics of work settings which are motivationally important. According to the Atkinson formula, the properties of the situa-

[15]Clyde Kluckhohn and Henry A. Murray, *Personality in Nature, Society, and Culture* (New York: Alfred A. Knopf, Inc., 1955), chap. ii.

[16]Robert White, "Motivataion Reconsidered: The Concept of Competence," *Psychological Review*, Vol. LXVI (1959), pp. 297–333.

tion as well as the motives of the person must be known in order to anticipate his behavior. Only those motives and preferences which are activated by the person's perception of the situation can directly influence behavior.

Aspects of the work situation which have either motive arousal properties or incentive value include the following:[17]

Motivationally Relevant Properties of Work Settings	*Sociotechnical System Referent*
1. They provide financial remuneration	Formal organization
2. They require the expenditure of energy	Technology
3. They involve the production of goods and services	Technology
4. They permit or require social interaction	Social system, formal organization, and technology
5. They affect the social status of the worker	Formal organization and social system

This list of possibly salient aspects of job situations makes the range of work-relevant motives more explicit.

Money

It is possible to speak of the importance of monetary rewards as means to satisfaction of basic physiological needs, but their functions are likely to be more complicated. Vroom points out that "the goods and services that are purchased with money go far beyond insuring survival. They serve, among other things, as an indicator of social status of the purchaser."[18] Remuneration may also have the function of confirming the self-worth of the person or serving as an achievement symbol. The need of money may not be an essential condition for work, however. From 60 to 90 percent of the subjects in a national survey reported they would keep on working if they inherited enough money to make earning unnecessary. The younger and better trained the respondents, the higher the proportion of them who responded they would continue working. The phenomena of dollar-a-year men and winners of British football pools who continue on their jobs also make it clear that money is not the only important incentive.

---

[17] Vroom, *op. cit.*

[18] *Ibid.*, p. 30.

Energy Expenditure

The principle of least effort is not clearly supported as an important factor in human motivation. There is considerable evidence to indicate that the expenditure of effort can be satisfying. The idea of the "Protestant ethic" includes the notion that some people find moral justification in hard work. Beyond this, work may be intrinsically rewarding. It may provide variety, an "optimal" level of sensory stimulation, the opportunity for demonstration of mastery, or the opportunity to innovate solutions to complex problems. Though the amount of satisfaction from work may be a function of the degree of objective success, some evidence also indicates that results from the investment of effort are more highly valued than those not requiring much energy. It is clear that work and satisfaction are not in themselves always in conflict.

Products

Some satisfaction may derive from the value assigned by the culture to the goods or services produced. If a worker views the product as useful and important or perceives that others evaluate the product favorably, he will tend to be positively motivated in its production. What Clark[19] describes as contribution opportunity increases as a worker sees his efforts contributing to the completion of the end product. Another form of product identification is illustrated by the worker who experiences the entire production cycle for a given product and enjoys satisfaction from the realization of a concrete and whole result from his individual efforts.

White[20] proposes that manipulation and mastery of the environment is innately satisfying to humans. In the modern work world, work roles are highly varied in their opportunities for meaningful impact on the environment. Some jobs provide only fragmentary tasks with no apparent link to a final product or visible end result. Other jobs provide opportunities for the worker to experience a sense of mastery and achievement. Satisfactions from task and product identification may not only reinforce quality performance but may have consequences for individual health and development beyond the workplace.

---

[19]James V. Clark, "Motivation in Work Groups: A Tentative View," in Paul R. Lawrence and John A. Seiler, *Organizational Behavior and Administration: Cases, Concepts, and Research Findings* (rev. ed.; Homewood, Ill.: Richard D. Irwin, Inc., and Dorsey Press, 1965).

[20]Robert White, *Lives in Progress* (New York: Holt, Rinehart & Winston, Inc., 1952).

Social Interaction

The importance of the social aspects of work roles has been documented by many survey and clinical studies. Individual differences are so important in this realm, that although some form of social interaction may be an important aspect of all work roles, the satisfactions are highly particular. One person may be attracted to a group because of his chance to influence other members of the group, another particularly enjoys acceptance and group inclusion, while a third may dependently want the group to be responsible for him, to provide limits and models for his behavior. Many are the uses of groups. While we should be cautious about gratuitously imputing peoples' motives, we should be aware that social interaction provides a broad range of opportunities for gratification.

Almost every work role involves membership in one or more groups. It is safe to assume that even where social satisfactions are not primary, they are generally significant. The work performance of even the intended isolate may be influenced by social factors. Social interaction provides a basis for testing reality, a normative framework for the development and alteration of personal values, and an acceptance and personal feedback important in the clarification and realization of identity. In jobs low in skill content, intrinsic attractiveness, or contribution opportunity, social factors may be central in maintaining performance and satisfaction.

Social Status

Work roles have status characteristics associated with both the workplace (internal status) and the larger community (external status). Income, assigned authority, age, seniority, skill, ethnic fit, and role in the informal system may all be factors in the determination of internal status and thus are status indicators. Workers who enjoy high and clearly defined status may find this an appealing aspect of their work role and thus a significant factor in their performance and satisfaction. When status indicators are inconsistent, however, ambiguities are created which diminish internal status as an incentive. The resultant social disorganization may, in fact, have negative motivational properties.

External status, though based on some of the same indicators as internal status, i.e., education, income, residence, family, and occupation, tends to have less direct impact upon motivation in the work place. Its influence is usually modulated through the internal status system. The relevance of external status factors to job satisfaction and performance is likely to be a direct function of the degree of fit between the social structures of the company and the community. Those at the extremes of the external status hierarchy, professionals and top managers, and those who are performing menial tasks, are most likely to be sensitive to the external status aspects of their positions.

Summary

In our efforts to understand task performance, job satisfaction, and job and career choices we need to take into account the motives, ways of thinking, and abilities of particular persons, the properties of particular work roles, and the relation between the characteristics of the person and the work role. The analysis of the work role must include its incentive and motive arousal properties as well as technical job content and skill demands. Behavior is a function of both the "built-in" preferences or predispositions of the person and the situational factors which engage or arouse behavioral tendencies toward overt expression.

Three Cases of the Influence of Human Inputs

In order to test out how human inputs or predispositions interact with work situations to produce behavior, three simple cases of organizational situations follow. Although none of them contains elaborate data concerning the sources of predispositions of characters in the case, each provides an opportunity to analyze the impact of those predispositions on behavior.

The cases have been organized in such a way that the reader may predict from his analysis of inputs what behavior would result, then check his predictions against what actually took place. Some of the inputs are described in Part 1 of the case. Then questions on how those inputs would be likely to influence behavior are listed. The actual behavior in Part 2 of the case may be compared with the reader's answers to these questions. This type of analytical exercise does not suggest that predictive perfection is a practical or even possible goal. It does suggest that the probability of error can be reduced somewhat by careful analysis of the interrelation of forces bearing upon the situation. Consequently, once the exercise has been completed, it is suggested that the readers reflect not only on how accurate his predictions were but also on what factors in the situation made prediction difficult.

The cases included here vary on a number of dimensions, including complexity and inclusiveness. One case, the last, is in five rather than two parts, since it involves changes in the situation whose effects the reader is asked to predict. Each of the cases has potential utility not only as an analytic exercise but also as an example of how human inputs influence behavior. The reader is invited to reflect on these cases to see how various ideas expressed in this chapter look in real life.

THE BRADDOCK COMPANY

Part 1

The Braddock Company was a large manufacturer of heat-generating equipment. Most of its products were conventional. In 1955, however, a nuclear division was inaugurated to do research and development in advance of what company management believed to be the inevitable swing toward atomic power estimated to be a decade away.

The nuclear division was composed almost entirely of highly specialized scientists with established reputations in their various fields. Almost all of them held doctorates. They were considered to be of extremely high occupational status among physical scientists working in industry. They were dedicated to the unalloyed pursuit of knowledge and had little patience with those who were not so dedicated. The division was physically separated from the rest of the company and appeared to be more like an academic institution than part of an industrial firm.

At the stage of technological development in the atomic energy field at the time of this case, there were few tangible products of the division's work. Almost all of its output was in the form of written reports addressed to the government (which financially supported most of the division's work), to a few potential customers, and to Braddock management. Because of the uneven technical sophistication of the readers of these reports, and in order to relieve scientific personnel from painstaking report preparation for which many of them were ill-suited, the division established a Technical Report Section.

The Technical Report Section's task was to rewrite, edit, illustrate, and publish the various draft documents prepared by the scientists. To carry on this task, it was necessary for some members of the section to work closely with the author-scientists to ensure that technical accuracy was not sacrificed to readability. The scientist-author was explicitly stipulated to be the final judge of a report's acceptability.

The work load of the section tended to vary widely, since report completion was based upon contractual commitments and, commonly, several reports were simultaneously required from different scientists working on related projects. Consequently, the Technical Report Section would often work for several weeks at overcapacity, then spend several weeks with little to do.

The section was divided among several specialties. The section supervisor scheduled incoming reports, assigned them to editors, and took care of administrative functions for the entire group. The editors edited or rewrote the reports. When the editor's work had been completed to the author's satisfaction, the report was turned over to a coordinator, who assigned it to typists and, if illustrations were required, to the illustrator. The coordinator served as a focus for a great deal of work interaction among editors, typists, and illustrator during final stages of a report's processing.

The members of the Technical Report Section were somewhat younger than the scientists. They were all liberal arts college graduates with a high interest in literature and philosophy. They displayed little interest in either commercial or technical affairs, though they all enjoyed the challenge of bringing clarity and style into a written composition, regardless of its particular content.

PREDICTIONS—Part 1

a) The work output of the Technical Report Section will usually (exceed management's expectations) (meet management's expectations) (fall behind management's expectations).

b) The quality of the work of the Technical Report Section will usually be of (high) (medium) (sometimes high, sometimes low) (low) quality.

c) The relationships among members of the Technical Report Section will be (close knit) (neutral) (hostile).

d) The relationships between members of the Technical Report Section and scientific personnel will be (close knit) (mixed—some friendly, some not) (neutral) (hostile).

e) The level of individual (work) (social) satisfaction among members of the Technical Report Section will be (high) (medium) (low).

THE BRADDOCK COMPANY

Part 2

A few scientist-authors openly sought the help of the Technical Report Group and showed willingness to accede to changes in grammar, style, and organization. In such cases, the editors made every effort to produce an outstandingly readable, accurate report. There was some inconclusive evidence that these reports received more favorable attention from readers.

Most authors, however, considered the Technical Report Section an obstacle in the pursuit of knowledge. Some were adamant that no changes be made beyond the addition or deletion of commas. Many, more simply, took no interest in the section's work, impatiently and cursorily examining its efforts and denying any change which could not be construed as purely grammatical. In such cases, the section corrected only the most glaring errors, paid no attention to readability or continuity, and gave minimum effort to illustration or reproduction format.

The members of the section discovered that not only did contractual arrangements cause work-load peaks but most authors failed to allow any time for editorial work. Peak loads were, thus, expediently managed by the section by doing a minimum of editorial work on late reports.

There was little social intermingling of scientists and report-writing personnel, on the job or off. Section members ate together and discussed Camus or Kafka, separating themselves both physically and emotionally from the scientists.

The report section showed interest in its work only on those few occasions when an author sought its help. The section dutifully met schedules, even when overtime was required, but showed no hesitancy to pursue individual literary interests when work was slack. The section's members seldom discussed their work with each other informally. A common point of view was: "What difference does it make whether a report is well written or not; most of our authors, and the readers, for that matter, wouldn't know good writing if they saw it. I'll bet those scientists haven't read a good book since freshman English. Why doesn't the company save its money and the occasional hard feelings engendered by our trying to write decent reports? They can easily slide by with poorly written ones."

POSTPREDICTION ANALYSIS

Refer to your predictions at the end of Part 1. How closely do they match the information above? Do inaccuracies in your predictions reflect inadequate analysis? If so, explain the analytical failure. If not, what additional information would you have needed in Part 1 to improve your predictive accuracy and how would you have used that information?

REINER COMPANY, INCORPORATED

Part 1

Reiner Company, Inc., a nationally known store situated in New York City, specialized in hardware, appliances, and gadgets for the home. On the second floor of the store, gadgets and high-cost cooking utensils were sold. Five experienced clerks worked here, two men and three women, all of whom had been at Reiner at least five years. The clerks were paid a base salary plus a 2 percent commission on net sales. Because of the great variety of items sold on the floor, the clerks often sought one another's help concerning the placement or future availability of goods. Mrs. Esposito, a woman who had been with the store 15 years and who had become the floor's most successful clerk, had the best overall knowledge of existing inventory. The clerks most often referred their questions to her.

Paul Richards, a college student, was hired as a salesclerk for the summer of 1960 to alleviate the service shortage caused by vacationing employees. Like all Reiner's temporary employees, he earned a straight salary. After a brief training period, he came to the second floor where he was assigned a "station" at the main counter. Like all the salesclerks, he kept his sales book and pencils at the "station," but his "area" of sales included the entire floor. At the request of the personnel manager, Mrs. Esposito took charge of Richards, scheduling his work shifts and teaching him selling techniques and inventory location.

From the start, the salesclerks freely offered Richards suggestions and assisted him with his sales. For the most part, feeling uncertain, he did not approach a customer until after all the other clerks were busy. Whenever he had difficulty in filling a customer's request, he would seek the help of one of the experienced clerks, who often would complete the sale for him. In these cases, the other clerk took credit for the sale on his own tally.

As the summer progressed, Richards became more confident of himself, developing a real interest in "the art of selling" and in experimenting with various sales techniques. He found he became bored when customers were few and made every effort to spend as much of his time as possible waiting on customers. Often an experienced clerk would tell a customer that he would be "right with her," leaving the customer to wait while another sale was processed. Even when other clerks were not busy, Richards noticed they never approached a "be right with you" customer. In an effort to keep well occupied, Richards would cut the customer's wait short by offering to help her.

PREDICTIONS—Part 1

From what I know of conditions at the Reiner Company, Inc., I would predict that:

a) Relations between Richards and the five other clerks at the end of Part 1 will be (worse than) (better than) (the same as) they were when he first started work on the floor.

b) The other clerks will (continue to give Richards extra help) (treat him as one of the group of experienced clerks) (ignore him) (take some other action in relation to Richards). If you select the last choice, state also what you expect that action to be.

REINER COMPANY, INCORPORATED

Part 2

Shortly after Richards began demonstrating his increased attempts at salesmanship, Mrs. Esposito informed him that the other clerks were finding his methods of selling very annoying. They had explained to Mrs. Esposito that they saw no need for the aggressiveness of his sales technique, particularly his servicing of customers another clerk was to be "right with," in view of the fact that he was not working on commission as the rest of them were.

Richards saw no reason to modify his efforts, since, as he told Mrs. Esposito, he wished to learn as much as he could. Soon the other clerks began to "borrow" the pencils which Richards used to write up his sales. Then his sales book was taken. When these attempts left Richards undaunted, the clerks began to refuse him information about inventory placement and availability. Sometimes, near the end of the day when customers were few, a clerk would obstruct him physically as he was attempting to reach a customer. This restraint became a group effort, as the clerks became openly antagonistic toward him.

POSTPREDICTION ANALYSIS

Refer to your predictions at the end of Part 1. How closely do they match the information above? Do inaccuracies in your predictions reflect inadequate analysis? If so, explain the analytical failure. If not, what additional information would you have needed in Part 1 to improve your predictive accuracy and how would you have used that information?

P. PAPADOPOULOS AND COMPANY

Part 1

Just after the turn of the century, Peter and John Papadopoulos and a third partner founded P. Papadopoulos & Co. in Salonica, Greece, and began to operate a business in the field of automobile engine rebuilding. All three partners brought to the business a high degree of technical skill. Following World War II and the end of the German occupation, the market for engine rebuilding expanded rapidly, while there were few companies bidding for this work.

Engine rebuilding was carried on in one 1,500-square-meter room (Exhibit 1). The room contained several heavy and light lathes, welding equipment, and grinding, boring, and drilling machines. Customers arrived with their automobiles at the side door of the shop, where they were met by one of the senior workers. First, the customer and the worker would discuss what needed to be done. Then the worker would give a price for the labor and parts and would fill in on a shop card the name of the customer, the date the engine was received, and the spare parts and work to be done on the engine. From that point on, it was the worker's responsibility to see the engine through the various stages of repair, to secure the parts from the spare-parts department, and to make sure the delivery promise was kept. He did not perform all the work himself as a rule. Although the senior workers all had had many years' experience with the company and knew how to operate all the machines, often they would exchange particular jobs for the sake of convenience. Furthermore, senior workers supervised junior men who performed minor elements of the work. There were 10 senior and 15 junior workers.

Exhibit 1

P. PAPADOPOULOS AND COMPANY

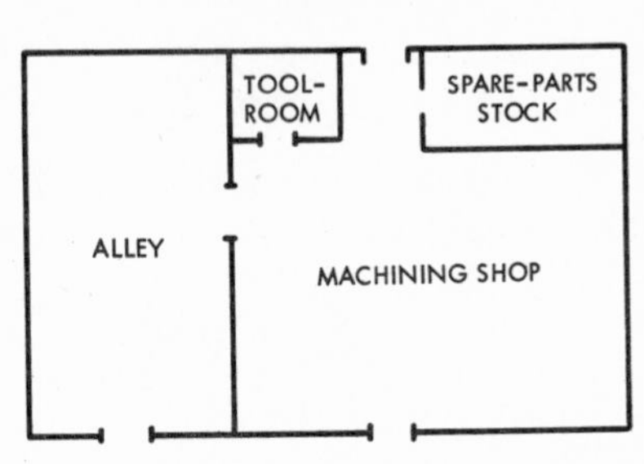

The informality of the system of job allocation placed a great deal of responsibility upon the senior workers. The fact that there was no particular assignment of machines to men meant that a great deal of interaction among the workers and constant agreement about the utilization of machines were necessary.

Mr. John Papadopoulos loosely supervised the senior workers, spending most of his time in his office on the second floor. Senior workers had learned most of their skills from Mr. Papadopoulos as apprentices during the early years of the company's existence. Mr. Papadopoulos took an interest in the personal affairs of the men.

PREDICTIONS—Part 1

From what I know of the procedures followed in the engine rebuilding room, I would predict that:

a) The senior workers would get (much) (some) (little) individual satisfaction from their jobs.

b) The productivity of the workers would be (high) (standard) (below standard).

c) The relationships among the senior workers would be (close knit) (neutral) (hostile).

P. PAPADOPOULOS AND COMPANY

Part 2

P. Papadopoulos and Company did a larger volume of business and was more profitable than any other engine-rebuilding company in Greece. The workers were extremely loyal to Mr. Papadopoulos and were united together on and off the job. Individual initiative was high, yet the men were always ready to assist one another. Senior workers called each other by their first names, whereas the rest of the personnel used the prefix "master" before their names.

POSTPREDICTION ANALYSIS

Refer to your predictions at the end of Part 1. How closely do they match the information above? Do inaccuracies in your predictions reflect inadequate analysis? If so, explain the analytical failure. If not, what additional information would you have needed in Part 1 to improve your predictive accuracy and how would you have used that information?

P. PAPADOPOULOS COMPANY

Part 3

In 1958, management realized that the engine-rebuilding business was passing into the hands of the small shops with low overhead costs, and that the future of large companies in this field was not promising. It was decided to switch to tractor manufacture, which would utilize the machinery and experience of the company. Tractor production began during the summer of 1962.

Exhibit 2

P. PAPADOPOULOS
AND COMPANY

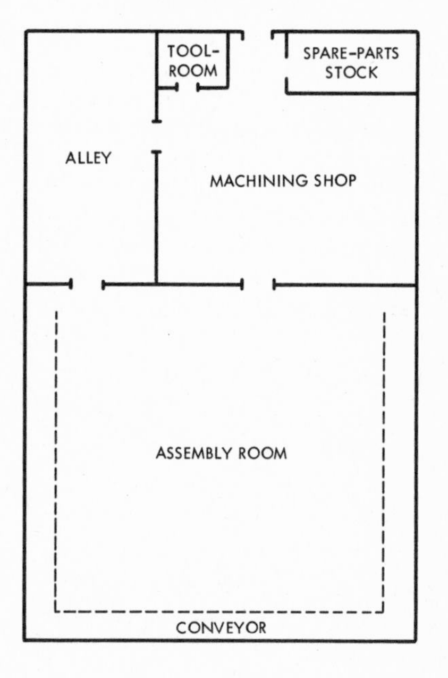

Many changes followed the switch to tractor production. New machinery was placed in the old machinery room (Exhibit 2). Each worker was assigned a specific job and a specific machine with which to work. An assembly line system was put into effect.

A new plant manager was hired. He was a recent graduate of an English engineering school and experienced in the technology of tractor manufacture. He was to manage the whole plant, replacing Mr. John Papadopoulos, who was to undertake other responsibilities.

PREDICTIONS—Part 3

From what I know of the procedures in the company and the changes in Part 2, I would predict that:

a) The workers' job satisfaction will (increase) (remain the same) (decrease).

b) Relations between the senior workers and the new plant manager will be (cordial) (neutral) (strained).

c) The productivity of the workers will be (high) (standard) (low).

P. PAPADOPOULOS AND COMPANY

Part 4

It was not long before a considerable amount of worker dissatisfaction became evident. This was expressed primarily in complaints about the new plant manager. The workers felt that they could do their jobs without "interference from the manager." The complaints increased toward the end of August, 1962, when one of the most skilled and trusted workers threatened to resign unless the new plant manager was removed. There was evidence that many other workers shared the same feeling.

Finally it was decided to fire the plant manager, and Mr. John Papadopoulos resumed management of the plant.

POSTPREDICTION ANALYSIS

Refer to your predictions at the end of Part 3. How closely do they match the information above? Do inaccuracies in your predictions reflect inadequate analysis? If so, explain the analytical failure. If not, what additional information would you have needed in Part 1 to improve your predictive accuracy and how would you have used that information?

PREDICTIONS—Part 4

From what I know of Mr. Papadopoulos, the organization, and the demands of the new technology, I would predict that:

a) The new job organization and production methods will very likely be (scrapped in favor of the earlier informal system) (revised somewhat to better meet the skills and needs of the workers) (maintained essentially as they are).

b) Mr. John Papadopoulos will (supervise the workers fairly closely) (seek the help of the workers in making certain changes but not supervise them very closely) (spend most of his time in the office, leaving supervision to the senior workers).

c) Productivity of the workers will (rise considerably) (remain the same) (drop further).

d) Morale of the workers will (rise considerably) (remain the same) (drop further).

P. PAPADOPOULOS AND COMPANY

Part 5

The change was a success. Mr. Papadopoulos sought the help of the machine shop workers in developing some new parts required by recent changes in the tractor design and in determining the methods of production for these parts. No changes in worker assignment or production methods were made. Worker morale and productivity rose considerably.

POSTPREDICTION ANALYSIS

Refer to your predictions at the end of Part 4. How closely do they match the information above? Do inaccuracies in your predictions reflect inadequate analysis? If so, explain the analytical failure. If not, what additional information would you have needed in Part 1 to improve your predictive accuracy and how would you have used that information?

CHAPTER 4

Behavior Reconsidered

IN CHAPTER 3 we examined in some detail the cognitive and emotional characteristics which people bring with them into organizations. We observed how properties of the organizational situation evoke or fail to evoke individual predispositions, i.e., how interdependent individual and organizational forces are in producing actual behavior. In a sense, Chapter 3 put the lens on the individual and proposed that a great deal of what goes on in organizations can usefully be explained through awareness of how individual development is expressed in current situations.

In this chapter we want to take one step up the ladder of behavioral complexity to the two-person relationship. In fact, the most ubiquitous property of an individual's environment is other individuals. It is the individual's perception of other individuals' demands upon him and responses to him which comprise by far the greatest evocation of the individual's behavior. In Chapter 5 we shall move up the ladder of human complexity one more step to group behavior, but we want to pause at least briefly before doing so to make sure we understand the most basic relationship of all, the interpersonal.

Thinking back to Chapter 2 and to our basic analytical framework, it will be recalled that the focus of our attention was on behavior. While we have to comprehend the inputs and outputs of behavior in order to make sense and understand the significances of behavior, it is behavior which, as managers, we wish to influence. We too easily can lose sight, in our quest for the gross patterns that emerge from the interrelation of inputs and outputs, of the dynamic, concrete confrontation of two individuals. And that confrontation *is* the locus of most behavior. While individuals respond to things and ideas, they seldom do so in isolation from others, and they seldom do so without those things and ideas having a clear association with other individuals.

Another way of underlining the fundamental character of two-person relationships is to take a more careful look at one of our behavior categories, interaction. When we analyzed the Utility Power Company case, we noted that team behavior was an important element in influencing productivity, satisfaction, and development. We talked of a "sense of belonging" and "cohesion" and "teaching-learning relationships" and so on. In every instance, what we were referring to was a pattern of behavior whose composition was particular instances of activity engaged in by an individual in relation to a specific other individual from which arose certain feelings and opinions. When we refer to cohesion, for example, what we mean in terms of behavior is that a series of interpersonal acts occurs in each of which the pairs of people involved behave with each other in such a way that each comes away feeling that he is accepted by the other. One man helps another lift a carton; an executive confides his personal troubles to a fellow executive; an engineer sits down for an hour with a draftsman, and they work out calculus problems together. What we want to do in this chapter is explore some ideas which can help us understand these specific interactions in such a way that we do not lose sight of their concreteness in the midst of our other goals of seeing larger patterns in organizational behavior. While we shall not examine all of the ideas which might be appropriate to this task, we shall discuss one set of ideas which will stand as a beginning for the comprehension of specific, two-person behavior.

Expectations

In the previous chapter, reference was made to how we develop hypotheses about the way the world works and about the way we think it will work. Our expectations are derived from our concepts for organizing the information which is available to us about what is going on. This book is attempting, in fact, to suggest the use of the system concept for ordering information. But the reader can supply his own still more personally meaningful concepts as examples. Although our concepts are cognitive in character, i.e., they have to do with our intellect, they are basically as much a result of our emotional experience as anything else. Although we may have a concept of competence which is important to us in the way we sort out behavior, that concept is likely to be a result of how we have come to *feel* about our own competence. It is also likely that we use the competence concept to select information about ourselves in relation to others in such a way as to help us *feel* that the world is manageable. If our early life experiences led us to distrust our abilities—perhaps because we had a father whose ideal we could never live up to—our need to strive for a sense of competence would be an important influence on the development of a competence concept in us. As we looked at the world, our concept might then help screen out some of the evidences which would weaken our sense of being competent—aiding us to view the math test we failed as unfair or inconsequential rather than as an indication of our incompetence.

It is in this connection between one's concepts and the preservation of his image of himself that the idea of "cognitive dissonance" has arisen. Simply stated, when we hold two conflicting ideas about something of importance to us, something has got to give. If I conceive of myself as competent in some activity and I am given some evidence of failure in that activity, either I must change the concept, translate the evidence into more favorable terms, or so preselect evidence that I avoid becoming aware that such conflicts exist. Belief and the experience we admit to awareness must jibe, or we experience discomfort.

Dissonance Problems and Interpersonal Behavior

The drive for consistency appears, then, to be a basic one. We human beings need to develop internally consistent ideas and ideas which give us a sound basis upon which to develop valid hypotheses about the outside world. Over time we develop expectations about what fits and what does not. Our tendency to do so is most pragmatic, since we cannot function at all without some sense of confidence that there is stability in the world, some sense of security that every new situation we encounter does not need to be treated as though we were approaching an unknown planet.

Edward Sampson[1] described the situation something like this. In order for people to coordinate their activities, as they must do in any social order such as a business or a school, each must have some knowledge by which to anticipate the behavior of those others upon whom he depends. It is important both that these pieces of knowledge be con-

---

[1]Edward E. Sampson, "Status Congruence and Cognitive Consistency," *Sociometry,* Vol. XXVI, No. 2 (June, 1963).

sistent with each other—so that the guidelines for action are relatively clear—and that these pieces of knowledge or expectation match rather closely what actually occurs—so that real coordination can take place.

Sampson goes on to describe two obstacles to consistent and valid expectations: The first obstacle occurs when an individual behaves differently at different times or with different people. The teacher who is supposed to be counselor and personal confidant at one time and disciplinarian and evaluator at another is difficult to contend with. Who will he be this time? He cannot even maintain a consistent picture of himself without great effort. The executive who dominates his subordinates, is a buddy to his peers, and is subservient to his superiors may be in a similar position, both from the way he looks to himself and from the way others see him. It is not uncommon to designate such people as untrustworthy, signifying our inability to predict their behavior with any satisfactory degree of assurance. And it is not uncommon for us to try to modify that part of their behavior which makes them unpredictable, or to avoid contact with them.

The second obstacle has to do with a particular method we use to predict what a person will do or how he should behave. We assume from what we know about his background, from his appearance, and from other cues about his social status that he will behave in a manner befitting such characteristics. If he is elderly, we probably expect dignity, forbearance, and paternal behavior. If he is highly educated, we might expect aloofness, intellectualization, and privilege. If he is new to an organization and of low job rank, we may expect him to be quiet, respectful, and obedient. There are a number of measures of him which we may use as quick shortcuts telling us how we may relate to this person. But what if some of his characteristics, say his advanced age, lead us to expect one kind of behavior and other characteristics, say his newness and low job rank, lead us to expect the opposite? It has been found that work groups whose members' characteristics lead to consistent expectations about their behavior tend to be more cohesive, more highly satisfied, and to some degree at least, more productive than those composed of members whose characteristics lead us to expect conflicting behavior. Apparently, the article suggests, the effectiveness of coordination depends greatly upon how clear the cues are about what to expect from other members of the group.

So, we need a stable base upon which to build our expectations of others. When our expectations of them are not fulfilled or are confused by conflicting signals, we tend to avoid those people as a way of reducing the discomfort we experience in the midst of confusion and conflict.

The Expectation of Reciprocal Exchange in Interpersonal Behavior

A basic expectation about how persons will relate to each other, one whose violation will create considerable cognitive dissonance, concerns the idea of reciprocity.[2] There is considerable evidence to indicate that there is a universal social rule to be found operating in all cultures. The rule states that what one is given he shall repay in approximate equivalence.[3] This statement implies that the conduct of human relationships can usefully be conceived as a process of exchange or trade.

Before we examine the implications of the norm of reciprocity, let's see what is involved in the exchange simile. The concept involves the idea that human and social systems engage each other to obtain what they want but do not have, at a cost less than the perceived value of that which is sought. Both parties to this social exchange[4] must perceive a direct or indirect "profit" from their relationship, or no interpersonal bargain can be struck. These statements may seem unduly commercial unless one conceives of all behavior, even the most altruistic, as satisfying to the individual's needs. Under this conception, marriage and labor-management relations are both more subject to the power of psychological expectation than they are to the legal structures built to govern them.

The commodities conveyed in interpersonal exchange range broadly from the employer-employee exchange of physical and mental effort and skill for money, power, and status to "goods" more widely exchanged, such as affection, interest, help, respect, responsibility, knowledge, emotional support, and love. However, since social exchange must, if dissonance is to be avoided, represent a balance between what is given and what is received, not only must we include goods with positive connotations but also those of a punishing character. Disrespect,

---

[2]A. W. Gouldner, "The Norm of Reciprocity, A Preliminary Statement," *American Sociological Review,* Vol. XXV, No. 2 (April, 1960), pp. 161–78.

[3]The universality of this rule may well be linked to the well-established animal instinct for the rights of ownership. For a provocative treatment of man's instinctual heritage, see Robert Ardrey, *African Genesis* (New York: Dell Publishing Company, 1961).

[4]G. C. Homans, *Sentiments and Activities* (New York: Free Press of Glencoe, 1962) chap. xvii. See also, by the same author, *Social Behavior: Its Elementary Forms* (New York: Harcourt, Brace & World, Inc., 1961).

spite, belittlement, disinterest, bodily harm, and withholding of expected benefits are all behaviors used to keep relationships in balance the way we expect them to be.

How social goods are valued also rests upon our expectations of what is fitting. Valuation depends only in part on the good, itself. It depends equally on who the giver and receiver are. Respect from one person is worth more than respect from another. Sometimes the endowment which the individual gives the goods he exchanges comes from his unique qualities, such as the endowment a wise person who knows us well may give to his praise of us. Other times the endowment is inferred by the symbols which we expect to represent certain personal qualities, such as age, education, socioeconomic standing and so on. We are likely to expect, for example, that approval from a man with many years' experience will be worth more than approval from a relative neophyte.

Actually, the balance of a social exchange is determined by the *relative* endowments of the participants. The president of a company, other things being equal, may expect far more recipient sacrifice in return for a favor extended to one of his juniors than he would expect in return for the same favor bestowed on a member of his club. The commodities which are in exchange have no social value independent of the relationship between the characteristics of the giver and the receiver.

These, then, are the basic premises underlying the expectation of reciprocity in interpersonal relationships. Let's look at some of the functions of the reciprocity expectation in operation. For one thing, no interpersonal relationship could begin without reasonable assurance that the initiator would not be exploited. Only if there is a valid assumption that an obligation is created by the act of giving would one normally engage in an attempt at exchange. The concept of debt bears a close relation to the start-up function of the reciprocity expectation.

Stability in social relations is another function of the rule of reciprocity. For one thing, the expectation of a continuingly rewarding exchange helps keep relationships open. And both creditor and debtor are bound, over time, to maintain contact until the debt is liquidated and the credit balanced. Unlike most commercial dealings, social exchanges are rarely subject to fine measurement. The stipulation of "approximate equivalence" means that, often, neither party is quite sure of who is in whose debt. Consequently, there is a tendency for exchange to be prolonged indefinitely, lest the books inadvertently be closed on an unbalanced account.

As the reader is clearly aware, however, the expectation of reciprocity is not always met. For some, the frequency of disappointed expectations becomes a dissonance managed by nothing but alienation, rejection, and withdrawal. For most, however, the occurrence of imbalance in social exchange is either sufficiently isolated or so infrequent as to be manageable. Two common sources of reciprocity breakdown are worthy of mention.

It happens that some people who are required by their jobs to enter into an interpersonal relationship have such different sets of expectations about the value of their endowments and their goods that, while each feels he is giving value, neither sees that he is getting commensurate value in return. For example, a production manager who believes that practical experience, with which he is well endowed, is the most valuable endowment with which to evaluate his contributions, inevitably runs afoul of the engineering supervisor who believes just as strongly that formal education is the most significant endowing quality. When one of these men accedes to a request by the other, he expects a far greater *quid* for his *quo* than the other believes is warranted. The chances are that they both experience dissonance, and both attempt to reduce it by forcing the other to change his expectations and, thus, reinforce the bases upon which their imbalanced exchange began.

A second type of breakdown in relationships can occur when one person is required by his job to act *as though* his endowments were greater than he actually feels them to be. The production control clerk who schedules the work of a fabricating department may be perceived by the foreman of that department as behaving like a superior rather than an inferior. In this case, there is no disagreement between the men as to expectations, but one party to the exchange is forced to behave inconsistently. Resolution of this imbalance often takes the form of extreme obsequiousness on the part of the clerk or extraordinary dominance on the part of the foreman, if the two are to maintain contact. There are many other sources of breakdown in relationships, but the foregoing are so common as to merit special mention.

Expectation, Dissonance, and Exchange in Two Cases of Interpersonal Behavior

In this chapter we have called attention to the fundamental importance of having a way to think about, and take into account, what goes on in specific, two-person interactions. We have suggested that we all develop a sense of consistency in our expectations of what should happen, in the absence of which we have to make things right, somehow. One source of uncomfortable inconsistency is to be found in the individual who behaves in conflicting ways so that we do not have a secure feeling about how to approach him. We feel the same insecurity about those whose characteristics—age, education, and so on—do not seem to fit together. We noted that there is an acultural expectation about interpersonal behavior, that it will be governed by reciprocal exchange. Reciprocity is determined both by what is being exchanged and by the endowments of those engaging in interaction. The goods of interpersonal exchange are more often expressions of affect than they are tangible commodities. We found that the expectation of reciprocity helped relationships to develop and to continue, and that without a mutual sense of the expectation of reciprocity operating in a relationship, interaction would falter, break off, or only continue under special guarantees.

To find such examples of successful or unsuccessful interpersonal exchange, one need only turn to his own associations with others and use the concepts set forth above to select information from the behavior taking place in those relationships. In addition, the following two short cases have been included here as descriptions of actual interactions upon which some of the foregoing ideas may be tested.

In the first case, Gordon Foundry Company, interaction seems to be oriented to finding some grounds upon which exchange could be started, but the dissonance which each party to the interaction represents for the other is severe.

GORDON FOUNDRY COMPANY[5]

Right after I had graduated from the Provincial Technical Institute, I accepted a position with the Gordon Foundries, a medium-sized firm located in a small town in one of the Eastern Provinces. It was a fine position, for I was the assistant to Mr. Smith, who was general manager and president of the family-owned company. I was anxious to learn the foundry business and since I was living alone it was not long before I literally lived in the foundry. We had many technical problems, the work was intensely interesting, and my boss was a very fine man.

The foundry workers were a closely knit group and in the main they were older men. Several had spent a lifetime in the foundry. Many of them were related. They felt that they knew the foundry business from A to Z and they were inclined to "pooh-pooh" the value of technical

[5]Copyright, 1956, by the University of Alberta. Reprinted by permission.

education. The president had mentioned to me when we discussed the duties and responsibilities of the position that no graduate of a technical institute had ever been employed in the Gordon Foundry. He added, "You will find that the men stick pretty well together. Most of them have been working together for more than 10 years, which is rather unusual in a foundry, so it may take you some time to get accepted. But, on the whole, you will find them a fine group of men."

At first the men eyed me coldly as I went around and got acquainted. Also, I noticed that they would clam up as I approached. A bit later I became aware of cat-calls when I walked down the main aisle of the foundry. I chose to ignore these evidences of hostility because I considered them silly and childish. I believed that if I continued to ignore these antics, the men would eventually stop, come to their senses and see the ridiculousness of their behavior.

One Saturday, about a month after I had started, I was down in the Enamel Shop. As I entered it I observed a worker who was busy cleaning the floor with a hose from which flowed water at pretty good pressure. It was customary to "hose down" the Enamel Shop every so often. I was busy near one of the dipping tanks when, all of a sudden, I was nearly knocked down by the force of a stream of water. The worker had deliberately turned the hose on me. I knew that he had intended to hit me by the casual way in which he swung around as though he had never seen what he had done.

The second case, The Young Foreman, also concerns a young man new to an organization. In this case, we find the young man caught between a number of different expectations for his behavior, satisfying any one of which appears to create dissonance for others. When you get to the description of the crisis at the end of the case, see if you can figure out why it worked out as it did.

THE YOUNG FOREMAN

In the summer of 1955, I was working for the North Harbridge Railway to earn money with which to pay for my next year of college. Quite a few college students in the area worked for the company every summer, doing cleanup work and laying track; but the majority of the men doing this work were permanent employees between the ages of 20 and 25. There were three other college men in the gang I was assigned to, and the four of us became quite close friends. The rest of the gang consisted of 11 fellows about 20 years old, from poor families, most of them without a high school diploma, and all of them tough and hard as nails. Our foreman was a fellow of about 35, who was known as a taskmaster of the first order. We knew him only by the name Chick. With the exception of our foreman, all of us had been hired at the beginning of the summer and were on the same basis, except that the four of us who were college students did not intend to continue our employment after the end of the summer, as did the others.

I always worked with the three other college students, Mac, Jack, and Doc, because we could carry on interesting conversations and swap stories which helped pass the time and make the job more enjoyable. In addition, the rest of the gang seemed fairly tight-lipped, in their own close group, and little, if at all, interested in talking with us. I made an effort to work harder than some of the other fellows, because I had gotten my job through a friend of one of the bosses and felt I had an obligation to him.

The summer progressed this way into early August. I frequently talked with the foreman, and we often joked or hurled friendly insults at one another. The rest of the crew did not very often engage Chick in this sort of banter, but they all seemed to get along with him well enough. Occasionally, when he had messages to deliver to various parts of the plant, or other crews needed an extra man for an emergency job, Chick would send me; but ordinarily, I worked with my regular crew and did the same work as they did. On one occasion, Chick sent Mac, Jack, Doc, and me on an emergency job to clean up some track where a "spill"[6] had occurred, and placed me in charge of the group.

Then, in the second week in August, Mac, Jack, and Doc quit working, so as to remain deductions on their father's income taxes as dependents. Thereafter, I spent more time talking to Chick, asking him questions about the plant and "shooting the breeze." I was able to do this and still hold up my end of the work, but I noticed some of the others on the crew seemed to resent and became cooler than usual toward me. I didn't worry about this, as they had never been very friendly, and I was satisfied that I was doing a satisfactory job. Chick sent me on an increasing number of errands and jobs, I think, because he knew that I was interested in learning more about the operation of the railroad. Some of these jobs involved nothing more difficult than walking around oiling switches, which meant I was my own boss for the day. On other occasions the jobs Chick sent me on were emergencies, in which case the work was considerably more difficult than my regular job.

The rest of the crew grew steadily cooler to me and frequently made snide remarks about "getting a soft touch from the boss," even when I was sent out on some of the tougher jobs. Adding to this atmosphere was the fact that when I went on these special jobs, I always had time to wash up before reporting back to the time clock, which the rest of the

[6]Coal had spilled from a car and blocked the track.

crew generally did not have the opportunity to do. Seeing me cleaned up when they came in at the end of the day did little to change their opinion of how hard I was working. I continued to ignore their attitude, for I knew I would only be working for another month and then would probably never see any of them again.

One very hot morning, Chick asked me if I would like to go outside the plant during lunch for a couple of beers. This was something he had always forbidden the crew to do; and as it was very hot, I readily accepted. Thereafter, we used to follow this practice about three or four times a week. This only served to make matters worse, and some of the crew became quite hostile toward me in their statements and actions. This bothered me quite a bit, as most of them were bigger than I was and considerably tougher due to the "struggle for existence" type of environment in which they had been brought up. One of them even went so far as to warn me that it might not be wise for me ever to let him catch me alone, or at least "when there weren't any bosses around."

One morning in early September, Chick told me to take four of the crew and the truck to another section of the yard to clean up a load of coke dust that had been spilled on the tracks. I wanted to think of some excuse for not going, because I was afraid of what might happen or that the men might just refuse to work for me. However, I felt I owed it to Chick to accept the responsibility he had delegated to me. I could think of no logical excuse except the truth, and I refused to lose face in this way. Chick told four of the fellows to get into the truck and go with me, and informed them that I was to be their boss for the remainder of the day. They climbed into the back of the truck, and we set off for our new job. On the way to the other side of the plant, I tried to think of some way to gain their cooperation, but could not. I realized that if I did the wrong thing, we would get little, if any, work done and that I might collect a few bruises for my trouble as well.

When we arrived at the coke spill, I explained to them what we had to do, and we started working. It was a blistering hot day, and coke dust is the dirtiest stuff imaginable to work with. The crew didn't like it at all, and it wasn't long before they were spending more time leaning on their shovels than using them. I also heard several remarks relating to what they thought of me and several sneers were passed in my direction. I realized that something had to be done or we wouldn't begin to finish the job, and we might all get in a good deal of trouble. I had continued to work while the others leaned on their shovels. At that moment, one of them made a very nasty remark about me and my relationship with the boss. With this, I completely lost my temper.

"Why, you dirty s.o.b's," I yelled. "I don't give a damn what you think of me; but as long as you're working for me, you're going to work your tails off, and anyone who doesn't like it can take his timecard and get the hell out!" I shouted this at the top of my lungs, and they all stood staring at me. I turned around and began to shovel as hard as I could, half expecting to get a shovel over my head.

A few minutes later, the five of us were working like demons, and we accomplished more that day than our whole crew of eight ever had done before.

CHAPTER 5

*Social Inputs**

HAVING, in Chapter 3, looked at the human inputs to organizational behavior—examining some ways of thinking about how individuals as biological-psychological-intellectual systems get to be the individuals they are and how their characteristics tend to influence the way they perceive the world, the way they form expectations about themselves and their environment, and the way they conduct themselves in relation to their perceptions and expectations—we were able to move on, in Chapter 4, to formulate ideas for thinking about the behavior of the simplest social system, two individuals in interaction. We focused on systems of interpersonal relationships by conceiving of them as processes of exchange, subject to rules of reciprocity.

We are ready, now, to take on the more complex task of understanding how the next higher level of social system, informal groups, influence organizational behavior. In so doing, we shall be using our ideas about individual functioning and interpersonal exchange to understand the many relationships involved in group behavior.

As the reader will recall from Chapter's 2 outline of the sociotechnical system, the social input is somewhat unique among the four inputs to organizational behavior. While the human, technical, and organizational inputs are most conveniently conceived as coming from *without* the system, the social input emerges in the sociotechnical system from the interaction of the other three inputs. At the time that an organization is formed and people are brought together in some chosen

*I am indebted to Assistant Professor Jay Lorsch of the Harvard Business School for the assistance he rendered in preparing an early version of this chapter.

organizational relationship to perform tasks within a technology, there is as yet no social input. It is only *after* people have begun to work together and their activities, interactions, and sentiments have begun to be influenced by human, technical, and organizational factors, that social groups begin to form, members and nonmembers are distinguished and shared ideas about what is proper behavior are developed. Once the emergence of a social system has taken place, however, the duties and rights of informal status positions, and other norms of behavior applicable to group members at large, act as influencers of behavior, just as human, technical, and organizational inputs do. So the characteristics of the informal part of the system not only are the channel through which many aspects of the other inputs make themselves felt, but social inputs exert their own unique influences on behavior, as well. We shall be referring to this dual functionality of social inputs throughout the chapter, and we will return to a more precise look at how social inputs fit into our analytical framework before we are through.

In many ways, group behavior is only somewhat complicated interpersonal behavior. Certainly, all of the notions about individual and interpersonal behavior are applicable to individuals and pairs of people when they are behaving in groups. But the complexity of the group situation brings a new dimension to behavior. When we move from two people to three or more, something like the notion of the "group mind" comes into play. Without falling prey to the mystique sometimes associated with this conception, let's see if we can think systematically about what groups are for and how they come to have the influence they do on organzational behavior.

The Attractions of Group Membership

People join groups because they can get some things from groups which they simply cannot get at all or in sufficient degree when they are acting alone. First, they get a wide variety of *social satisfactions.* All of us have experienced the enjoyment of being accepted by a group of people whom we like and respect. Without doubt each of us has also undergone the uncomfortable experience of being rejected in some way by a group whose good opinion we sought (at least before the rejection). More commonly, we are strangers trying to figure out how to behave in the midst of a group of people who know each other well. Through experiences like these, experiences of acceptance or belonging on the one hand and rejection or alienation on the other, it is not difficult to realize the potency with which groups influence behavior.

There are many other social values to be derived from group membership beyond the sense of belonging, as basic as that sense may be. An accepted member can seek and attain special signs of esteem from other group members. He can "play out" his desire to influence others through the attainment of special group roles, such as spokesman, joker, organizer, and so forth. Furthermore, the group provides a uniquely rich opportunity for the individual to test out the effectiveness of his social skills and to try on new behavior in a relatively certain and perhaps helpful atmosphere. Group membership imbues those who possess it with a special image in the minds of those who do not. Sometimes this stereotypical effect enhances the individual's status. Sometimes it has the opposite effect. Even when it is in the negative, however, a group's membership may still be attractive due to the power it lends to the individual's exchange with others, but that kind of attraction will be discussed later. So, there are countless ways in which groups provide social satisfaction to their members. We need not try to be exhaustive here, since the reader's own experiences will already have expanded the list.

The second type of attraction in group membership arises from the fact that groups offer the individual an expanded *environmental control.* Groups can magnify one's ability to cope with the world. Both formal and informal groups are formed on the premise that, for certain tasks at least, groups are more potent than individuals. In designing its organization, management tries to put people together who need to communicate easily or who, by precepts of job design, need to be proximate in order to work on common objects. Groups emerge informally because their members observe that, while individuals may easily be dismissed by more powerful individuals, groups of individuals have to be reckoned with.

However, the formal groups which technology and organization dictate never coincide exactly with the informal groups which emerge in the organizational system. It is unlikely, first of all, that the members of an informal and a formal group will be the same, since interpersonal compatibility is not the major (and often not even a minor) criterion for formal group composition. Some member of the formal group is likely to be unacceptable to others, while individuals outside the formal group may be invited into the informal group on favorable interpersonal grounds. And, second, the goals and rules for conduct of formal and informal groups virtually never coincide, since they originate in different places and from people with different points of view. In fact, formal and informal goals and rules for conduct may be quite incompatible. It is not unusual, for example, for one function of a group's membership to be to frustrate some expressed or implied aspect of the formal organization. Blue-collar groups may band together to defeat the purposes of a particular wage incentive system, as did the group of egalitarian miners who pooled their varying production bonuses each payday and redistributed the money on a share-and-share-alike basis. White-collar employees engage in group activities which, though different in form, have goals not unlike those of the miners. Men in middle management often conform to an agreement to withhold certain kinds of information from their superiors. The electrical equipment industry's price-fixing scandals of a few years back are a case in point.

How functional the behavior of an informal group is for the goals of the formal organization, then, depends on the particular mix of human, technical, and organizational inputs to the system. That there will be informal activity which is functional for the informal group's sense of being influential over its environment, however, is certain. Even the most benign organizational environment challenges those who inhabit it to compete for scarce resources such as approval, budgetary allotments, space, and so on. The group which fails to enhance its individual member's capacity to obtain these resources is in danger of dissolution, no matter how bountiful it might otherwise be in providing social rewards. An informal group which has formed around a production unit, for example, must help its individual members fend off the attempts by engineers or sales personnel to make what to production are arbitrary demands or find its members disaffected and the group in a state of collapse.

The fact of the matter is that an informal group cannot survive without achieving some simultaneous success in satisfying both social and environmental needs. One without the other is impossible. Without a group's members having a sense of social support from other members, the group cannot make use of its numbers in dealing with the environment. Without some effective influence over its environment, the group has no umbrella with which it can protect its social values. More central to the indivisibility of coping and social activity, however, is the fact that social rewards are often derived from coping activities and coping rewards commonly are a by-product of social activity. A group elevates its leaders and casts its rules of behavior, compliance to which brings the esteem and affection of group members, in accord with the demands of the environment. Similarly, the more effectively a group fends off attempts to attack it, the greater the esprit and sense of belonging which emerges among group members.

A classic example of the interdependence of social and coping behavior comes from the Bank Wiring Observation Room research at the Western Electric Company,[1] conducted during the depression of the 1930's. Workers perceived management to be in the process of raising output standards and discharging workers who could not meet those standards. This perception persisted despite management's rather extraordinary efforts over several years to retain the work force intact. The perception continued into later depression periods when layoffs did take place, although management assured workers that seniority was the criterion by which men were chosen for layoff. Basing their actions on what appears to be a myth, the informal group which emerged in the bank wiring room, where the research focused its study, developed a specific measure of a "fair day's output," and group members limited their productivity to points near that level. Reportedly, they believed that in so doing, the more highly skilled would not profit at the expense of naturally slow workers. (It may be surmised that this myth persisted in the face of contrary evidence because the members of the group could not abide the feeling of dissonance which could have come from evidence that their group was impotent in dealing with a severe threat to its existence.)

Those who conformed to the informal standard and who were highly skilled were given positions of leadership. Only conformers were included in the games, jokes, and everyday conversations of the group, while nonconformers were punished by exclusion and derision. A great many of the activities of the group were simultaneously functional for coping efficacy (as the group defined it), through their reinforcement of work restriction norms, and for social satisfaction, through their reinforcement of membership qualifications and feelings of cohesion. The "work" of dealing with its environment gave the group something to talk about and to be interested in together, while the games and conversation helped strengthen the sense of unity among group members which was essential for an effective restriction of productivity. Coping gave content to social activity; social activity supplied the collaboration required for coping.

Social Control

Coping and social rewards are obtained only because group members act in consort, according to a relatively consistent understanding of a set of rules and of the corollary sanctions for enforcing compliance

---

[1]F. J. Roethlisberger and W. J. Dickson, *Management and the Worker* (Cambridge, Mass.: Harvard University Press, 1938).

to the rules. These rules and sanctions alert each member to the group's interests and to the role he is expected to play in achieving those interests if he is to enjoy the rewards of the group. They provide a degree of certainty that the group will be a group rather than a collection of individuals. The informal rules governing group behavior are generally referred to as *norms.* A norm is a sentiment or idea in the minds of group members about what they and others in the group should do in a given set of circumstances. A norm is not necessarily, or even very likely, the actual behavior of all group members all the time, since norms are standards of what behavior should be. Furthermore, norms generally specify a range of acceptable behavior (for example, productivity between —5 percent and +5 percent of a standard amount; or being unprepared at a meeting once in awhile but not too often) within which a member can vary without risk of censure.

Norms are operational rules for specific activity in a specific situation. As such, they are the action counterpart of generalized values which the individual brings with him to the situation. Values are absolute ideals; for example, charity is an ideal, but one who values charity can never perfectly realize that ideal. Norms, on the other hand, are more limited prescriptions for behavior, such as "help those who stick by the group but withhold charity from those who don't." Norms express the pragmatic resolution of conflicting value positions under the concrete conditions of specific life situations. The norms and underlying values of the group operate in a fashion similar to the maps and constructs of the individual, i.e., inconsistency between a group's norms or ideals and its experience will motivate members of the group to act so as to restore a sense of consistency.

The most common method for reducing group members' feelings of dissonance between norms and actual behavior is to punish deviant members. Although these sanctions sometimes involve withholding coping rewards, for example, failing to protect a member from external threat, they more frequently are social in character. Common social punishments are sarcasm, invective, jokes, disregard, and ostracism. The Bank Wiring Observation Room study[2] contains clear examples of group sanctions in operation. The authors of this study pointed out that only those whose productivity closely approximated the agreed-upon level were included in invitations to the group's social activities or were offered help on the job. Those whose output greatly exceeded or fell

---

[2] *Ibid.*

well below standard were punished by such obvious sanctions as "binging," i.e., striking the guilty party on the arm. Binging's efficacy depended less upon physical pain than on the disapproval which it signified. Similarly, workers who did more than the accepted level were derided as "speed king" or "slave."

Another example of social control in operation is described in Blau's study of a federal regulatory agency.[3] In this agency the informal group of agents were constrained by a norm stipulating that the more competent investigators should help less competent agents on cases with which the latter were having difficulty. This practice was contrary to the formal rule that agents should confer only with supervisors. Blau concluded that informal consultation did contribute to the effective operation of the agency because it improved the quality of the agents' decisions. There were dysfunctional consequences, however, particularly in the weakened authority of supervisors. The practice was functional for maintaining group cohesion, since the agents developed stable, reciprocal exchange relationships. Less competent agents received help in dealing with clients, in exchange for which they gave more competent agents social approval and esteem.

The federal agency example calls our attention to the fact that different group members may seek different rewards from their membership. The more competent agents needed little help from the group in dealing with clients, but they did desire the social rewards which resulted from group leadership. Their adherance to the helping norm gave them this reward. The less competent agents needed help in coping with the client and were quite willing to support the leadership position of the more competent agents in return for this aid and for satisfaction of their needs for belonging and for appearing competent before their supervisors. Despite the different needs which members may bring to groups, the interdependence between coping and social activities makes it mandatory that all members in good standing participate in most, if not all, of the activities, interactions, and sentiments of the group.

But the various needs which members bring to groups do not always work out with such complementarity as they did in Blau's study. Finding a viable basis for exchange between group members depends partly on how strong an individual's needs are for membership in a particular group. The strength of this need determines how closely he will try

[3]Peter M. Blau, *The Dynamics of Bureaucracy* (Chicago: University of Chicago Press, 1955).

to hew to the group's norms and, thus, how secure his membership position will be. A good example of how impotent group controls can be is to be found in the study of a commission-incented retail selling group[4] whose members were paid according to the dollar sales each had made. There was a norm in the group against one salesman making sales at the expense of other salesmen. According to the norm, salesmen were supposed to take their turn in waiting on customers. The salesmen made it clear that high production could be achieved only by violating this norm. In an effort to find out why some salesmen were able to deviate from the norm in spite of the hostility and ostracism of the group (top producers received 10 times as many expressions of hostility as did other salesmen), the researcher asked each man to give the name and occupation of friends outside the organization. Eight salesmen named outside friends who were of higher social position than themselves. Of these eight, seven were among the eight high producers in the group. High producers apparently were able to withstand the hostility engendered by their deviance because they related more closely to persons of higher occupational rank than to members of their work group. Their "reference group," i.e., the group whose values they referred to in making judgments of behavior, was not the one in which they worked.

Let's interpret these findings by using some of the ideas we have been exploring. Many of the salesmen possessed common expectations about how to cope with a retail selling situation, depending on coordinated action for coping success. Some other salesmen, however, had different expectations, involving behavior acceptable to people of higher social status than their fellow salesmen. They were not looking to their sales mates for approval. Thus, attempts by the others to reject these men had no power. Rejection by fellow salesmen created little or no dissonance for the high producers, since being high producers, and consequently high earners, enabled the deviants to behave in consonance with their high-status conceptions of themselves. Even if getting along with other salesmen had not cost them high income, it is likely that conforming to the norms of "merely average salesmen" would have been too inconsistent with the high producers' beliefs about themselves as salesmen-out-of-the-ordinary. Thus, the difference in expectations among these salesmen made reciprocal exchange relations impossible and, at the same time, rendered impotent the sanctions of the social group. In

[4] C. J. French, "Correlates of Success in Retail Selling," *American Journal of Sociology,* Vol. LXVI, No. 2 (1960).

every informal group whose behavior we may try to understand, we will find that people are arrayed widely across a continuum from "in" to "out." While those on the "in" end of the spectrum will, in various ways, conform to group norms, those on the "out," either because they do not value group membership or because they are incapable of behaving as desired, will not conform. Attempts will be made by the "ins" to get the "outs" to increase behavior favorable to the group. Typically, when we find deviation taking place, group members will focus a great deal of their activity on the deviant, perhaps first trying to entice the violator to see the rewards inherent in conformity, then punishing him when he breaks rules. After a period of time, however, if compliance is not forthcoming, the group may resign itself and seal the deviant off from group activity and interaction, in an attempt to isolate him.

Group Structure: Differential Positions and Relationships within Groups

Although we have given our attention so far to the characteristics of group membership in general, it has been obvious from our discussion that members of groups are not and could not be duplicates of each other. As individuals bring their individual differences to groups, the group assigns different statuses or positions to each individual. We have already referred to deviants, isolates, members-in-good-standing, and leaders. These are some of the basic statuses in a group, though there are often many others. Each status position has a role or set of behavior which it is expected the person holding the status position will perform. In the case of deviant and isolate statuses, the attendant role behavior is implied by the status title. A member in good standing, as has been noted, is expected to observe the group's norms. The leader, as we shall discuss shortly, is expected to personify the values and norms of the group. Furthermore, the leader, because of his status, has certain privileges not common to the roles of other group members. For one thing, he is allowed to ignore some of the group's norms, at least some of the less important ones. In exchange for his valuable services, he is rewarded by a loosening of the rules. So, rules not only have duties or obligations but also connote rights and privileges.

Of course, people occupy not only the status or statuses associated with a particular face-to-face group but also those coming from the larger society in which they hold broader status positions. Each of us holds many of these: student, student at a particular school, father, son, husband, engineer, Midwesterner, "WASP" (white, Anglo-Saxon, Protestant), and so on. Thus, each of us has a set of statuses, each with its own associated behavioral expectations. Furthermore, each status has not just one role but many. The student is expected to behave one way with instructors, another with fellow students, yet another with businessmen with whom he may come in contact. Each status has its set of roles, and each of us has his set of statuses.

Viewed over time, each of us passes from one set of statuses and roles to another as part of his life cycle, his education, his mobility, and his personal development. Some part of the sequence of status and role is peculiar to each of us as individuals, but other parts are so common as to be integral parts of the structure of society. Typically common sets are: dependent child–student–citizen; medical student–intern–resident–practitioner; trainee–junior executive–executive.

". . . operating social structures must somehow manage to organize these sets and sequences of statuses and roles so that an appreciable degree of social order obtains, sufficient to enable most of the people most of the time to go about their business of social life without having to improvise adjustments anew in each newly confronted situation."[5] These are the organized expectations which spring from the individual sets of expectations which were discussed in previous papers.

Since each person is subject to such a complex set of role expectations, he is bound to find himself responding to some conflicting pressures. In the retail selling group study, the high producers were subject to the conflicting expectations of the selling group and of their higher status friends. They chose to resolve the conflict by rejecting one group in favor of the other. They could deviate from their work group's norms because other membership made membership in the work group a hazard rather than an asset. But belonging to two groups which demand diametrically opposed behavior often confronts the individual with a more difficult dilemma. What if he desires the acceptance of both groups? The internal conflict to which the individual is subjected under these conditions is readily exemplified by the supervisor who aspires to membership in the management group, yet who keenly feels the need for friendship with his subordinates (particularly when they were recently his peers). The greater the disparity between the values and norms of the two groups, of course, the more conflicted will the individual be and the more difficult will it be for him to find a resolution of the opposing forces which are acting upon him.

---

[5]R. K. Merton, *Social Theory and Social Structure,* (Glencoe, Ill.: Free Press, 1957), p. 370.

The status of informal group leader, it has been noted, reflects apparently conflicting attitudes toward conformity. The fact that informal leaders have high rank in the group means they are highly regarded by the members who have accorded them that rank. Thus, they have a great deal to lose if they break norms and are punished. To maintain leadership, they must hew closely to the group's expectations. On the other hand, "rank hath its privilege." The services which the leader provides the group give him in return not only respect and allegiance but also certain rights. Because he has confirmed his reliability by past performance, he can break some norms with impunity. While certain major norms, often those connected with coping, are so important that all members are expected to rigidly comply, other norms develop which are less central to the group's existence. Some norms, in fact, appear to have a ritual quality, the only reason for their existence being to test the allegiance of group members. "In" jokes or special language are common examples of what is expected of members ritually. Group leaders often hold themselves aloof from this type of activity, leaving the observance of rituals to lieutenants. The evidence indicates, then, that while the well-established leader must adhere to major norms, he is freer to break peripheral ones than other group members because he has built up such a large stock of social credit.

The status of newcomers presents the opposite picture. Having no group acceptance, newcomers have little to lose by breaking norms. Up to the point where deviance results in ostracism, they suffer only continued low rank for their deviance. In a sense, exchange between them and the group has yet to be established. However, if a newcomer decides he wants the group's rewards, thus offering a basis for exchange with the group, he is extremely vulnerable to social controls. Since he has little to offer in terms of past performance, he must be rigorous in his compliance with all group norms, including some of the ritual ones which higher ranking members may be ignoring. If, however, the newcomer does not highly value group rewards, he may continue to deviate and to remain a low-ranking member. In either case, the exchange between the newcomer and the group is balanced at a high or low traffic level.

Social Inputs as a Function of Human, Technical, and Organizational Inputs

We have on occasion in this chapter made implicit reference to the interdependence of the four inputs to organizational behavior. Let's summarize, complicate, and give emphasis to this interdependence by looking at how the cohesiveness of a group and its power to control member behavior depend on human, technical, and organizational factors.

Human Inputs. The idiosyncratic backgrounds of individual group members are clearly reflected in a group's particular set of norms and role assignments. Through the differences among a group's members come the potentially complementary contributions which make the group more than the simple sum of its parts. Conversely, the degree of similarity among members has a distinct bearing on the kind and amount of cohesiveness which develops within the group. It was noted in the previous chapter that congruence among the status characteristics of group members not only was a predictor of the amount of cohesion in the group but also, up to a point, of the productivity of the group. Apparently, if a group's members are so much alike that they are nearly indistinguishable, cohesion detracts from, rather than stimulates, productivity. In this extreme of cohesion, either the group does not possess a productive complementarity of skills or the group tends to focus so heavily on social activity that it neglects to attend to the demands of the environment. We can, then, expect to find cohesion where we find relatively homogeneous human inputs. We can expect to find both cohesion and effectiveness in groups whose members are much alike on grounds important for interpersonal solidarity but are complementarily different in terms of the skills required for coping with the group's environment.

Technical Inputs. One of the most obvious influences on a group's cohesion and internal control is the degree of physical proximity between members. Proximity has a great deal to do with the ability of group members to communicate with each other. When all members are within view of each other and where the noise level is low, there is a constant sense of "groupness" and a great potential for members to observe and sanction the behavior of their fellows. When physical conditions limit easy communication, alternate methods are often sought. Frequently, these methods take the form of lunch or coffee-break gatherings. Where noise is a factor, substitute signals may be employed. But the physical conditions which most facilitate cohesion are those permitting close physical proximity and easy communication.

Organizational Inputs. Not only is physical proximity an important factor in keeping people psychologically together but how the work is divided up has a significant influence, too. If members of a group sense a close interdependence among them for the satisfactory completion of a task, they are constantly reminded of their closeness by the routine work which they perform. If their combined efforts add up to a tangible result with which they can easily identify themselves, their sense of cohesion is magnified. If payment methods depend on group output, cohesion will be increased even further. And if their formal leader treats the group as a group instead of as a cluster of discrete individuals, cohesion will be reinforced even more. As we have noted, the greater the sense of cohesion, the more potent is the group in controlling member behavior.

Social Inputs and the Analysis of Behavior

It only remains for us now to spell out how our ideas about social control and structure can most effectively be used in the analysis of specific organizational systems. We have just indicated how social inputs may be linked to the other three inputs, and that is a first step in indicating how to fit social factors into an analysis. But how do we put together what we can find out about social inputs and then derive a relation between these inputs and behavior?

First of all, we can fairly assume that there are some informal rules for behavior and that those rules are having some effect on behavior. So, we need to spell out as best we can what the social norms are. A helpful way to do so is to list norms in the same form that we can imagine people in the situation reporting them to us if we were on the spot and had their confidence. "We should talk in meetings when we have something to say which won't put the other guys in a bad light." Or, "If you want to get along here, show what you can do, don't talk about it." Often norm statements have to be derived from observing the behavior of people we know to be "in," particularly looking for patterns or repetitions of basic behaviors for evidences of norms. Once we know what the norms are, we can look to see how behavior in a problem situation may be a function of these norms.

But knowing what the norms are is not the only important requirement of a sound analysis. So is knowing where people fit into the social side of things. It makes a lot of difference in planning action, for example, whether we try to deal with the group leader or with an isolate. In one case we can expect the leader to guide his behavior by reference to the beliefs and desires of his group. Whatever influence we may be able to exercise with regard to the leader will tend to have broad results throughout the social system. Information from an isolate, on the other hand, will have narrower, though not necessarily less important, implications, and our influence will certainly relate to a smaller part of the system. Furthermore, when a problem arises, it will be useful to look and see if someone is caught between conflicting sets of expectations. If so, adding pressure to the conflict may turn out to be the least effective thing we could recommend. So, we will find it advisable to spell out the various statuses of the people involved in the situation and to stipulate what role behavior is expected of those statuses.

Finally, we will want to assess how influential the social inputs are. Norms may be relatively unimportant in determining behavior if group cohesion is weak. We may, for example, find that group norms are, in fact, quite functional for productivity but, because of some blocks to group solidarity, those norms in comparison with other inputs, are having a weak effect on productivity. In such a case we might try to reduce those blocks to cohesion over which we have some control. Similarly, if the group is strong, working through its leadership structure will be important. If it is weak, however, we may want to adopt a different strategy.

Thus, finding out what the norms and status positions are, how strong the group is, and what influence other inputs have on these social characteristics should help us to assess the situation and, at the same time, develop sound ideas for taking action to reduce the effects of behavior which are dysfunctional for the goals we want to achieve.

Four Cases of Social Influence

Four simplified descriptions of organizational behavior in widely varying contexts are included here for the purposes of exemplification and analytical practice. The cases have been organized in such a way that the reader may predict from his analysis of inputs what behavior can be expected to result. He may then check his predictions against what actually took place. Some of the inputs will be described in Part 1 of the case. Then questions on how those inputs would be likely to influence behavior will be listed. The actual behavior in Part 2 of the case is to be compared with the reader's answers to these questions. This type of analytical exercise does not suggest that predictive perfection is a practical or even possible goal. It does suggest that the probability of error can be reduced somewhat by careful analysis of the interrelation of forces bearing upon the situation. Consequently, once the exercise has been completed, it is suggested that the reader reflect not only on how accurate his predictions were but also on what factors in the situation made prediction difficult.

The cases included here vary on a number of dimensions, including complexity and inclusiveness. One case, the last, is in four rather than two parts, since it involves a change in the situation the effects of which the reader is asked to predict. Each of the cases has potential utility not only as an analytic exercise but also as an example of how social inputs influence behavior. The reader is invited to reflect on these cases to see how various ideas expressed in this chapter look in real life.

THE MOLDING UNIT

Part 1

Production in the molding unit of the Becker foundry was controlled by the movement of a conveyor belt. During each cycle the workers made four molds apiece. The workers were each stationed before a molding machine, with the conveyor moving behind them (Exhibit 1). Empty boards stacked in sets of four were brought toward them on the conveyor. Each worker would remove his four boards from the conveyor, place a mold on each board, and replace mold and board on the conveyor while it was stationary. Then a bell would sound, and the conveyor would move on. The molds were poured in the next stage of production. The boards remained on the conveyor after the mold had been poured and the casting dumped off. Further down the line, men stacked the empty boards so that they would be in easy reach for the molders during the next cycle.

Like all production workers in the foundry, the molders were Negroes, and had little formal education. The foreman was white, as was all supervision in the plant. The molders appeared from their jokes and laughter to have achieved an easy camaraderie. Some of their joking served to haze less skilled workers. Turnover in the unit was low.

John Roberts, a recent college graduate and a trainee in the foundry's management training program, had spent a day watching the operation of the molding unit with the foreman when he asked if he could try one of the machines. Although union regulations forbade nonunion molds being poured, the foreman assigned Roberts a vacant machine position, instructing the pourers to pass his molds by.

At first the trainee was unable to fill his section of the conveyor during the cycle time. Everyone on the line could see his production, since the conveyor passed all the work stations, but they ignored him, and those who usually stacked the boards for the molders left his on the conveyor as they were.

Finally, Roberts managed to fill his section of the conveyor almost every time. Shortly thereafter, Roberts noticed one of the operators, as he rode by on the conveyor, smear grease on the handle of the sand hopper which was above the trainee's machine. Roberts, who was working at the time, gave no indication that he had noticed the man or what he had done. Needing more sand for the pattern, he started to reach around the handle of the hopper to grasp it above where the grease was. Then he changed his mind and grasped the greasy handle.

Exhibit 1

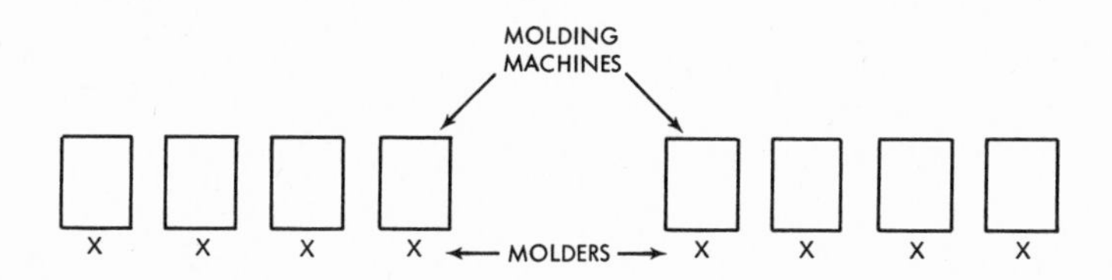

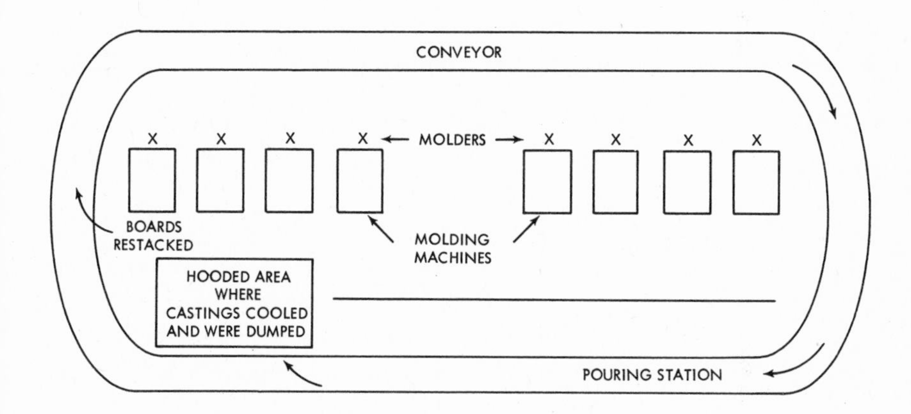

PREDICTIONS—Part 1

From what I know of the molding operation described in Part 1, I would predict that:

a) The operator who smeared grease on the handle did so (by accident) (purposely to try to get rid of Roberts) (purposely to find out what Roberts would do) (for some other reason).

b) The operator who smeared grease on the handle did so (with the disapproval of the other operators) (without the awareness of the other operators) (with the approval of the other operators).

c) If Roberts wants the respect and liking of the group of operators, he should now (leave the production line) (take the grease smearing as a joke but stay on the line) (pay no attention to the grease and go on working).

THE MOLDING UNIT

Part 2

As Roberts took hold of the hopper handle, he became aware that everyone else had stopped work to watch him. They all knew he had "gotten the grease." Suddenly he broke into laughter, and at this everyone around him began to laugh. A short time later the men began showing him easier ways of removing the pattern and of turning the mold, so that he soon was able to fill his section of the conveyor on every cycle. His boards also started coming back to him in a stack. This was the last day of his assignment to the molding unit, but his later visits to the department always produced friendly greetings from the men and questions about when he would return to take one of the machines again.

POSTPREDICTION ANALYSIS

Refer to your predictions at the end of Part 1. How closely do they match the information above? Do inaccuracies in your predictions reflect inadequate analysis? If so, explain the analytical failure. If not, what additional information would you have needed in Part 1 to improve your predictive accuracy and how would you have used that information?

THE THIRD NATIONAL CITY BANK

Part 1

The night transit proof department was the check-processing center for the Third National City Bank. This department processed the checks of the eight area banks which used Third National as a clearing center. Through these facilities the banks received credit on their checks a day or two sooner than if the regular Federal Reserve clearing channels had been used.

Late each afternoon, trucks would arrive at the bank with the checks that had been deposited that day in each of the area banks. These checks were enclosed in bundles within cloth bags. Wrapped around each bundle was a tape total listing each check and the total dollar value of all the checks.

Upon their receipt each of the checks was microfilmed in order that the bank might have a record of all the items it had received. After microfilming, the checks were forwarded to the IBM proof machines. These machines had compartments to which the checks were sorted according to their destination. When each check was sent to a compartment, the dollar value was simultaneously recorded on a master tape and on a tape of the specific compartment to which the check was directed. After the bundle of checks had been sorted, the tape total sent by the area bank was checked with the total recorded on the master tape of the machine. If the dollar values on both tapes were not equal, the operator had to check whether he or the area bank had made the error. This was done by matching each item listed on the master tape with the original tape total. Since most bundles contained approximately 500 items, the checking of errors could be a very time-consuming process. The process could be even more taxing if the order of the listed checks on the bank tape did not correspond to the sequential order on the IBM master tape.

After all the checks had been run and the final total of each machine had proved to the total listings of the checks received from the area banks, each compartment was emptied, and the checks were secured by a rubber band with the corresponding compartment tape total. Then all the bundles were placed according to their compartment in cloth bags. These bags were sent by armored carrier to their respective destinations.

The skill necessary to operate an IBM proof machine could be readily acquired within a one-week training program. During this time the operator learned how to interpret the transit number imprinted on each check and learned which compartment in the machine corresponded to a certain transit number. Operation of the machine keyboard could also be easily learned. The finger dexterity required to record the dollar values of the checks could be readily acquired with continued practice. After a month of operation, the average operator would attain enough proficiency to process 600–800 checks an hour.

The bank management required the crew to remain on the job until every check had been processed. This was necessary since a one-day delay in receipt of credit for the checks would, in view of the $20 million volume processed each night, result in significant lost interest earnings. If the checks were not cleared, the bank might find it necessary to borrow from the Federal Reserve in order to meet its reserve requirements.

The bank had found that the best source of manpower for the night crew was the pool of young men who attended the five colleges within the city. Many of the young men found it necessary to work part time in order to meet the expense of their education. Therefore, although the job paid only slightly above the minimum wage, the bank had found that it could obtain the workers necessary for the operation.

The supervisor of the night crew was 24-year-old Douglas Dobek, who had left State College after attending for one year. Douglas had worked in the department for three years. He was paid on a straight salary, while all the other members of the crew were paid on an hourly basis. Douglas hoped to be recognized by bank officials as a candidate for further responsibility. Therefore, he was anxious that the proof department operate efficiently by performing its nightly work load in the least possible hours.

Since he was anxious to complete the work as soon as possible, Douglas moved constantly about the room all evening directing the work. When the first load of checks arrived from the armored carriers, Douglas would cut open the bags and tell the microfilmer which checks to film first, even though all the checks had to be processed before any could be sent out. Throughout the evening Douglas would constantly reassign the check bundles from operator to operator.

At times when everything seemed to be progressing smoothly, Douglas would sit down at a machine and process checks. When an operator found it necessary to leave his machine for a few minutes, Douglas would take the vacant machine over and rapidly run checks.

The six operators of the proof machines and the operator of the microfilmer were all juniors in college. Three of the operators attended State College and the remaining four attended Barton College. All of the operators expected to remain with the bank until they graduated from college.

The seven operators had all attended the same high school, and in college they were all majoring in education.

PREDICTIONS—Part 1

From what I know of the night crew operations described in Part 1, I would predict that:

a) Productivity of the crew would be (high) (average) (below management's standard).

b) The leadership style displayed by Douglas Dobek would be basically (functional) (dysfunctional) for work-group performance.

c) Relations between the crew members and Douglas Dobek would be (cordial) (neutral) (hostile).

d) Crew members would (get along well with each other) (get along well with some but not others) (not get along well with each other).

THE THIRD NATIONAL CITY BANK

Part 2

When Douglas left the room, the operators slowed down and joked about his behavior. The seven operators were very friendly with one another. On weekends they participated in group games such as basketball and touch football.

When school was in session, the operators chose to keep their work hours to a minimum. During the summer months and at other vacation times, however, the operators were anxious to obtain as many hours' pay as possible. One way to increase the number of working hours was to increase the incidence of errors. The operators congregated in the washroom before going to work and determined what sort of errors would be made that night. Some nights the microfilmer would run the checks in a manner that would allow them to fall out of sequential order. The operator who received the bundle would then make an error in listing the checks. If two or three errors were made within a night, one to two extra hours were gained.

During the latter part of July, Douglas compared the daily and weekly check-processing figures of the summer and winter months. He discovered that although the volume of processed checks had declined, the group was working more hours per week than it had during the peak winter months.

POSTPREDICTION ANALYSIS

Refer to your predictions at the end of Part 1. How closely do they match the information above? Do inaccuracies reflect inadequate analysis? If so, explain the analytical failure. If not, what additional information would you have needed in Part 1 to improve predictive accuracy and how would you have used this information?

76th RADIO COMPANY

Part 1

The 76th Radio Company was an Army communication unit that had been transferred from the United States to Korea in the early stages of the Korean War. In 1954, the company was geographically located in central Korea and was responsible for several vital communication links between frontline combat units and rear headquarters.

The effects of decreasing draft calls were particularly noticeable in the 76th. Although the unit was authorized for a complement of 234 men, it seldom contained more than 160. Furthermore, decreases in Defense Department funds had shortened training times for many technical skills so that what new personnel did arrive were ill equipped for duty and required additional training.

The 76th was located in an extremely isolated area. The campsite was centered on a plateau surrounded by rugged mountains. Only one road serviced the area. During the winter of 1953, a blizzard had closed the road, necessitating supply airdrops for a two-week period. The unit seldom had visitors except for an occasional inspector from higher headquarters. A daily run delivered working supplies, rations, and mail.

Its isolated location worked many hardships on the 76th. Being at the end of the line, literally and figuratively, it was the last to receive supplies, often causing the men to feel they were not getting a "fair share." For example, most of the men possessed only one pair of boots, when two were authorized and considered essential. Supply shortages were common in operations, too. Occasionally, transmitters or receivers would go on "downtime" due to lack of a tube or other component.

The men lived in tents, most of which were virtually in pieces and only minimally successful in keeping the elements outside. Below zero temperatures were not uncommon in the tents in winter.

The shortage of supplies, equipment, and personnel created arduous working conditions for the men. Often they were required to work 14 to 16 hours a day to perform necessary maintenance and to keep circuits open. There was little time for leaves or passes. The men worked in portable metal huts measuring 6 feet by 10 feet by 6 feet. Lack of heat in the winter and ventilation in summer made temperatures inside the huts vary seasonally between zero and 130 degrees. It was the usual procedure for two or three men, depending on manpower availability, to work a "shift" together. Eight-hour shifts were normal, but lack of personnel resulted in 12, 14, and 16-hour shifts. During work hours the men had no contact beyond their shift mates and supervisor. At the end of a shift the men usually went directly to their tents. Tent personnel assignments were left to the option of the men.

After visits to other units to see friends from previous assignments, the men would report to their buddies how others were improving their working and living conditions. Some "sister" units of the 76th located closer to headquarters were installing modern plumbing, and one unit was living in a permanent building that had central heating. The men of the 76th were well aware of the fact that all other units in the command lived and worked under much better conditions than they did.

Major William Wilson, commanding officer of the 76th, had held this position for 15 months and was due for a transfer to the States within a month. He spent much of his time trying to secure additional equipment and supplies to support the unit mission and to add to the men's personal comfort. Since it was impossible to persuade higher headquarters to put anything resembling a "permanent" structure in such an isolated position, Major Wilson had little success in this area.

Major Wilson's administration was not characterized by tight military discipline. So long as work shifts were covered, the men were relatively free to govern their own lives. For example, the work uniform was whatever was comfortable, ranging from loafers, sweat socks, and a variety of other civilian garments to cut-down khakis in the summer. Major Wilson habitually wore a baseball cap and a civilian shirt.

PREDICTIONS—Part 1

From what I know of the operations of the 76th described in Part 1, I would predict that:

a) Morale in the 76th would be (high) (medium) (low).

b) Operational efficiency in the 76th would be (high) (medium) (low).

c) The leadership style displayed by Major Wilson would be (functional) (dysfunctional) for work-group performance.

d) Off-duty activities would be (more than) (about) (below) average in number and would receive (above average) (average) (below average) support.

e) Relationships between the 76th and other units would be (close knit) (neutral) (hostile).

76th RADIO COMPANY

Part 2

Morale was extremely high in the 76th. When other commanders visited Major Wilson, they always told him that many men in their units wanted to volunteer for transfer to the 76th. None of the transfers was ever approved, however, as each CO was reluctant to let anyone, regardless of skill or personal choice, leave his unit. However, only one member of the 76th had requested transfer during Major Wilson's command and that request had been granted.

The efficiency of the 76th was a model for the remaining units in the command. In loss of circuits, operational speed, and other criteria by which unit efficiency was judged, the 76th had the best record in the theater.

The men were inventive in keeping communications "in" and working at top speed. Exchanging parts with friends in other units was a common practice. Frequent "scrounging" raids were organized. The shift supervisor, usually a noncommissioned officer, would organize and plan these raids. Scrounging parts and supplies from sister units was not considered theft and was accepted practice among all Army units. Usually, however, it was confined to supply personnel. In the 76th practically everyone was an accomplished scrounger, and the unit achieved a far-ranging reputation for its successes. The men usually got the cooperation of their friends in other units. These "accomplices" comprised most of those in other units who had asked for transfer to the 76th but had been turned down. When scrounging raids proved unsuccessful and a critical shortage developed, the men would resort to outright theft to keep the circuits in. There was an intense pride in their record, and everyone in the company strived to maintain and better their ratings.

In general, the men working together in a hut lived together in a tent, though this rule was often violated. There was an advantage to living with one's workmates since, with one shift occupying the tent while the other shift worked, the oil stoves could be kept burning in winter.

The men had converted some of the 76th's land into an athletic field. They had built facilities for basketball, volleyball, softball, horseshoes, and so forth. One energetic golf enthusiast had designed and built a small ninehole golf course in his spare time. After that, the entire area became jokingly known as the "country club." A great deal of enthusiasm attended many of the intramural contests, and these contests were marked by spirited and vigorous if unskilled, play.

The men took advantage of the unit's loose discipline in a variety of ways. Many took two- and three-day "unofficial passes," swapping work shifts with their buddies. No one wore a regulation uniform on any occasion. Everyone called Major Wilson "Bill."

POSTPREDICTION ANALYSIS

Refer to your predictions at the end of Part 1. How closely do they match the information above? Do inaccuracies in your predictions reflect inadequate analysis? If so, explain the analytical failure. If not, what additional information would you have needed in Part 1 to improve your predictive accuracy and how would you have used that information?

THE HARLOW COMPANY

Part 1

The Harlow Company was the oldest and one of the largest major automobile dealerships in Kansas City. Established in 1916, it was still owned by the founding family in 1961. The company had established an excellent reputation in the Kansas City area for reliability, trustworthiness, and service to its customers. It was said that one could always count on getting fair treatment from the Harlow Company.

The sales force of the Harlow Company consisted of two managers and 12 salesmen. The managers hired and fired all sales personnel, ordered new cars, and authorized all car sales. The salesmen were hired to sell both new and used cars. The sales force was broken down into four groups of three men each. Two groups were always at work simultaneously, one group operating at the used car lot, the other at the new car showroom. The two groups working the morning shift would be "off" in the afternoon, returning to work again in the evening, when they would switch locations with each other. The next day these two groups would be off in the morning and evening and on in the afternoon.

The managers, both 40 years old, had been with the company since 1949. Six of the salesmen had been with Harlow for eight years, the rest for at least two. When hiring a salesman, the managers placed particular emphasis upon the man's appearance, youthfulness, command of spoken English, and desire to sell. A man with these attributes and a willingness to comply with the Harlow system needed no prior experience.

The Harlow system was unique. The management had laid down definite rules and policies that were considerably different from those of other Kansas City dealerships. Although managements in other dealerships did not like their men to drink at lunch or between shifts, they rarely took any disciplinary action against such a practice. This was not the case at the Harlow Company. Any salesman caught showing up for work with liquor on his breath was discharged immediately.

The company also practiced a rigid system of "ups." An "up" was the vernacular for a salesman's turn to wait on a customer. The men on each shift drew lots to determine the order of "ups." In car dealerships it was tempting for a salesman to jump out of turn and wait on what was obviously a bona fide "buyer." This practice, known as "skating," was very common throughout automobile agencies in Kansas City. A person who was a good "skater" could make out very well for himself at the expense of his fellow workers.

The pay plan used by the company was unique not only to the Kansas City area but to the Midwest as well. The plan gave Harlow salesmen the chance to make two to three times the amount made by salesmen in other dealerships in the area. In addition to this pay plan, the top man for each month received a $50 bonus, and the members of the top group were invited to take their wives out for dinner at a fashionable restaurant at the company's expense. The company also gave each salesman a Christmas bonus based on the profits of the preceding year.

Working conditions at the Harlow Company were pleasant. The showroom was modern and well ventilated. Each salesman had his own desk where he could visit with customers and keep his order books and appraisal sheets. The used car lot, situated a block away from the showroom, provided similar conveniences.

PREDICTIONS—Part 1

From what I know of conditions in the Harlow Company, I would predict that:

a) There would be (a great deal of) (some) (practically no) competition among the sales force.

b) The productivity of the sales force would be (high) (standard) (below standard).

c) Social interaction among the sales force would be (high) (medium) (low) (1) during working hours, and (2) off the job.

d) The morale of the group would be (high) (medium) (low).

THE HARLOW COMPANY

Part 2

The morale of the sales force was high. There was a great deal of friendly kidding and joking both among the individual members of each group and among the various groups. Usually the two groups from the morning shift got together for lunch, and after the evening shift they met at a nearby tavern for a few beers to discuss the day's events before going home. Several times during the year the salesmen and their wives got together for a picnic, barbecue, or some other social event.

Though nominal, the monthly prizes gave incentive to the sales force, and a healthy competition had developed both among individuals and among the various groups. However, productivity was high for the sales force as a whole. No one salesman was consistently the top man, nor was any one salesman consistently at the bottom. If a man was having a bad month, the others on the shift would watch his technique, listen to his pitch, and then try to offer helpful suggestions. Usually by the end of the month the top salesman would have sold only three or four cars more than the bottom man.

POSTPREDICTION ANALYSIS

Refer to your predictions at the end of Part 1. How closely do they match the information above? Do inaccuracies in your predictions reflect inadequate analysis? If so, explain the analytical failure. If not, what additional information would you have needed in Part 1 to improve your predictive accuracy and how would you have used that information?

THE HARLOW COMPANY

Part 3

In February of 1962, a 55-year-old man named Ben Johnson came to replace one of the salesmen who had left to take a job as manager in another dealership. Although somewhat older than the others, Ben, with his white hair and "fatherly" appearance, projected the kind of personal image which was apt to inspire the customer's confidence. He had had considerable experience in the automobile business, having spent roughly 30 years selling cars. During his interview he had produced several letters of recommendation from previous employers saying he was an excellent producer.

Ben *was* an excellent producer. In the six months he worked for the Harlow Company, he was the top man four times. However, Ben's behavior and attitude deviated from that which the Harlow management expected of its employees. He frequently showed up late for work and with alcohol on his breath. (He cured the latter with gum.) He had to be asked to help move cars on and off the showroom floor and to do other jobs which the other salesmen had always done willingly. When asked to do a favor, Ben could find a thousand excuses for not doing it.

Ben's selling techniques also violated Harlow policy. He conferred with his customers in clandestine whispers, persuading them that they were the recipients of special favors. Sometimes he would make his 9's look like 8's. This practice allowed Ben to quote $895 to his customer but to receive sales authorization from the sales manager on the basis of a $995 price. When the papers were drawn up at the $995 figure, Ben would tell the customer that he had misquoted him the price, that he was very sorry, and the extra $100 would hardly be noticeable in his payments. At this point the customer either went ahead with the deal or walked out in a huff. Such incidents always arose as an apparent misunderstanding between Ben and the customer, and management had no tangible evidence of deliberate misrepresentation.

Ben also "skated" a lot of "ups." Frequently he would jump out of turn to wait on a customer, talk to him for a while, and then walk him to the door. If asked, he would explain that the person had been an old friend of his rather than a customer, and he would keep to his scheduled "up." As often as not, a week later he would sell the "old friend" a car.

PREDICTIONS—Part 3

From the changes described in Part 3, I would predict that, compared with the conditions existing before the changes:

a) Relations between the original salesmen and Ben will be (cordial) (neutral) (strained).

b) The morale of the original salesmen will (increase) (remain the same) (decrease).

c) The original salesmen will be (more competitive) (as competitive) (less competitive).

d) The productivity of the original salesmen will (increase) (remain the same) (decrease).

e) Social interaction among the sales force will (increase) (remain the same) (decrease) (1) during working hours and (2) off the job.

THE HARLOW COMPANY

Part 4

It soon became evident that Ben's behavior was undermining the morale of the sales force. Frequent complaints about Ben's "skating" were voiced, and several remarks were made directly to Ben. However, Ben did not reform. Even his fellow workers' most pointed remarks and criticisms left him unfazed. Before long the joking and friendly bantering tapered off. Everyone appeared tense and nervous. The luncheon and evening get-togethers occurred very seldom. When they did, it was primarily to complain about how bad sales were, how someone wished he were on another shift, or what good jobs other people had at other dealerships.

The competitive spirit died out completely. Productivity for the sales force as a whole reached an all-time low. Ben was the only person who was really selling; he was by far and away the best producer. Despite severe criticism from management, sales for the group continued to drop off.

Finally, one morning it was announced that Ben had been fired. He had come to work the previous evening under the influence of alcohol. By noon that day the old camaraderie had returned to the group. As the week progressed, sales shot up. Intergroup and intershift competition developed again. By the end of the month, sales were back to normal "pre-Ben" levels.

POSTPREDICTION ANALYSIS

Refer to your predictions at the end of Part 1. How closely do they match the information above? Do inaccuracies in your predictions reflect inadequate analysis? If so, explain the analytical failure. If not, what additional information would you have needed in Part 1 to improve your predictive accuracy and how would you have used that information?

CHAPTER 6

*Technical Inputs**

by Paul R. Lawrence

TECHNOLOGY as a general element of culture has a pervasive and powerful influence on all aspects of human affairs. This chapter will examine technology as an input to the functioning of organizational systems. The empirical observation that technology has an important influence on the behavior of people in organizations is as true for technology when it is defined in the narrow sense of knowledge and techniques relevant to the production of physical goods, as when it is defined in the broader sense to include all systematic techniques which lead to the output of ideas, marketing projects, accounting reports, training programs, and other organizational activities which support the production of goods and services.

In examining the influence of technology, we must again keep fixed in mind that technology and other system inputs are interdependently related. A useful way to begin our examination of technology, in fact, is to explore three basic ways in which technology influences behavior through its effects on other inputs. First, technology is a determinant of the human inputs required by an organization and, thus indirectly, of the predispositions of employees. Second, technology is a determinant of certain gross features of organizational structure and procedure. Third, technology is an immediate determinant of individual and group job designs and, therefore, indirectly a determinant of social structure and norms.

---

*I am indebted to Professor Paul R. Lawrence of the Harvard Business School for preparation of this chapter. During one phase of the development of these ideas, he was assisted by Assistant Professor Gene W. Dalton.

Technical and Human Inputs

The fact that different technologies are relevant to different kinds of business creates the obvious need for different kinds of people to operate those businesses. A chemical company cannot operate without securing the services of a certain number of chemical engineers, for example. These men bring into the firm not only a predisposition for solving certain types of technical problems but also a wide variety of other shared beliefs and ways of behaving which the firm must take into account. They will share some expectations about the kind of work they may properly be assigned to do, about the degree of deference they should enjoy, and about other aspects of their working climate. The organization cannot safely ignore these expectations. They have emerged from common professional training but also from more fundamental, early-life predispositions which led these individuals to seek an engineering career in the first place. Firms may, and often do, develop indoctrination programs designed to modify the expectations of groups of employees about how work should be conducted, to bring them more in line with the organization's preexisting methods and beliefs. Such attempts to create conformity will prove to be self-defeating, however, if they go so far as to weaken the bases upon which the employees' expertise is founded. Adjustment of an engineer to the organization's expectations, for example, may cause him to adjust away from the capacity to keep up with new technical developments and to solve new engineering problems. So, shaping an organization around the predispositions of its needed human resources is by no means a simple case of "keeping everybody happy." It also involves creating the work climate most conducive to carrying out effective specialized work.

Because in recent years business has needed to recruit the more technically specialized managers and professionals, like our exemplifying chemical engineers, at an accelerating pace, it has become acutely aware of the impact of the predispositions that these highly trained people bring with them. This trend, however, should not cause us to lose sight of the fact that technology is highly related to the predispositions of employees in the less formally trained blue- and white-collar segments of the work force. In his company's early days, Henry Ford spoke with considerable gratification of the predisposition toward conscientiousness among the "Wayne County farm boys" who were attracted to his assembly plants by the "$5 day." It is worth noting, however, that the second and third generations of auto workers, coming from an urban factory background, now are displaying different predispositions. In a recent study of industrial workers, Turner and Lawrence[1] distinguished among blue-collar workers from a variety of industries which they studied, those from "city" and those from "town" subcultural backgrounds and compared their attitudes toward work. In general, they found that so-called town workers were predisposed to seek more complex and challenging work assignments, while city workers as a general group were inclined to want more routinized and less demanding jobs in which they could make a simple exchange of time for economic rewards, meantime complicating their lives in other ways outside of work. We shall have more to say later about the linkage between worker predispositions and job design.

In concluding our review of this aspect of the relation between technology and predispositions, we need to be reminded that, while our generalizations about the predilections of different segments of the work force are useful, they need to be constantly revised as conditions change. Our stereotypes of groups have a way of persisting long after they lose their accuracy. For instance, there is now some limited evidence that the latest wave of young people who are coming into blue-collar factory work bring different expectations with them. These new urbanites, some of them high school dropouts, though exhibiting a veneer of cynicism toward organized work, lack the passivity of their predecessor urban workers and, for this reason, may be searching for opportunities to become more involved in complex tasks.

Technical and Organizational Inputs

The body of technical knowledge relevant to the work of any given organization acts as an important environmental influence on the organization's structure, i.e., on the way in which the work of the organization is divided up. This point is quickly conceded as obvious, but what is often missed by managers and organizational analysts is the power and pervasiveness of the impact of this variable on the day-to-day operation of the entire network of organizational variables. The fact that this is a long-term influence that often works in subtle ways sometimes obscures its importance. With the perspective of history, many examples can be drawn of the relation between these elements. We tend to take the present form of automobile companies for granted

---

[1]Arthur N. Turner and Paul R. Lawrence, *Industrial Jobs and the Workers* (Boston: Harvard Graduate School of Business Administration, Division of Research, 1965).

without analyzing the following causal sequence: Knowledge of precision metalworking plus knowledge of internal combustion engine mechanics led to the possibility of manufacturing automobiles with interchangeable parts and, in turn, to the feasibility of mass-producing those parts. Mass production and mass markets made it possible to achieve economies through large-scale manufacturing units and assembly line procedures. From these characteristics came the final step of centralized decision making, detailed and narrow job definitions and mechanistic, hierarchical leadership styles which have become characteristic of the auto industry. This chain of causation is, of course, an oversimplification of a more complex process. The last step in the chain above was reported in an intensive study of automotive organizations.[2] In this study, technical, organizational, and social phenomena were found to be highly interrelated.

The experience of the automobile industry illustrates how certain technical facts guide an industry's choice of overall production methods and how, in turn, these methods have a profound effect on attributes of the organization's structure. It makes a great deal of difference in the way a business is organized, for example, whether it deals with a continuous process technology such as in the oil or chemical industries; with a job shop or small-batch process such as in fashion clothing manufacturing; with a custom, one-of-a-kind, process such as in shipbuilding; or with a mass-production process such as in household appliance manufacturing. These gross technical differences are closely associated with different ways of dividing up the work of the organization into its major subsystems. This, in turn, influences the kind of control and coordination issues a management system must address.[3] For example, contrast the organizational implications of a technology such as oil refining with one such as missile production. They both are science-based industries characterized by relatively fast rates of change in relevant technical knowledge. But oil-refining technology is implemented by a continuous process manufacture of large quantities of a standard product through the use of expensive, special-purpose equipment. Missile manufacture is a small-batch production of very complex products utilizing relatively general-purpose manufacturing equipment.

---

[2]Arthur N. Turner, "Management and the Assembly Line," *Harvard Business Review,* September-October, 1955.

[3]For further analysis of the effects of different ways of subdividing the major units of a complex organization, see E. J. Miller, "Technology, Territory, and Time," *Human Relations,* Vol. XII, No. 3 (1959).

Implicit in these technical processes are quite different ways, for instance, of coordinating research and development work with production work. In the oil case, these two specialized functions are apt to be differentiated along both formal authority and physical location lines, each a large separate unit significantly influencing the other only in regard to infrequent new-plant investment and design decisions. In the case of missiles, the research and development function is often coterminous with the production function, the same people and formal organizational units often carrying out both functions. Technology, then, is highly determinate of who interacts with whom and around what types of activities.

The organizational consequences of these technical differences can be seen even more dramatically in contrasting the influence of mass-production methods with either continuous or job shop methods. The contrasting effect of these processes was highlighted by extensive research on this topic reported by Joan Woodward.[4] She finds that companies using mass-production processes tended to follow such mechanistic practices as clearly defining and specifying all the duties and responsibilities of each position, using written communication in preference to verbal communication, and having highly specialized functions for the different members of management. This was in contrast to both continuous and job shop processes where opposite practices tended to be followed. Furthermore, the companies with the best performance records were those whose practices were modal for each type. Thus, the effectiveness of organizational practice depends upon the type of technology which is characteristic of each industry, rather than upon some absolute, ideal division of labor, managerial style, incentive system, or other facet of organizational input.

The effects of technology on organizational structure seem also to be related to the rate of change in the body of technical knowledge. For decades, certain industries, such as coal mining, drew on a relatively unchanging body of technical knowledge and, as a consequence, adopted organizational structures and processes that reflected this stability. If, for any of many reasons, the body of relevant knowledge begins to change rapidly, organizations are faced not only with adopting new technical methods but also with adopting new organizational structures appropriate to the new technology, and, particularly, with adopting structures which can accommodate to the quicker tempo of successive

[4]Joan Woodward, "Management and Technology," *Problems of Progress in Industry*, No. 3 (London: H. M. Stationery Office, 1958).

changes. This linkage between rates of technical change and organizational structure will be examined in more detail in Chapter 7.

Technological Inputs, Individual Satisfaction, and Social Behavior

The third way in which technology, broadly defined, influences the behavior of people in organizations is through the specific design of each employee's task. In order to achieve a desired technical result, for example, two parts fitted together and attached in a specified manner, someone must engage in certain behavior. These task requirements influence the employee's response to his job and to other aspects of the organization in important ways. It is a matter of common observation that different jobs vary widely along such dimensions as required skill and knowledge, variety versus repetitiveness, autonomy of choice, and so on. These job attributes are built into the way jobs are initially designed and into the way they evolve over time. Although jobs are designed by managers who can exercise some degree of choice in such matters as the fineness of the division of labor, job design decisions must be made within certain rather narrow limits of technical feasibility.

In a study of job design and its impact on the behavior of blue-collar workers, industrial jobs were compared in terms of (1) the amount of variety in the activities prescribed for the job; (2) the amount of discretion or autonomy about job activities permitted and required of the incumbent; (3) the frequency and diversity of interaction with others demanded by the job; (4) the amount of opportunity for optional interaction built into the nature of the job; (5) the length of learning time for job proficiency; and (6) the amount of responsibility that needed to be assumed by the incumbent as measured by the likelihood of serious error, the uncertainty in regard to proper corrective actions, and the length of time that elapsed before the results of the work were known. These six attributes of jobs are useful ways of describing the physical and, to a lesser extent, the organizational constraint of particular jobs. The way these six dimensions of individual tasks influence behavior has not been fully researched, but the evidence of their importance is clear. For instance, careful studies have been made by Walker[5] and his associates that compare the behavioral con-

[5]C. R. Walker, *Modern Technology and Civilization: An Introduction to Human Problems in the Machine Age* (New York: McGraw-Hill Book Co., 1962); C. R. Walker *Toward the Automatic Factory* (New Haven, Conn.: Yale University Press, 1957); and C. R. Walker and R. H. Guest, *The Man on the Assembly Line* (Cambridge, Mass.: Harvard University Press, 1952).

sequence of the attributes of automobile assembly line work with the the work of tending control equipment in an automated steel rolling mill. These job differences seem to induce quite different worker attitudes and behavior and, in turn, this has a marked influence on supervisory styles and organizational structures and procedures. These and other studies indicate to date that jobs that score low on the six dimensions tend to induce mechanistic hierarchical patterns of organizations. Jobs that score high tend to induce organic participative patterns.

These studies also indicate, as was noted earlier, that individuals and cultures differ in their predispositions to favor and find satisfaction in work that is psychologically involving and complex (high on the six dimensions) or in work that is simple and routine (low on the six dimensions). In particular, cultures associated with the Protestant ethic (or its cultural equivalent), which looks upon work as a good in itself, seem to predispose work forces to seek and enjoy complex work. These cultural influences are more apt to be found in the United States among work forces of town and rural background, whereas work forces from urban settings, either because of different cultural predispositions or by longer acculturation to low-content industrial work, are more likely to find satisfaction in low-content jobs with infrequent changes and distractions. These recent findings suggest a way of accounting for earlier discoveries which seemed contradictory. For instance, a study of factory work in England[6] indicated that workers preferred nonconveyor to conveyor work and longer rather than shorter cycle times. On the other hand, several careful observational studies, such as those reported by Baldamus[7] indicated that many workers found satisfaction in the "traction" or rhythm of low-content work, so long as interruptions and pressure were not too great.

Technology affects behavior not only through the design of individual jobs but also through its collective effect on jobs throughout departments and plants. For instance, when the technology suggests bringing together a large number of workers in a single area to do the same work, say operating punch presses, a resonating effect can occur. Any problem that a single worker might pass off as relatively unimportant can be blown up into major proportions by many operators sharing their grievances and thereby reinforcing and escalating each other's sense of injustice.

---

[6]S. Wyatt, and R. Marriott, *A Study of Attitudes to Factory Work* (London: Medical Research Council, 1958).

[7]W. Baldamus, *Efficiency and Effort* (London: Tavistock Publications, Ltd., 1961).

The facts of technology can also put certain work groups into a highly strategic position vis-à-vis the flow of work through an entire production system. Such groups tend to develop quite different characteristics from groups that are more peripheral to the work flow.[8] It has been demonstrated in many different work groups, including bomber crews, that the physical proximity of work positions, as determined by technology, can have a powerful effect on the pattern of human relations and, in turn, on productivity. Furthermore, research in a variety of work settings reveals that people generally expect higher status members of an organization to initiate activity for lower status members. Difficulties arise when the opposite occurs. Sometimes the technical work flow creates such incongruous situations. One such incongruity was described by Whyte in his study of how restaurant waitresses experienced chronically bad relations with cooks whenever it was necessary for waitresses to give cooks verbal food orders. An impersonal system of placing orders helped eliminate the problem.[9]

In general, research on worker proximity and interdependence suggests that people take a more responsible interest in task performance when they are required to interact within a small group to accomplish complementary aspects of an overall task which, itself, is definable, visible, and reasonably complex. A clear example of this general finding is Rice's study reporting the favorable results of reorganizing an Indian textile mill, following such guidelines.[10] Under these technical conditions people can simultaneously fulfill their needs for social interaction and for making a contribution to a larger purpose.

The Interdependence of Technical, Human, Organizational, and Social Inputs: A Review

Effects of the three general types of technological influence, i.e., technology as a body of knowledge, technology as a gross determinant of organizational structure, and technology as a specific determinant of group and individual job designs, may be compatible and reinforcing or they may be inconsistent and conflicting. The interdependence between technology, human characteristics, formal organizational structure, and informal social structure often remains obscure until a technological

---

[8] L. B. Sayles, *Behavior of Industrial Work Groups* (New York: John Wiley & Sons, Inc., 1958).

[9] W. F. Whyte, *Human Relations in the Restaurant Industry* (New York: McGraw-Hill Book Co., 1948).

[10] A. K. Rice, *Productivity and Social Organization: The Ahmedabad Experiment* (London: Tavistock Publications, Ltd. 1958).

change highlights the interdependence with a dramatic impact. Let's look at an example.

In a traditional woodworking shop, where much of the work requires skill and judgment, both formal and informal relationships tend to be established along lines consistent with the demands of the task and the technology available to perform it. Older, experienced craftsmen who can produce more and better work than new men are paid more for their work. They train and otherwise initiate activity for younger men, due to the skills they have developed over the years. The most experienced and skillful men are logical choices for supervisory positions. The impact of technology under such a circumstance is easily overlooked because everything seems to "fit." But the effects of technology are highlighted when the specifics of the technology change in such a way that old relationships are reversed, attenuated, or strained. If new automatic woodturning equipment is introduced to the woodworking shop, a number of changes will result. An inexperienced man, after a short period of instruction will be able to produce the same or a greater quantity and quality of work than an experienced man had been able to produce formerly. Pay differentials disappear. The instruction and skills of older men are no longer so valuable to younger workers. Older experienced men may even find themselves being told what to do by a young, low-seniority engineer. We can easily visualize some of the disturbances which might result. Rewards would now be "out-of-line" with prior expectations concerning the value of age and experience. A man who is of low status along most of the dimensions which have been important in the shop is now initiating action for high-status men. We can imagine the kinds of efforts which will be made by the social system of the shop to restore a state of equilibrium.

Most of the technological changes we have described in the woodworking shop illustration affect status relationships. But we could as easily have focused on changed spatial patterns which would have obstructed prior social exchanges and necessitated the development of new ones. The same kind of change takes place when a company moves to a new building with a different configuration of office spaces. Prior helping relationships may be made impossible by walls and desk arrangements. In a chemical plant where continuous-operating equipment is introduced for the first time, formerly independent work shifts will now find that their work depends on what other shifts have done. Yet, they may lack the social mechanism for handling the inevitable problems which will arise out of their new interdependence.

The above discussion may imply that management behavior is perfectly constrained by technical inputs. That is, of course, a serious overstatement of the case. The beliefs and customs of managers markedly influence the way in which technological variables effect actual behavior. Management may seek technologies with high change rates, or it may avoid them. It can set up research and development departments whose guiding policies channel the direction and degree of technical advances. Furthermore, it can, within the constraints of technology, try to maximize either the complexity or the simplicity of individual jobs. It can set up organizational structures and foster leadership styles that are compatible or incompatible with technological influences. Management's decisions involving technology are sometimes influenced by outmoded customs of business or by arbitrary applications of so-called principles of management, as well as by careful situational analysis of the risks and opportunities of alternative approaches.

However management seeks to mediate the influence of technology on the behavior of people in its organization, one fact is universally clear—the particular technological choices with which it favors its organization will be clearly reflected in the form of that organization and in its social structure and norms. At bottom, the assigned activities and interactions—those stipulations for behavior which grow out of the nature of technology and management's choices among alternative organization structures—combined with the individual predispositions of the organization's members (themselves preinfluenced by the skills required by the nature of the technology) will determine broadly who can socially relate to whom and what sentiments will emerge. Thus, technology directly and, through organizational structure, indirectly forces some people into contact, separates others, and provides the basic work activities and groupings around which social structure, norms, and actual behavior emerge.

Three Cases of Technical Influence

In order to permit the reader to test out his understanding of the ideas included in this chapter and to see ways of fitting them into the basic analytical scheme of the book, several cases of organizational behavior have been included with this chapter. The cases, as previously, have been designed so that predictions of actual behavior can be made from prior examination of human, social, technical, and organizational inputs. After Part 1 of each case, questions governing predicted behavior are suggested. Study of Part 2 of the case will make it possible to determine the accuracy of predictions. The third case included here, Harlan Shoe Company, is in four parts rather than two, since a change in inputs was made by the company. Therefore, two sets of predictions can be made on this case.

It should be emphasized again that these so-called prediction exercises are not to be construed to mean that predictive perfection is either a practical or possible goal. They do suggest that careful, systematic analysis of interrelated forces can decrease the probability of incorrectly interpreting events and, thus, increase the chance that the consequences of one's actions will be those which are intended.

THE TUDOR CORPORATION

Part 1

The Tudor Corporation had recently built a new plant for producing large orders of color cards for the paint, cosmetic, and automotive industries. Well over 1.5 million color brochures were to be produced in the plant each year displaying the ranges of colors available in the customers' line of paints, lipsticks, cars, and the like. The new plant was located in a town of 2,000 people in a generally rural area. The town has but two other smaller industries.

The company's production organization was divided into 11 departments. One of these departments, referred to as the bindery section, employed 15 women, who were responsible for the final operation before shipping the color cards. The mechanical equipment in the bindery consisted of folding machines and drying ovens (see Exhibit 1). There were six folding machines used for scoring, slitting, perforating, and folding brochures. Each was operated by a pair of women. One woman, called the "feeder," placed a tissue on each card and then "fed" the cards into the rollers of the folding machine. This job involved some judgment as to acceptable quality and considerable dexterity in the speed with which the cards were fed. The feeders were not required, however, to have extensive knowledge of the mechanics of the machine or of the folding process. Feeders were given a relatively high degree of attention by the bindery manager because of their control on quality and quantity of production through the department. Frequently, the feeder would stop the machine if in her judgment it was not producing good folds.

The second worker on the folding machine was called the "packer." She stood at the delivery end of the machine and banded the folded cards into packs of 25, after which she placed the packs in cartons for shipment. Her production was governed by the feeder. The job of packing entailed less dexterity and therefore less experience than feeding. All jobs in the bindery, however, paid the same hourly wage. The output of the girls on each folding machine was recorded separately by the foreman, taking the size, shape, and number of folds on each particular card into account. No work contacts were required of the folding girls other than minimal contacts with the other girls on the same machine.

The third job in the department was "pulling," which was done by a girl who sat on a stool at the end of each of three 120-foot drying ovens and pulled the cured cards out of the conveyorized wickets of the oven. Generally, a puller had to remain at her position to pull the cards as they came from the ovens, although it was possible to get a

Exhibit 1

THE TUDOR CORPORATION

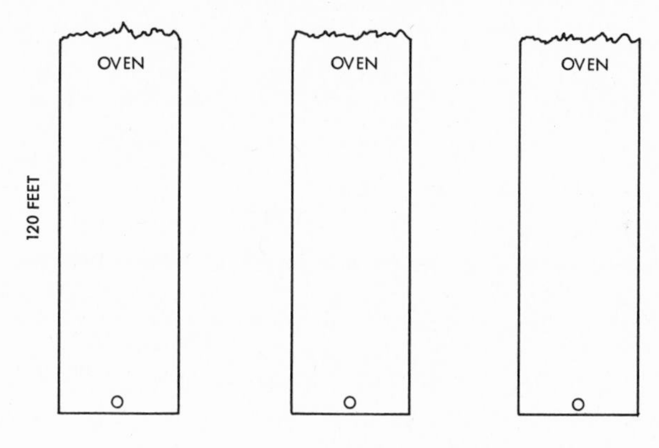

IN-PROCESS STORAGE AREA

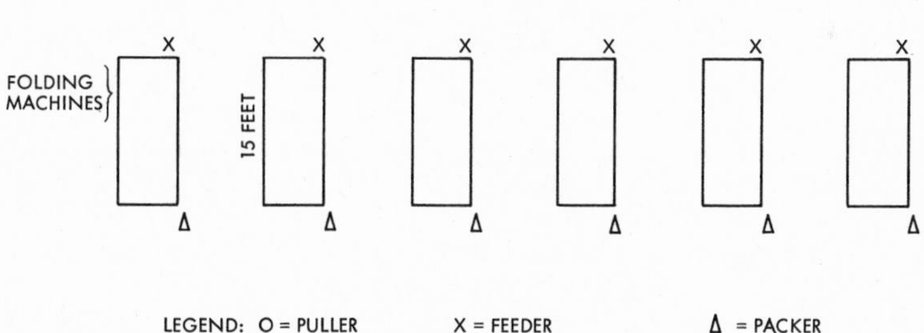

LEGEND: O = PULLER X = FEEDER Δ = PACKER

few minutes ahead by walking along the conveyor and pulling cards before they came to the end of the conveyor. The cards were stacked in piles and were transported to the folders at the end of each day by a man from another department. The manner in which the pullers stacked and counted their piles had an effect on the way the feeders were able to handle the cards. No interaction was required between individual pullers or between pullers and folders. This job required even less skill than the folder jobs and was characterized by a high degree of monotony. Conversation was not possible, due to the distance between pullers. The proximity of the ovens caused the area to be unpleasantly warm.

The bindery manager rigidly controlled the work habits of the women. All the girls had to take their lunch breaks at the same time and all ate their lunches on the premises. Coffee breaks were staggered so that only one or two girls were resting at a given time. Very little talking or joking on the job was allowed by the manager, even though conversation was inherently difficult because of machine noise. He rarely spoke to the pullers or packers but occasionally called out a general announcement to the group at the start or end of the work period.

PREDICTIONS—Part 1

From what I know of the operations of the bindery section described in Part 1, I would predict that the workers in the bindery section would:

a) (All eat lunch together as a group) (would tend not to eat lunch with other girls in the same section) (would eat together in sub-groups [if so, which one?]) (would evolve no definite pattern of lunch partners).

b) (Generally tend to get along well with the other girls in the section) (get along well with some girls in the section, but not others) (generally have difficulty getting along with others in the section).

If you predict the second alternative, which girls would you expect to get along well together and which would not.

c) (Be well satisfied) (be moderately satisfied) (be dissatisfied with their jobs).

If you do not predict a uniform level of satisfaction, identify, and explain the differences you predict.

d) Rate as follows on these performance measures:

Relative labor costs per unit output (high) (moderate) (low) labor costs

Relative absentee rates (high) (moderate) (low) absenteeism

Relative turnover rate (high) (moderate) (low) turnover

THE TUDOR CORPORATION

Part 2

The feeders, packers, and pullers all ate their lunches separately in their own job groups. To a limited extent the workers in each of these groups helped out members of their own job group, but they did not help members of the other job groups.

A certain degree of tension grew up between the groups. The pullers felt that they should not have to do all the unpleasant work but that all the women should take turns pulling. The feeders, on the other hand, felt that they should never be asked to do other work.

Frequent disputes arose about the manner in which the pullers stacked and counted their piles. The feeders felt that the pullers vindictively piled the cards in a manner which delayed the folding.

The pullers would try hard to get ahead of the conveyorized wickets so that they could have time to go over to talk to, and sometimes help, other pullers. The pullers also made frequent trips to the water fountain and lavatory to escape the boredom of their jobs.

The labor costs per thousand folds in the new plant were higher than they were in the bindery of an older plant that the company operated in a metropolitan area. Absenteeism was high. In spite of the fact that most of the bindery girls felt they were fortunate to have good-paying jobs in a farm area, several of the women quit without explanation.

POSTPREDICTION ANALYSIS

Refer to your predictions at the end of Part 1. How closely do they match the information above? Do inaccuracies in your predictions reflect inadequate analysis? If so, explain the analytical failure. If not, what additional information would you have needed in Part 1 to improve your predictive accuracy and how would you have used that information?

THE ABC TACTICAL FIGHTER WING

Part 1

The ABC Tactical Fighter Wing was composed of two geographically separate units. The first and largest was based in the United States. The other smaller unit was based overseas.

The U.S.-based unit consisted of approximately 75 jet fighter-bomber-type aircraft in three operational squadrons. The aircraft were maintained by a consolidated maintenance squadron with crew chiefs to service, inspect, and maintain them, and specialists to repair complex aircraft systems such as the electronic, armament, and hydraulic systems.

The crew chiefs worked overlapping nine-hour shifts. The first crew (including crew chiefs and specialists) arrived at 0630 to preflight and launch the aircraft on the early missions. Both crews were on duty after the first flights landed to perform maintenance, to service, and to launch the aircraft on a second flight. After the aircraft were launched a second time, the first crew was free to leave. The second crew remained on the job until all aircraft were landed, postflight inspections were made, maintenance was performed, and the aircraft were serviced for flying the next day.

Each experienced crew chief was assigned responsibility for specific aircraft. These assignments frequently changed. Because of shift work and periodic alert duty, the assigned crew chief often could not be present when maintenance was being performed on his aircraft.

The specialists, who received special proficiency pay, were under centralized control and were dispatched to an aircraft whenever a complex system discrepancy was reported. Normally, the specialists worked in pairs on an aircraft without the assistance of a crew chief. The specialists had little contact with pilots. They worked on aircraft which were out of commission in shops which were located some distance away from the squadron operations building.

The overseas unit consisted of a detachment of men and aircraft based near a gunnery and bombing range. The detachment consisted of 12 aircraft, 12 crew chiefs, and approximately 25 specialists. Because of the stringent bombing and gunnery mission requirements, each aircraft was normally flown two or three times each weekday, and sometimes once on Saturday if the detachment fell behind its training schedule. Maintenance men worked 10 to 15 hours a day to fulfill the required sortie rate. Crew chiefs were assigned specific aircraft and were present whenever that aircraft was flown. They worked along side the specialists to perform maintenance on their aircraft.

PREDICTIONS—Part 1

a) Aircraft in-commission rate of the overseas detachment will be (higher than) (about the same as) (lower than) that of the U.S.-based unit.

b) Social relationships among maintenance personnel of the overseas base will be (more congenial than) (about the same as) (less congenial than) those among U.S.-based personnel.

c) Social relationships between flying personnel and members of the maintenance crew of the overseas base will be (more congenial than) (about the same as) (less congenial than) those between similar personnel at the U.S. base.

d) Overall individual satisfaction among maintenance personnel at the overseas base will be (higher than) (about the same as) (lower than) among personnel based in the United States.

THE ABC TACTICAL FIGHTER WING

Part 2

The aircraft in-commission rate of the U.S.-based unit was low, and flight abort rate was high. Aircraft in-flight emergencies were numerous, and the wing's accident rate was high in comparison to that of similar units. Because of the low in-commission rate and missions canceled due to weather, the wing often flew training missions on Saturdays and Sundays to meet training requirements. Morale was low among maintenance men. Men with many years' service frequently remarked, "This is the worst organization I have ever been in." Much bitterness arose between the maintenance men working on the line and the supervisors working in the dispatch office.

Specialists sometimes left panels undone after they had worked on an aircraft. This often had serious consequences such as an instrument panel falling into a pilot's lap on take off or an external panel blowing off in flight. The responsibility for these errors frequently fell on the pilot and crew chief because their inspections did not uncover the discrepancy before the flight.

The in-commission rate was very high at the overseas detachment, and the abort rate was lower than at the home base. Pilots frequently conferred with specialists to gain additional insight into a system which would help improve their bombing and gunnery scores. Most maintenance men were proud of the performance of the aircraft and took an active interest in the bombing and gunnery scores recorded by the pilots flying their airplanes. Crew chiefs often spent extra time cleaning and polishing "their" aircraft. The pilots felt that their good flying records depended on good maintenance, and they periodically rewarded the maintenance men with a "beer bust." Morale was high, and many single airmen volunteered for extra tours of duty with the detachment.

POSTPREDICTION ANALYSIS

Refer to your predictions at the end of Part 1. How closely do they match the information above? Do inaccuracies in your predictions reflect inadequate analysis? If so, explain the analytical failure. If not, what additional information would you have needed in Part 1 to improve your predictive accuracy and how would you have used that information?

HARLAN SHOE COMPANY

Part 1

The Harlan Shoe Company operated the largest chain of retail shoe outlets in the United States. The company stored its men's and boys' shoes in a warehouse located in Newark, New Jersey.

Retail outlets sent orders to the Newark warehouse twice a month under normal business conditions, and three times a month during the Easter and back-to-school rushes. When orders were received, they were

Exhibit 1

HARLAN SHOE COMPANY

FLOOR PLAN, DISTRIBUTORS' SECTION

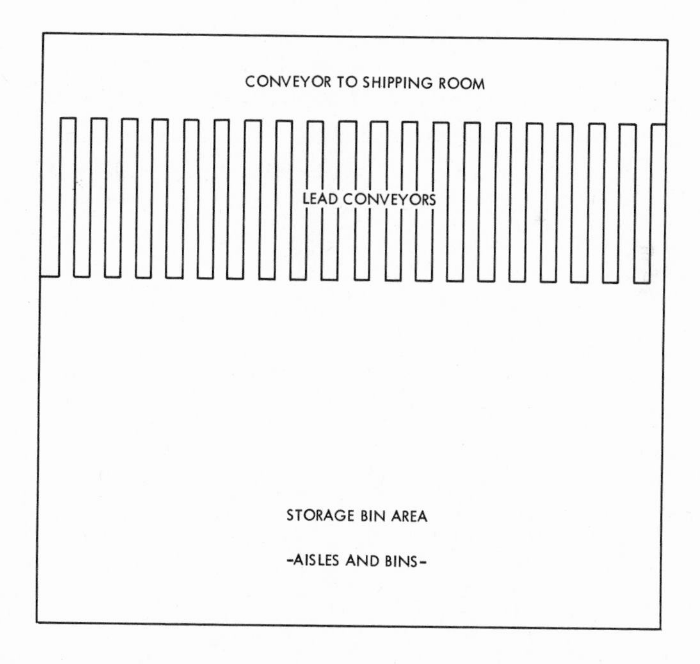

handed out, one at a time, to 20 clerks known as distributors. A distributor's task was to select from the shoe bins the styles, quantities, and sizes specified on the order. He deposited the shoes he had "pulled" from the bins into cartons placed on a cart. When he had finished pulling his order, he wheeled this cart to one of the 20 conveyor belts (see Exhibit 1). This distributor then checked the shoes he had pulled against the order to make sure he had the correct styles, quantities, and sizes. It was often necessary to return to the bins to obtain a pair of shoes previously overlooked or to exchange a size pulled incorrectly. Once the order was perfect, the distributor wrote out an invoice for it and placed the shoes on the conveyor, which carried them to the shipping department. Except for the return to the bins to correct a mistake, the checking function consumed approximately the same amount of time as the pulling function.

The distributors could be divided into two main groups. One group consisted of 10 veterans of World War II who had been with the company for 15 years. They belonged to the same Legion Post. The second group was made up of younger workers, including a few recent high school graduates. All the distributors were paid an hourly rate, but this varied according to seniority.

PREDICTIONS—Part 1

(When and if you predict behavioral differences between the two sub-groups, specify each subgroup.)

a) The productivity of the distributors in terms of (1) quantity, and (2) quality would be (high) (standard) (below standard).

b) Social interaction (1) among the older distributors, (2) among the younger distributors, and (3) between the older and the younger distributors would be (high) (medium) (low) during working hours.

c) The morale of the distributors would be (high) (medium) (low).

HARLAN SHOE COMPANY

Part 2

In general the 20 distributors worked at a leisurely pace which was adequate for the normal influx of orders; however, overtime was necessary during the two rush periods. The quality of their work was more than satisfactory.

The two groups of workers adapted somewhat differently to the job situation. The members of the older group arranged with the foreman to obtain their orders at the same time in the morning, and they worked at the same pace throughout the day. Thus, they were almost always working adjacent to each other in the bin area, and they used adjacent lead conveyors. The men took advantage of this opportunity to talk and joke with each other.

The younger group clustered together on the job to a much lesser degree (although they often saw each other after work). They worked faster and usually handled more orders per day than the older group.

Despite the differences in adaptation, there was a minimum of friction between the two groups. The men got along well with each other and morale was high.

POSTPREDICTION ANALYSIS

Refer to your predictions at the end of Part 1. How closely do they match the information above? Do inaccuracies in your predictions reflect inadequate analysis? If so, explain the analytical failure. If not, what additional information would you have needed in Part 1 to improve your predictive accuracy and how would you have used that information?

HARLAN SHOE COMPANY

Part 3

During the period 1958–1960, Harlan opened 100 new retail outlets in various parts of the country. The volume of work required of the distributors in the Newark warehouse increased considerably. The shipping superintendent and the foreman of the distributors decided that the increased work load could not be met under the present system. They therefore instituted several changes.

Under the new system the distributors would be divided into two groups of 10 each. The first group would be the pullers; they would select the proper shoes from the bins and leave them at one of the conveyors. The other 10 men would be stationed at the conveyors. They would perform the checking function, including the correction of all errors made by the pullers. The pullers would be instructed to take great care in their activities so that the checkers would not often be required to leave the conveyors to correct mistakes. While the checkers were at their stations, they would be physically separated from each other by the conveyor belts. Since high stacks of shoe boxes would be on these belts almost continuously, the line of vision between the men would be blocked.

The superintendent and the foreman felt that the increased worker specialization under the new system would increase speed considerably. Furthermore, it would mean fewer workers in the aisles and would thus decrease congestion. Since 10 rather than 20 conveyors would now be needed, there would be additional storage space for the new style lines about to be introduced.

To provide additional incentive, a bonus plan was introduced into the wage structure. Pullers and checkers would receive an hourly rate on a seniority basis, as before, but they would also receive a bonus per 1,000 pairs of shoes handled.

The foreman let the senior workers choose the job they would prefer. The older group met one night at their Legion Post and decided to become checkers, since the physical effort would be less.

(Once again, when and if you predict behavioral differences between the sub-groups, specify those differences.)

a) The distributors' work performance will (exceed) (meet) (fall behind) managements' expectations.

b) Social interaction (1) among the older distributors, and (2) among the younger distributors will (increase) (remain the same) (decline).

c) Morale will (increase) (remain the same) (decline).

d) New changes (will) (will not) be necessary. If you predict the first alternative, explain what these changes should be and why you would expect them to succeed.

HARLAN SHOE COMPANY

Part 4

Several weeks after the new system had been put into effect, the foreman was beset by problems. Shop output and quality of work was way below what had been expected. Furthermore, the checkers had begun to complain bitterly. The pullers, they asserted, raced through their job in a careless manner in order to collect a greater bonus. The checkers' frequent trips to the bins to correct the pullers' mistakes made it more difficult for the checkers to earn a good bonus. The morale of the whole group decreased considerably; the jovial atmosphere and frequent conversations disappeared.

POSTPREDICTION ANALYSIS

Refer to your predictions at the end of Part 3. How closely do they match the information above? Do inaccuracies in your predictions reflect inadequate analysis? If so, explain the analytical failure. If not, what additional information would you have needed in Part 3 to improve your predictive accuracy and how would you have used that information?

CHAPTER 7

Organizational Inputs

by Ralph M. Hower
and
Jay W. Lorsch

AS WE INDICATED in Chapter 2, we find it useful for analytical purposes to classify as organizational inputs the following major elements:

1. The pattern of formal relationships and duties—the organization chart plus job descriptions or position guides.
2. Formal rules, operating policies, work procedures, control procedures, compensation arrangements, and similar devices adopted by management to guide employee behavior (including that of executives) in certain ways, within the structure of formal relationships.
3. Leadership style or supervisory behavior—the way the boss deals with the people around him.

We shall generally refer to (1) and (2) above as organizational structure and to (3) as leadership style. An important characteristic of this group of variables is that they are frequently altered by managers, more so than any other input to the system. Let's look at some examples of management action regarding each of the three types of organizational inputs. A decision is made that functional specialists (for example, personnel men or those responsible for quality control) are to be grouped together and are to report to a top executive or, conversely, that they are to be scattered among operating divisions and are to report to line supervisors at lower levels. A policy is established of paying by results (through monetary incentives) or by salary in amounts determined by status and length of service. The supervisor assigned to the group is a disciplinarian, or good at giving technical assistance, or effective in delegating responsibility.

One must recognize that these variables are not discrete and independent. We shall see that with these, as with other elements in the system, we are compelled to treat organizational inputs as interdependent variables, influenced *by* other variables as well as acting *upon* them. As is described in the chapter on technical inputs, certain organizational structures and practices appear to be more appropriate than others for different technical tasks. In other words, formal organizational structures are to some extent shaped by purely technological considerations. Within these general technical requirements, however, management usually has some latitude as to the particular structural details and desired formal relationships that it may prefer for getting work done. For example, a leader with a directive, controlling nature, to refer to one aspect of the human and organizational input interdependency, is likely to set up structures and procedures which differ from ones established by a leader with a permissive predisposition, even though they are both concerned with essentially the same products and technology. And, of course, structural and other decisions will affect, and be affected by, the social groupings and informal codes which emerge in the system.

Formal Organization Structure

Organizational structures and procedures are statements of intent—"the way things ought to be." In themselves they have no reality beyond that of any blueprint, until the people concerned behave more or less in the way prescribed. The extent to which people conform to the "supposed-to" pattern will vary from organization to organization, from subsystem to subsystem and from time to time, in accordance with the influence of other variables. Rarely, if ever, is there strict compliance with the official blueprint. Those familiar with life in business and governmental organizations usually agree that any organization chart, procedures manual, or policy book is in some degree already out of date by the time it appears, because of the changes which continually take place within the internal and external environment. Nonetheless, the prescribed structure, by marking out the "legitimate" allocations of responsibility and authority among the specialized functions and levels within the hierarchy, normally does have a strong influence upon the pattern of actual behavior and relationships, even though various unofficial or informal modifications develop in the course of day-to-day activities.

Not all organizations have formally prescribed structures. It is sometimes alleged that a particular company has no organization chart and is proud of the fact. Often there are explicit reasons for the absence of a specific structure or even for the absence of tightly patterned authorities and responsibilities. One reason is that the company's leadership style eschews tight control, for example. Even in small and informal groups, however, a persistent pattern or structure usually emerges as the members develop ways of completing their tasks.

The fact that organizational structure is supposed to govern the way people work means that its form is intended to relate in some way to the task to be accomplished. That is to say, one important determinant of organizational structure and practice is the nature of the work to be done. It prescribes relationships and behavior, and it guides or constrains activities into patterns which someone thinks will effectively yield an end product—proper quality and quantity at a reasonable cost and at the desired time. Whether or not the structural design in fact contributes to that result will depend ultimately upon its suitability to the work at hand. As we shall presently see, the structure's suitability depends upon a number of variables, among them the nature of the technology and the degree to which the task is simple or complex. Before we look at this important relationship we want to examine several other factors which may help to shape organizational inputs.

Culture and Organizational Inputs

There is reason to believe that the cultural environment, operating through human inputs, is an important variable influencing certain aspects of organizational structure. Only a few years ago the ratio of administrative personnel (line and staff administrators and supportive employees, such as clerical workers) to production workers in the Volkswagen organization in Germany was 1 to 10. The comparable ratio for Renault was 1:5, and for two automobile firms in England, it was 1:3 and 1:4. Harbison and others reported a 1:50 foreman-to-worker span of control in a German steel plant, whereas an American steel plant of comparable size, product, and number of employees showed a 1:15 ratio—a really striking difference.[1] Undoubtedly these ratios in some degree reflect differences in attitude of workers and managers in the three countries toward authority, discipline, and the like.

A recent study by Crozier[2] provides a greater understanding of this

[1]See data assembled in William M. Evan, "Indices of the Hierarchal Structure of Industrial Organizations," *Management Science,* Vol. IX, No. 3 (April, 1960).

[2]Crozier, Michael, *The Bureaucratic Phenomenon* (Chicago: University of Chicago Press, 1964).

point. He indicates that the types of organizational structures (bureaucracies) which typically exist in various countries can only be understood in the cultural context of each country. For example the typical French organization emphasizes centralization of decision making, isolation of levels in the hierarchy from each other, and individual loneliness. This, Crozier asserts, is consistent with French cultural characteristics. In contrast he describes the typical Soviet organization as relying on hierarchy, suspicion, and control, which he indicates is consistent with Russian cultural traits. When he also compares the Soviet and French types of organization with the typical American organization, he sees the latter as relying much more heavily on functional specialization and due process, consistent with what he believes to be certain American cultural traits. Clusters of human inputs, then, expressed through the culture of the organization's members, tend to influence in general but profound ways the broad outlines of an organization's structure and leadership style.

Management Ideology and Organizational Inputs

Another important but somewhat more transitory influence on organizational inputs is the current management literature which instructs the administrator on how to organize or how to lead the participants in his organization. For example, the works of certain early management theorists (Fayol, Gulick, Mooney, and others) have been translated by some managers into immutable principles about how to organize.[3] Similarly, certain generalizations about leadership style have recently become popular as a result of reports of behavioral science findings (for example, MacGregor's).[4] The tendency for managers to translate such findings or theories into working generalizations, without regard to the explicit or implicit conditions surrounding the original statements, is not surprising when you realize how complex and uncertain our current knowledge about organizational inputs is, and yet how crucial it is that managers behave wisely in this area. However, reliance on such principles will result in a functional relationship between organizational structure and task performance only when most

[3] Luther Gulick, "Notes on the Theory of Organization" in *Papers on the Science of Administration,* ed. L. Gulick and L. Urwick (New York; Institute of Public Administration, Columbia University, 1937); James Mooney, "The Principles of Organization," *Papers on the Science of Administration,* (rev. ed.; New York: Harper & Bros., 1947); and Henri Fayol, *Industrial and General Administration* (London: Sir I. Pitman & Sons, 1930).

[4] Douglas MacGregor, *The Human Side of Enterprise* (New York: McGraw-Hill Book Co., 1960).

of the conditions present in the original study are also present in the manager's actual situation. Mooney generalized from his experience in running automobile plants, and thus, a manager who tries to organize a research laboratory along the lines laid down by Mooney, though working with a simple organizational prescription, will be using one which does not fit either the predisposition of his scientists or the requirements of the task they are supposed to perform.

Organization Structure and Leadership Style

Thus far we have examined two factors, culture and ideology, which are external to the sociotechnical system and which shape organizational inputs. Now let's take a look at how leadership style and organizational practices and structure within the system are interrelated. As we have suggested, formal structure is often shaped by the ideas of the man in charge. It is also true that within any given structure, as a result of supervisory behavior or group influences, patterns of relationships emerge which are different from the relationships and behavior which the formal structure says should apply. What happens is that leadership style and managerial attitude shape *both* what is supposed to happen *and* what actually does happen in a variety of ways.

A study by Barnes[5] of two departments, similar in size and technology but parts of two different electronics firms, provides detailed evidence on this point. The contrasting departmental structures he examined, plus the contrasting managerial behavior which accompanied them, led to contrasting patterns of interaction and sentiment among the people concerned. These patterns, in turn, contributed to substantially different levels of task performance and satisfaction among the people concerned:

> Company A's management tended to stress management control and to limit engineer autonomy, interaction opportunities, and influence. In comparison, Company B's management tended to support subordinate autonomy, interaction opportunities, and upward influence. The goals of productivity and practicality were strongly tempered by the company's long-standing concern for individual rights and individual development.

The structures of the two departments studied by Barnes were different, each shaped by the department head according to his own predispositions. Department A was divided into a number of sections, each

[5]Louis B. Barnes, *Organizational Systems and Engineering Groups* (Boston: Harvard Graduate School of Business Administration, Division of Research, 1960).

with a senior engineer in charge, several engineers reporting to him, and technicians in turn reporting to engineers:

> Job-assignment and follow-up procedures placed each section member in a position of dependency, low autonomy, low opportunity for interaction, and low influence potential. Work procedures were dominated by section leader schedules and section leader quality control. These procedures also helped establish downward influence patterns while the resulting high dependency helped to discourage subordinate influence.

In Department B, in contrast, all engineers reported to one supervisor and all technicians reported to a foreman of technicians: There was almost no departmental structure. When an engineer needed help, the foreman of technicians assigned a technician to work with him. From then on, the two worked directly with each other, sharing responsibility for the quality and timely completion of the project. Each had a backlog of several projects on which he worked at any given time. Each, therefore, had a variety of tasks and a series of continuing work relationships with people in the department other than his direct supervisor. The procedures:

> . . . stressed autonomy, opportunities for interaction, and mutual influence. By structuring job assignments so that individuals became less dependent on an immediate superior. Supervisor B helped to build open system relationships. . . . Relatively broad departmental experience plus an area of specialization made each engineer a potential source of technical help and influence. At the same time, each engineer and technician built up further backlogs of knowledge and technical competence.

Structure, procedures, and supervisory style in each of the two departments tended to reinforce one another. From Department A, with what was regarded as "businesslike" direction, results emerged which were universally unsatisfactory. From Department B, with less precise structure, controls, and authority, came results which were relatively more satisfactory to upper management, engineers, technicians and customers. Without inferring that loose structure is a panacea for all organizational ills (we'll soon see it isn't), it is apparent that structure and leadership style have some relationship.

A still more recent study[6] reports on the restructuring of relationships in the product development laboratories of a large industrial firm.

[6]Louis B. Barnes, Gene W. Dalton, and Abraham Zaleznik, "The Authority Structure as a Change Variable." Paper presented at the 57th annual meeting of the American Sociological Association, August, 1962, in Washington, D.C.

One of the problems in modern industrial organizations which grows out of technological progress and increasing technical specialization, is how to reconcile hierarchical power ("line" or position-based authority) with professional expertise (knowledge-based authority). An experiment was conducted in the study's product development laboratories with the intent of redistributing power between scientists and supervisors throughout the laboratory hierarchy. The outcome of this attempt was an increase in autonomy, involvement, productivity, and satisfaction for senior scientists and junior managers but not for other members of the organization. Senior managers, who lost some hierarchial authority, were unhappy, and junior scientists (the most numerous group) were neutral or negative, depending upon whether junior managers encouraged autonomy below them or not. At issue was an increase in professional authority in relation to hierarchal authority, a contest in which the latter usually has the advantage. The authors conclude that "if professional authority is to increase, it must be aided by, and at the expense of, hierarchal authority." The study demonstrates the close connection between organizational structure and leadership behavior. While structural design may be a function of effective behavior, changes in managerial behavior are needed to make structures do the job they were designed to do.

Perhaps one of the most clear-cut instances of the impact of leadership behavior is reported in a study by Robert H. Guest.[7] An automobile plant employing 5,000 people was studied in 1953 and again in 1956. In the interval the plant manager had been replaced. Everything else in the situation was almost exactly the same as before: structure, product, processes, subordinate management personnel, and the organizational structure above the plant manager in the company of which the plant was a part. In a period of two and a half years the plant was turned around from being a poor performer (the worst among seven comparable plants) to an excellent performer, the best in the division. The process by which this was done is fully described in the book and cannot be easily summarized here. In essence the new manager shifted behavior from one of transmitting pressure downward to one of encouraging lateral and upward communication, plus advancing support from the top in solving various problems, many of them technical, which confronted his subordinates. That the change was not solely a

---

[7]Robert H. Guest, *Organizational Change: The Effect of Successful Leadership* (Homewood, Ill.: Richard D. Irwin, Inc., and Dorsey Press, 1962).

function of the manager's personality is evident from the way new patterns were institutionalized. When the new manager was promoted and another took his place, the improvements continued. The entire organization had developed ways of working together which were no longer dependent upon one man (though doubtless a poor plant manager might well again wreck the show if he were to influence a reversion to the unsatisfactory pattern of 1953).

Organizational and Technical Inputs

Having described several factors which shape organizational inputs and the interrelation between organizational structure and leadership style, let's look at some research findings which point to the relationship between the nature of the organization's task or technology and its organization structure and leadership style. Many of these experiments[8] are based on the premise that organization structure is in effect a communication network, with information, instructions, and commands flowing in prescribed channels. A variety of networks has been tested experimentally; the wheel (all information from the "spokes" clearing through the man at the hub and in some instances activities being directed by him); the closed chain or circle (each performer exchanging information with a performer on his left and right around a circle); the each-to-all network; and so on. Such networks have been tested with tasks ranging from the very simple and highly repetitive to the relatively complex and uncertain. Data have been collected on quantity, quality, and speed of output, together with the satisfactions derived by participants under different arrangements.

---

[8]This portion of the present paper owes much to the summary of research reports prepared by D. J. Hall which was included in his "Tentative Proposal for and Experimental Study of Work Group Structure and Behavior," unpublished, 1963. The principal sources used in this note follow:

1. Bernard M. Bass, "Experimenting with Simulated Manufacturing Organizations," *ONR Technical Report,* No. 27 (1961).
2. Alex Bavelas, "Communication Patterns in Task-Oriented Groups," *Journal of the Acoustical Society,* Vol. XXII (1950), pp. 725–30.
3. R. Carzo, Jr., "Organizational Structure and Group Effectiveness," *Administrative Science Quarterly,* March, 1963.
4. Robert L. Chapman *et al.,* "The System Research Laboratory's Air Defense Experiments," *Management Science,* Vol. V (1959), p. 250.
5. Arthur M. Cohen, "Changing Small Group Communication Networks," *Administrative Science Quarterly,* Vol. VI (1962), p. 443.
6. Murray Glanzer and Robert Glaser, "Techniques for the Study of Group Structure and Behavior; Empirical Studies of the Effectiveness of Structure in Small Groups," *Psychological Bulletin,* Vol. LVII (1961), pp. 1–27.
7. Harold Guetzkow and Herbert A. Simon, "The Impact of Certain Communica-

It is much too soon to reach firm conclusions, since the data are not always significant and sometimes seem to reveal contradictory results. Carefully evaluated, however, they suggest certain tendencies which may be summarized as follows:

1. The effect of structural design depends partly upon the nature of the task (whether simple or complex, repetitious or varying, and so on).
2. For simple, prescribed tasks, the wheel structure (i.e., a centralized communication structure) is efficient, even with an unpopular man at the center. Peripheral group members (the "spokes") are relatively dissatisfied with their jobs but this does not impair their performance. (This finding contradicts some popular views about structure and morale.)
3. For more complex tasks, the circle or each-to-all structures seem to be superior in results and satisfactions.
4. The circle network seemed to facilitate quick adaptation of the work group to sudden and confusing changes in task.
5. Structured groups have difficulty in performing in an environment which is subject to sudden and unpredictable change.
6. Repetition in any type of network leads to improvement in task performance.
7. Groups persist in using an inefficient problem-solving system, once they see that it at least enables them to reach a solution.

---

tion Nets upon Organizations and Performance in Task-Oriented Groups," *Management Science,* Vol. I (1955), pp. 233–50.

8. G. A. Heise and G. A. Miller, "Problem Solving by Small Groups Using Various Communication Nets," *Journal of Abnormal and Social Psychology,* Vol. XLVI (1951), pp. 327–35.
9. Harold J. Leavitt, "Some Effects of Certain Communication Patterns on Group Performance in E. E. Maccoby, T. M. Newcomb, and E. L. Hartley (eds), *Readings in Social Psychology* (New York: Holt, Rinehart and Winston, 1958).
10. J. Macy, Jr., L. S. Christie, and R. D. Luce, "Coding Noise in Task-Oriented Groups," *Journal of Abnormal and Social Psychology,* Vol. XLVIII (1953), p. 401.
11. Harold Pepinsky *et al.,* "Team Productivity and Contradiction of Management Policy Commitments," *Journal of Applied Psychology,* Vol. XLIV (1960), p. 264.
12. Pauline Pepinsky *et al.,* "The Effects of Task Complexity and Time Pressure upon Team Productivity," *Journal of Applied Psychology,* Vol. XLIV (1960), p. 34.
13. Marvin E. Shaw, "Some effects of Problem Complexity upon Problem Solution Efficiency in Different Communication Nets," *Journal of Experimental Psychology,* Vol. XLVIII (1954), pp. 211–17.
14. M. E. Shaw and A. R. Rothchild, "Some Effects of Prolonged Experience in Communication Nets," *Journal of Applied Psychology,* Vol. XL (1956), pp. 281–86.

While these experiments can be seen as experiments in structural design, it should be apparent that in the small-group setting it is often difficult to separate the effects of structure and the behavior pattern of the leader. Thus, in a sense, these experiments can also be seen as dealing with leadership style as a variable.

8. A group tends to develop a "tradition" or pattern of behavior in the course of its work, even when unstructured, and this pattern tends to persist. That is, the group will often apply past experience in a new situation whether it is appropriate or not.
9. However, a group rapidly changes its structure when the task greatly increases in complexity, and shortcuts are found when task pressures on the existing structure become too great.

In spite of the tentative nature of these experimental findings, there seem to be a consistent set of conclusions which can be drawn from them. Members of groups which are engaged in certain and routine tasks seem to perform most effectively when their organizations have a more controlling structure. Groups which are engaged in more uncertain and problematic tasks appear to function most effectively with a structure which is less controlling. While these experiments have been conducted with small groups working on contrived tasks, the validity of these conclusions for large organizations working on real tasks is demonstrated by several recent field studies.

In the report of a study of 110 industrial firms in the vicinity of London, Woodward[9] found that certain structural characteristics varied between firms having different types of technologies. For example, the number of levels in the management hierarchy was higher in mass-production firms (median of four levels) than in unit or job shop production firms (median of three levels) and substantially higher than either of the above in process industries (median of six levels). On the other hand, the span of control at the first level of supervision (number of persons reporting to a first-line supervisor) increased from a median of 21–30 people in unit production to a median of 41–50 people in mass-production operations, and then dropped sharply to 11–12 people in continuous process firms. While Woodward does not relate these differences explicitly to variation in the certainty of the task, she does report that the most effective firms within each processing technology tended to have structural characteristics which were near the median for all firms in their class of technology. This suggests, then, that there is some relationship between effective task performance and an organization structure which fits the technology.

An even clearer confirmation of the fact that there is a relationship between organization structure, the nature of the task and effective organizational performance is provided in a field study by Burns and

[9] Joan Woodward, *Industrial Organization Theory and Practice* (New York: Oxford University Press, Inc., 1965).

Stalker.[10] These researchers report that of British firms entering the electronics industry after experience in more stable industries, those which were effective in dealing with the uncertainties of rapid technological and market change in this new industrial environment were the ones which had developed less controlling, or what the authors labeled "organic," structures than less effective firms which tended to rely on the more controlling or "mechanistic" structures which had served them well for more stable markets and technologies.

Although in the Burns and Stalker study there do appear to be discernable structural and procedural differences between mechanistic and organic organizations, the most significant difference the authors found was in *the way people behaved* in the two types of organizations—how they looked upon structure and operated within it.[11] In the mechanistic system the structure is used to a large extent to protect the existing status and "political" control possessed by individuals and groups, rather than to advance the economic and technical goals of the company. In the organic system the structure is largely a means to company ends—a rough guide which if it is to survive, must aid in the solution of problems facing the company as a whole. To this end, direct interactions and communication at the operating level are not only permitted but, indeed, are actually stimulated, so that sales, development, and production can better cope with their external worlds. One paragraph contains the barest gist of Burns and Stalkers' findings:

> According to the evidence supplied by these studies, and the interpretation of it given here, both the organization of the internal interpretive system and the direction of the commercial, technical, and productive capacities of that system in the interests of the firm are conditional for their success on an appreciation of the rate of change affecting the tasks of the concern: i.e., of the number and importance of new technical and market circumstances confronting the firm from day to day. *As the rate of change increases in the technical field, so does the number of occasions which demand quick and effective interpretation between people working in different parts of the system. As the rate of change increases in the market field, so does the need to multiply the points of contact between the concern and the markets it wishes to explore and develop.*[12]

---

[10]Tom Burns and G. M. Stalker, *The Management of Innovation* (London: Tavistock Publications, Ltd., 1961).

[11]For a description of a similar approach see "The 'Rational' and 'Natural-System' Models in Organizational Analysis" in Paul R. Lawrence and John A. Seiler, *Organizational Behavior and Administration: Cases, Concepts, and Research Findings* (rev. ed.; Homewood, Ill.: Richard D. Irwin, Inc., and Dorsey Press, 1965).

[12]Burns, and Stalker, *op. cit.*, p. 231.

The ability of the organic systems to respond quickly and appropriately to both technological necessities and market opportunities enabled them to forge ahead. Conversely, the tendency of mechanistic systems to resist change and to "wall off" the new activities which were grafted onto the existing organizations, it is clear, deprived them of success. Since all the companies were contending in essentially the same markets and the same technological field, it is evident that there is no automatic adjustment of structure and procedure to external variables. The key to the differences in the two systems seems to lie mainly in the behavior of top management—in its ability to establish and maintain a pattern of readiness for change. This pattern stresses the importance of technical competence, rather than traditional authority, in working out solutions. Also, given the inevitable intensification of specialization that has emerged, this pattern permits and encourages widespread communication and cooperation.

The organic and mechanistic characteristics which seem to be differentially appropriate for these two major sets of task conditions set forth above, i.e., simple and certain versus complex and ambiguous, are summarized in Exhibit 1. In examining them it is important to bear

Exhibit 1

Organizational Characteristics	*Types of Organization Structure*	
Index	*Organic*	*Mechanistic*
Span of control	Wide	Narrow
Number of levels of authority	Few	Many
Ratio of administrative to production personnel	High	Low
Range of time span over which an employee can commit resources	Long	Short
Degree of centralization in decision making	Low	High
Proportion of persons in one unit having opportunity to interact with persons in other units	High	Low
Quantity of formal rules	Low	High
Specificity of job goals	Low	High
Specificity of required activities	Low	High
Content of communications	Advice and information	Instructions and decisions
Range of compensation	Narrow	Wide
Range of skill levels	Narrow	Wide
Knowledge-based authority	High	Low
Position-based authority	Low	High

SOURCE: This exhibit is an adaptation of one prepared by Paul R. Lawrence and Jay W. Lorsch in an unpublished "Working Paper on Scientific Transfer and Organizational Structure," 1963. The latter, in turn, draws heavily on criteria suggested by W. Evans, "Indices of the Hierarchical Structure of Industrial Organizations," *Management Science,* Vol. IX (1963), pp. 468–77, Burns and Stalker, *op. cit.,* and Woodward, *op. cit.,* as well as those suggested by R. H. Hall, "Intraorganizational Structure Variables," *Administrative Science Quarterly,* Vol. IX (1962), pp. 295–308.

in mind that the two types of structure really represent two theoretical ends of a continuum and that most organizations will actually fall between these two polar conditions. Note that they describe a wide variety of organizational factors, such as control and reward procedures, formal reporting relationships, operating procedures, job descriptions, and so forth, all of which relate to two broad types of organization structure.

In essence, then, the findings of both these field studies, particularly those of Burns and Stalker, support the conclusions drawn from the experimental studies cited earlier. Organizations coping with a highly certain task will perform more effectively with a controlling or mechanistic structure, while those dealing with a less certain and less predictable task will perform more effectively with a less controlling or an organic structure.

The studies of Burns and Stalker and Woodward are primarily concerned with the relationship between organization structure and the organization's task. There is, however, a recent study which points to the relationship between the task and the second important aspect of organizational inputs—the style of the leader's behavior. Fiedler[13] has assembled data from a variety of situations in such a way as to relate leadership style to a group's effectiveness in performing different types of tasks. His findings are too complex and tentative to report in detail here, but some examples are worth noting in relation to our discussion of the interdependence between task and organization structure. He has found, that in groups which are dealing with a highly certain task, and where the leader has friendly relations with his subordinates but a very weak power position, with few rewards and sanctions at his disposal, a more controlling, active leader is most effective. On the other hand, in groups which have a very uncertain task, and in which the leader has good relations with his subordinates and a weak power position, a more permissive, passive, and considerate leader is most effective. These are just two examples of a number of possible situations involving different degrees of task certainty, different qualities of leader-member relations, and differing degrees of positional power and different types of leader style which have been examined in Fiedler's work. There are two important points to be made in regard to the issues raised by Fiedler's study. First, it seems clear that there is room for different styles of leadership behavior as a means of achieving effective group perfor-

---

[13]F. Fiedler, "Engineer the Job to Fit the Manager", *Harvard Business Review,* Vol. XLIII, No. 5 (September-October, 1965), p. 115.

mance in different situations. One of the important variables which seems to be related to the effectiveness of a leadership style is the certainty of the group's task. To this extent Fiedler's work is consistent with our prior examination of the relationship between organization structure and task. However, Fiedler's work also suggests that the relationship between task and organization structure may be mediated and complicated by the interpersonal and social factors which pertain between the leader and his subordinates. Unfortunately, knowledge about the precise quality of these intervening variables is still highly tentative.

There is one important complication in the relationship between the organization's structure and its task environment which we have as yet ignored. The fact is that the internal and external environments of organizations are not homogeneous. Different parts of the environment may be more or less certain than others. For example, if we look at a typical manufacturing firm, we can see that the part of the environment with which manufacturing managers deal, i.e., plant technology, raw materials, and the labor force, may be relatively certain, while the part of the environment with which research scientists or design engineers are concerned, i.e., scientific knowledge, may be highly uncertain. The market part of the environment with which sales and marketing managers are primarily concerned may have a degree of certainty which differs from either of these other parts of the company's overall environment. A recent study by Lawrence and Lorsch[14] points to this fact and examines the organizational consequences of the different degrees of certainty in departmental tasks within a large organization.

The different functional departments of production, sales, and research in the two organizations examined in this study all had different structures on the continuum from organic to mechanistic. These differences appeared to have been related to differences in the certainty of the tasks of each department. Production departments, with the most certain task, had the most controlling or mechanistic structure. Research units, with least certain tasks, had less controlling or organic structures. Sales departments, which were performing a moderately uncertain task, had a structure which fell between the extremes of the other two departments. Similarly, the managers in these departments developed different interpersonal and leadership styles which seemed generally con-

---

[14] J. Lorsch, *Product Innovation and Organization* (New York: Macmillan Co., 1965). See also J. Lorsch, and P. Lawrence, "Organizing for Product Innovation," *Harvard Business Review,* Jan-Feb, 1965, Vol. XLIII, No. 1 (January-February, 1965), p. 109.

sistent with Fiedler's findings, based as they were on differences in the tasks of each department.

Lawrence and Lorsch's findings are consistent with those cited above but, in addition, they suggest that when we think about the relationship between organizational inputs and the environment we must consider not just the certainty of the total environment, as Burns and Stalker have suggested, but also the certainty of different *parts* of the environment.

Differentiation and Integration in Complex Organizational Systems

The study by Lawrence and Lorsch emphasizes the fact that the formal structure divides the members of the organization into departments, each of which has a different task in coping with its part of the environment. The specialized departments involved in different tasks develop, in addition to the different formal department structures and interpersonal styles already alluded to, unique points of view appropriate to their respective specialized activities. The major difference between departments revealed in their study can be briefly diagrammed along four dimensions as shown in Exhibit 2.

Exhibit 2

MEASURES OF DEPARTMENTAL DIFFERENTIATIONS

Department	*Primary Environmental Orientation*	*Primary Time Orientation*	*Orientation toward Co-Workers*	*Degree of Formality in Departmental Structure*
Research	Science	Long	Permissive	Low
Sales	Market	Short	Permissive	Medium
Production	Plant	Short	Directive	High

The specialization of function and the differences which emerge are important for the effective operation of the separate sales, research, and production units, but they also tend to contribute to misunderstandings and differences of opinion which inevitably arise in organizations. In the organizations which were the subjects of this study, the dominant issue around which these conflicts developed was the innovation of new products and processes. To meet the need for coordination and resolution of differences, each of the two companies studied established a separate, "new-product department," a formal organizational device aimed at coordinating research and development, sales, and production. Each also made use of permanent cross-functional teams or committees to provide a flow of information between departments and to facilitate collaboration among them. Thus, the structure of these organizations not only divided up the work of members, it also provided a means for achieving coordination between the specialized departments. While we traditionally have thought of the managerial hierarchy as the principal organizational device for facilitating integration, managers in the organizations studied by Lawrence and Lorsch found it necessary to develop other mechanisms in the form of coordinating departments and teams to help coordinate the highly specialized departments.

Despite the fact that there were apparent similarities between the formal coordinating departments in the two organizations studied, there were subtle but important differences in the location and composition of the units in the two companies. There were likewise differences in the way they dealt with other departments and in the behavior of higher executives. Each of these elements, formal structure, interaction process, and supervisory behavior, interacted and reinforced the other and produced distinctly different consequences for the two companies.

In Company A the differences between the three departments, as measured along the four dimensions shown in the previous exhibit, tended to be more extreme than those between departments in Company B, although they were similar in general configuration. The departments in Company A appeared to be more highly specialized and better able to perform their specialized tasks. Because of the differences among them as to structure and orientation, however, one might expect that they would experience greater difficulty in achieving the high degree of requisite coordination.

However, the potential for greater coordinative difficulty in Company A was more than offset by certain structural and procedural differences which provided better overall collaboration in A than existed in B. The new product department in Company A, in addition to its coordinating function, was involved in technical service and market development activities. In Company B the new product department, besides coordinating R.&D. sales, and production, was directly involved in market planning and the coordination of sales activities. The result was that in Company A the new-product department occupied a middle position, in structure and orientation, between the three departments it was to link—as close to any one as to any other, concerned about all three parts of the company's environment, and able to deal with both the short-range problems of sales and production and the long-range problems of research. In Company B the new-product department tended to be highly oriented toward the market and toward short-range time concerns. Thus, it was not in an intermediate or balanced position between the three departments which it was supposed to coordinate. Company A executives perceived members of the coordinating department in their company as being familiar with the problems, procedures, and ways of operating in the three departments it linked. In Company B there were complaints that the coordinating unit was too much involved in day-to-day detail relating to current sales and, thus, was unable to develop long-range plans.

As we have indicated, there were differences of opinion to be reconciled between the specialist departments in both companies. In each company certain of these disagreements were handled by a cross-functional coordinating committee. The companies differed in interaction process and leadership behavior, as well as in the structural position of their coordinating committees. Company B operated with tighter spans of control, more specific rules, and a higher degree of mechanistic structure. The authority to make decisions for product innovation was at a higher level in Company B than in Company A. In the latter the coordinating teams were primarily composed of managers who had the detailed market and technical information necessary for decisions. They were the only ones who attended the meetings, and they had the authority to make those decisions. In Company B, by contrast, committee members did not have the authority to make final decisions, and often they did not have the knowledge to do so, either. They often brought to meetings both their superiors who had the authority to decide and subordinates who possessed the required technical and market knowledge. There were two to three times as many participants in Company B meetings as in those of Company A.

Furthermore, the established norms in Company B sanctioned withdrawal from disagreements and conflict. Thus, many decisions were ignored, delayed, or referred "upstairs" where they could be decided. The committee members in B appeared to lack the time and inclination to work through their differences. In Company A, on the other hand, the norm was to resolve differences at the committee level by fighting through disagreements constructively. "These things take several meetings to work out, but we are never really stalemated. We have decided in our committee that we won't be stalemated. There is more than one way to our ends. . . ." And this attitude in Company A's coordinating committees was reinforced by higher management. By its patience and its manifest expectation that the committee would achieve a working agreement, it kept decisions about innovation at relatively low operating levels. Company A's record clearly revealed more effective coordination and a significantly higher rate of product innovation and profits than was evident in Company B. The evidence strongly indicates that formal structure, the nature or process of coordination, and leadership style in Company A contributed to its greater success.

The Test of Consistency in Organizational Systems

In management circles in the past, as we have already suggested, there has been great concern about designing organizational structures, and leadership behavior has been thought about as if there were one best way to approach these issues. The more recent research findings reviewed here suggest that another approach may be more consistent with our view of organizations as systems. Questions of organizational structure and leadership style have to be answered in terms of what is most consistent with the other elements in the sociotechnical system.

In our discussion we have particularly stressed the importance of a fit between organizational inputs and the organization's environment or task. The need for consistency between organizational inputs and the predisposition of the organization's members is equally important, as is the need for consistency between organizational inputs and the norms and traditions of the organization. The relationship between organizational and human inputs has been touched on in Chapter 3 and between social and organizational inputs in Chapter 5. At this juncture, however, we should make the additional point that evidence on what constitutes a functional relationship between members' predispositions and norms on the one hand and organizational inputs on the other suggests that if the organizational inputs are consistent with the demands of the task, they will also provide an important satisfaction of members' needs. Rice[15] has indicated that when organizational units are structured in accordance with the demands of the task, their members derive important psychological and social benefits. When the unit's structure fits the demands of the task and when leaders adopt a style which meets task requirements, there is a greater probability that

[15] A. K. Rice, *Productivity and Social Organization* (London: Tavistock Publications, Ltd., 1958), pp. 186, 198.

members will find that many of their needs, such as those for achievement and affiliation, are satisfied by their being able to engage in productive work within a compatible work group. It is practically inevitable, of course, that no particular set of organizational inputs can be completely consistent with task requirements and still satisfy *all* of the needs of an organization's members. These nearly unavoidable inconsistencies influence the emergence of what has been called the informal organization.[16] We are suggesting, however, that norms and social controls will be less divergent from the characteristics of the formal organization, when organizational inputs are consistent with task requirements.

Planning and thinking about organizational inputs in a way which recognizes both the need for consistency between system elements and their obstinate tendency to be in conflict is a difficult but unavoidable job. Organizational inputs include those variables over which managers often have more direct control than they do over other elements in the system. They are not the only variables in the system which managers can alter, but they are often the most accessible.

Summary

Organizational inputs may be classified as the pattern of formal relationships and duties; as formal rules, policies, and procedures; and as leadership style. The first two, structure and ways of doing business, are expressed as "oughts," and they are never perfectly realized. The culture of an organization's members, and current thinking about organizational practice, heavily influence organizational inputs. The structure and procedures of an organization are intimately related to the leadership style which exists in an organization. Although the influence of human and social inputs on those of organizational character is strong, the relation between technology and organization is a primary focus of this chapter. Different types of task require different types of structure, procedure, and style. Broadly speaking, simple and certain tasks require formalized and controlled or mechanistic organizational inputs, while complex and ambiguous tasks require informal and participative, or organic, inputs. Different parts of an organization usually have different types of tasks which require different organizational inputs. This makes effective intermediate groups necessary for interdepartment coordination. Intermediacy is determined by coordinate groups possessing bal-

[16]Fritz J. Roethlisberger, and William J. Dickson, *Management and the Worker* (Boston: Harvard University Press, 1943), pp. 379–84.

anced orientations in terms of each department's environment, cognitive time span, leader style, and degree of formality. At bottom, however, consistency, not only between elements of the organizational inputs but between all four inputs, is the most significant factor influencing organizational behavior.

Three Cases of the Influence of Organizational Inputs

Three simplified descriptions of organizational behavior in widely varying contexts are included here for the purposes of exemplification and analytical practice. The cases have been organized in such a way that the reader may predict from his analysis of inputs what behavior would result, then check his predictions against what actually took place. Some of the inputs will be described in Part 1 of the case. Then questions on how those inputs would be likely to influence behavior will be listed. The actual behavior in Part 2 of the case may be compared with the reader's answers to these questions. Part 3 describes changes in inputs, and questions the readers on his predictions of behavioral changes. Part 4 gives information by which Part 3's answers can be checked. This type of analytical exercise does not suggest that predictive perfection is a practical or even possible goal. It does suggest that the probability of error can be reduced somewhat by careful analysis of the interrelation of forces bearing upon the situation. Consequently, once the exercise has been completed, it is suggested that the reader reflect not only on how accurate his predictions were but also on what factors in the situation made prediction difficult.

SPECIALTY CHEMICAL COMPANY

Part 1

The Specialty Chemical Company employed approximately 2,200 hourly personnel to operate its plant on a three-shift basis. The plant was divided into several operating departments with each department containing several process units. Department A's organization chart is shown in Exhibit 1.

Exhibit 1

SPECIAL CHEMICAL COMPANY

ORGANIZATION CHART—DEPARTMENT A

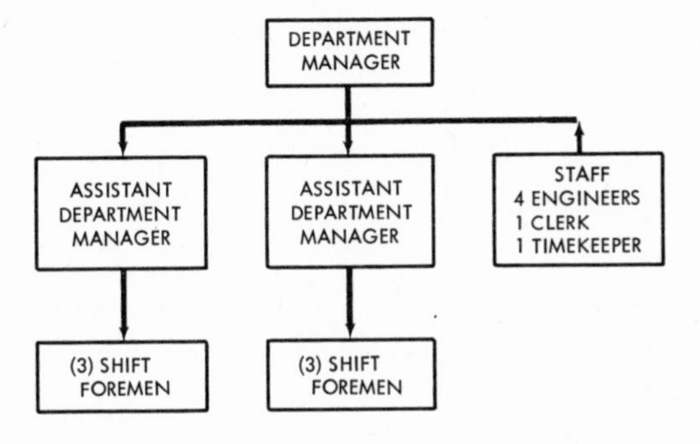

The operating departments' offices were located in the plant close to the units under their supervision. The main office building was just outside the plant's main gate.

The department manager was responsible for all phases of the department's operation and reported to the process superintendent in the main office building. He worked closely with other department managers in helping to plan the entire plant's operation.

The assistant department managers were responsible for the day-to-day operation of the unit within the department. They reported directly to the department manager.

The engineers were assigned to the operating department by the main office technical department. One engineer specialized in solving maintenance problems and worked closely with the assistant department managers and the hourly personnel who performed routine maintenance in the department. The other engineers worked on technical problems connected with the day-to-day operations and when time allowed worked on long-range technical studies (for example, development of mathematical correlations to describe the operation of the units).

The workday followed a routine pattern. The assistant department managers looked over the previous day's records that were sent to the office from the individual operating units. They noted any changes that had occurred during the night and made mental notes of items to check. One of the engineers usually calculated miscellaneous operating information such as the change in quantity of available raw material and the excess capacity left in the final product storage tanks. Any special problems that came up were discussed, and one of the engineers followed up on any details needing further investigation.

The office atmosphere was very relaxed. Coffee was available at all times. The department manager usually drank a cup of coffee and read *The Wall Street Journal* while the assistants reviewed the previous day's operation. He then checked with the assistants for a brief review and discussed any general future events which might have bearing on the department.

At the time these observations were made the department manager had just been promoted to his present position. He had been with the company for 15 years and had once worked as an engineer for one of the present assistant department managers. He was an excellent technical man and was highly regarded by all who had worked with him. His management philosophy, which he openly stated, was based on his belief that a good engineer will find his own problems and should require little supervision.

When the main office requested a special technical survey, he would mention the problem to one of the engineers and specify the deadline, if one had been set.

PREDICTIONS—Part 1

From what I know of the operation of Department A, I would predict that:

a) Productivity of the department in terms of (1) quantity, and (2) quality would be (high) (standard) (below standard).

b) Department members would be (highly) (moderately) (dis-) satisfied with their jobs.

c) Projects would be completed (ahead of) (on) (behind) schedule.

SPECIALTY CHEMICAL COMPANY

Part 2

Morale in the department was high. The engineers worked overtime (without pay) to complete projects ahead of schedule. They were careful to check and recheck every detail, because the department manager seldom rechecked the work that was sent out of the department. During off hours, the engineers joked, drank beer, and went bowling with the department manager.

The production of the department increased 15 percent under the new department manager. The hourly men, many of whom had regarded the previous manager as a sneak, were glad to see the new department manager when he made his rounds. He had told them that operating the plant was their job, and they took pride in doing their work well.

POSTPREDICTION ANALYSIS

Refer to your predictions at the end of Part 1. How closely do they match the information above? Do inaccuracies in your predictions reflect inadequate analysis? If so, explain the analytical failure. If not, what additional information would you have needed in Part 1 to improve your predictive accuracy and how would you have used that information?

SPECIALTY CHEMICAL COMPANY

Part 3

During a personnel reshuffle, a new man was brought in as department manager for Department A. He had held similar managerial positions in the company's two other plants. He, too, had served in Department A as an engineer under the same assistant department manager.

Under the new regime, Tuesday afternoon became "meeting" time. The entire department staff met to report on the various active projects. Originally, the meeting was designed to keep everyone up to date, but it soon turned into a briefing session during which time each engineer was told his duties for the next week.

In the mornings the department manager would arrive five minutes early to go over the previous day's "log sheets." When the assistants had gone over the sheets, he would question them regarding various details. Then he would visit each engineer's desk, checking on the man's progress.

A detailed account was now kept on all supply items such as pencils, flashlights, padlocks, and note pads. Hourly personnel were required to sign for such items. They were also required to call the office for permission to bring maintenance equipment into the operating area.

PREDICTIONS—Part 3

From what I know of the operation of Department "A" and the changes described in Part 3, I would predict that:

a) Productivity of the department in terms of (1) quantity, and (2) quality would (increase) (remain at the same level) (decline).

b) Department members would be (highly) (moderately) (dis-) satisfied with their job.

c) Project would be completed (ahead of) (on) (behind) schedule.

SPECIALTY CHEMICAL COMPANY

Part 4

Morale in the department dropped to a very low level. The new manager soon had the behind-the-back nickname of Captain Queeg. The engineers carried ball bearings which they banged together imitating the manager's habit of clanging his loose change.

The technical work issued by the department became progressively less complete. The engineers cared less and less about the accuracy of their work. Two months later, one engineer requested a transfer to another department. Production on the operating unit dropped 10 percent from its previous level.

POSTPREDICTION ANALYSIS

Refer to your predictions at the end of Part 3. How closely do they match the information above? Do inaccuracies in your predictions reflect inadequate analysis? If so, explain the analytical failure. If not, what additional information would you have needed in Part 3 to improve your predictive accuracy and how would you have used that information?

CARTER STEEL COMPANY

Part 1

The Carter Steel Company's industrial engineering (IE) department employed approximately 65 people. The department was subdivided into three sections, one specializing in standard costs, one in incentives, and one in methods. Each section performed its special function for all of the manufacturing departments. However, since the work of any one section usually created work for another, each line department (open hearth, sheet mill, tin mill, wire mill, rolling mill, maintenance and transportation) was assigned a "departmental IE" who acted as liaison between all of the IE sections and his particular operating department. This form of organization had existed for many years. Each engineer had become highly specialized in his skills and point of view. This tendency toward specialization had been reinforced by Carter Steel's gradual growth and the relatively stable technology in the steel industry.

The IE sections were physically separated from each other by 7-foot partitions. There was little formal contact between members of the various sections except at the start and completion of a project. Customarily, one and sometimes two men from each section were assigned to a project. They would usually have little contact with anyone within the section other than their supervisor during the course of a project.

Procedures and rules within the department were relatively informal. Coffee and lunch breaks were left to the men's discretion. Supervisory pressure was not heavy except when projects fell behind schedule.

All of the men in the department were college graduates and had general industrial engineering training and experience. Most were married, had children, and commuted from the suburbs surrounding the town in which Carter Steel was located. Although the ages of these men varied from 23 to 60 and experience from 1 to 25 years, the great majority of the men were between 25 and 40 years old with from 5 to 15 years experience. Supervisory status and pay grade correlated closely with age and experience. Promotion depended upon vacancies in superior grades. Salaries were competitive for Carter Steel's region.

PREDICTIONS—Part 1

From what I know of the operations of the IE department described in Part 1, I would predict that:

a) Productivity of the IE department would be (high) (standard) (below standard).

b) Members of the IE department would be (highly) (moderately) (dis-) satisfied with their jobs.

c) Members of the IE department (would) (would not) engage in group activities (inside) (outside) the department. (Briefly describe what group[s] you predict will exist if you predict the second alternative.)

CARTER STEEL COMPANY

Part 2

The productivity of the IE department was considered adequate by Carter management, generally. However, some of the line departments complained that IE projects seemed to drag along slowly at times and that they had to ride hard on the IE's to be sure that various phases of projects were carried through. A few men in line management asserted that most of the IE's were rather conservative in their solutions to manufacturing problems and that they resisted ideas for improvement which were originated by production men.

The IE's, themselves, were relatively satisfied with their jobs. Some who were qualified for promotion, particularly those who had at first risen rapidly through the ranks, were frustrated because their progress had slowed or stopped.

The social organization of the department took several forms. Most men commuted in car pools whose membership was dictated more by suburban geography than by IE subsection assignments. Members of the car pools and their familes engaged in extracompany social activities. At work, however, the sections were usually the focus of nonwork activities such as "flips" to see who paid for coffee and a number of card game groups which met during lunch.

The members of the department generally liked their supervisors, though some were more highly respected than others. There were strong values, particularly among the younger men, for dealing assertively with the line departments, for avoiding "pickiness" over details, and for "modern" methods.

POSTPREDICTION ANALYSIS

Refer to your predictions at the end of Part 1. How closely do they match the information above? Do inaccuracies in your predictions reflect inadequate analysis? If so, explain the analytical failure. If not, what additional information would you have needed in Part 1 to improve your predictive accuracy and how would you have used that information?

CARTER STEEL COMPANY

Part 3

Early in June, a rumor spread through the department that a reorganization was about to take place. Supervisors would comment only that such rumors had cropped up from time to time but nothing had ever happened. Nevertheless, the productivity of the department declined, any project requiring more than a few days' work being put off "until after the reorganization."

In late July, after the weekly Friday afternoon supervisors' meeting, the supervisors informed their sections that beginning the next Monday the department would begin reorganizing its sections so that each would correspond to one or more of the manufacturing units. Each line department was to have a corresponding IE section to which former specialists in standard cost, incentive, and methods were to be assigned. However, the men were now expected to be able to deal with all aspects of a department's project, since each man was by now assumed to be familiar with the established systems and procedures by which the department functioned. It was hoped that the new organization would allow new men to become familiar with all aspects of the department's work. A few senior specialists were to be assigned to a staff group under the chief IE, to be of service to the departmental sections. Because of the new staff group and the greater number of IE sections under the new organization, a certain number of promotions were necessary.

The reorganization required physical relocation of IE's so that all men assigned to one department would have desks together. The operation of the move was left to the IE's themselves, although plans called for nearly every man to move. Few of the old spatial relations were to remain unchanged. However, no renovation of office facilities was planned.

PREDICTIONS—Part 3

From what I know of the operations of the IE department and the reorganization described in Part 3, I would predict that:

a) Department members would (welcome) (tolerate) (oppose) the reorganization.

b) The eventual outcome of the reorganization would be (an increase) (no change) (a decrease) in the productivity of the IE department.

c) Group activities inside and outside the department would (remain as before) (change). (Briefly describe the nature of the changes you predict if you choose the second alternative.)

CARTER STEEL COMPANY

Part 4

During the first few weeks after the reorganization, there was constant friction among the men over possession and location of desks, chairs, and filing cabinets. Since many of these items had been shared by men who were now to work in different areas, the problems were slow in working themselves out. However, they finally subsided.

Some imbalance in work load soon became evident. A few sections found themselves overstaffed and underworked. No section was found to be undermanned, although no new personnel had been hired. The overstaffed groups became frustrated by their lack of work. Management expected that normal attrition would solve this problem.

Social reorganization was often awkward and slow. Most of the card-playing groups disintegrated and were reformed with new members. Car-pool groups, however, remained unchanged. After several months, a new set of social relationships had become established around the departmental sections. These appeared to be somewhat more intensive than those which had existed in the specialty sections.

The new work sections displayed an autonomy which was formerly lacking. The problems of communication between specialties on a project disappeared. The chief IE and his assistant were called on less frequently to solve coordinative difficulties but were often asked to evaluate and approve innovations in departmental operation. Line department complaints became less frequent. The men in each section appeared to be taking renewed interest in their work. Management interpreted the increased productivity of the IE Department as a sign of the reorganization's success.

POSTPREDICTION ANALYSIS

Refer to your predictions at the end of Part 3. How closely do they match the information above? Do inaccuracies in your predictions reflect inadequate analysis? If so, explain the analytical failure. If not, what additional information would you have needed in Part 3 to improve your predictive accuracy and how would you have used that information?

DANIELS COMPUTER COMPANY

Part 1

Daniels Computer Company's memory engineering department was composed of four sections: magnetic, electronic, mechanical, and electrochemical. The customary development work undertaken by the department involved well-known principles of memory design. Each section carried on its phase of development in logical sequence, using the results of the previous section as a starting point. The members of each section were expert in their own fields. The sections were close-knit socially. The manager of the department left technical direction to section supervisors, reserving for his own responsibility the securing of essential services and maintenance of the development schedule. The department rarely failed to meet its schedule or technical requisites.

In July, 1962, the memory department was assigned the development of a memory incorporating several new design concepts which had never been experimentally evaluated. The functioning of the special computer which was to incorporate the new memory depended upon the most advanced memory device possible within the limits of the new concepts. Development time was one-half the length of more routine developments.

The memory department manager selected the four most competent project engineers from the four sections to work on the special project. Each project engineer was directed to select five engineers and five technicians to work with him on the project. Because of time limitations and the unknown aspects of the new memory concepts, the four groups were to work on their own aspects of design simultaneously. Each team, remaining in the geographic confines of its home section but independent of its former supervision, commenced immediately to test design schemes and components relevant to its own division of the technology. The project group members quickly became enthusiastic about their new assignment. The department manager left technical supervision to the project engineers of each group.

PREDICTIONS—Part 1

From what I know of the special project operation described in Part 1, I would predict that:

a) The four project engineers (would) (would not) work well together to coordinate the work of their separate sections.

b) Enthusiasm among the members of the four special groups would (increase) (stabilize) (wane) as the project developed.

c) Work on the special project would (progress smoothly) (be uneven, though satisfactory) as time went on.

d) Social relationships will tend to be (project-wide) (special-group oriented).

DANIELS COMPUTER COMPANY

Part 2

In late August, 1962, the project engineers of the four special groups met for the first time to explore the technical prerequisites each had discovered. The goal of the meeting was to establish parameters for each group's subsequent design effort. It quickly became apparent that each group had discovered concept limitations within its own area which were considered by that group to be controlling. Inevitably, the position of any one group required considerable extra work by one or more of the others. The meeting concluded without compromise of original positions.

In the ensuing weeks, all four groups worked desperately to complete certain design segments before complementary segments were completed in other groups. Haste was believed necessary so that the tardy group would have to reformulate its designs, basing them upon that which was already completed. Development of the new memory proceeded in this fashion until the project engineer of the slowest group proved experimentally and theoretically that several designs completed by other groups imposed technologically impossible conditions upon his area of design. A number of personal frictions developed between the groups at this time, with aspersions cast concerning the competence of out-group members. Even department members not formally involved in the special project became involved, siding with their section mates. Enthusiasm for the project on the part of group members waned.

POSTPREDICTION ANALYSIS

Refer to your predictions at the end of Part 1. How closely do they match the information above? Do inaccuracies in your predictions reflect inadequate analysis? If so, explain the analytical failure. If not, what additional information would you have needed in Part 1 to improve your predictive accuracy and how would you have used that information?

DANIELS COMPUTER COMPANY

Part 3

On November 1, 1962, an engineer with considerable memory design experience was hired from outside the Daniels Company to become chief engineer for the special project. The four project engineers were directed to report to the new man. After examining the work of each group, the chief engineer indicated the basic approach to be taken in designing the new memory. Outstanding technical conflicts between groups were summarily dismissed by reference to the new approach. Each group was given a clear set of design instructions within the overall design plan. Firm design time schedules, based on project group interdependence, were set. Frequent progress reports were required of each project engineer.

PREDICTIONS—Part 3

From what I know of the special project operation and the changes in that operation described in Part 3, I would predict that:

a) The four project engineers (would) (would not) work well together to coordinate the work of their separate sections.

b) Enthusiasm among the members of the four special groups would (increase) (stabilize) (continue to decrease).

c) Progress of the special project would be (ahead of) (level with) (behind) the planned development time schedule.

d) The leadership style displayed by the chief engineer would be (functional) (dysfunctional) for total work-group performance.

e) Social relationships will tend to be (project-wide) (special-group oriented).

DANIELS COMPUTER COMPANY

Part 4

For several weeks after the chief engineer set the direction of the project, the project engineers vied with each other to see who could catch the chief engineer in error. Considerable time was spent in experimentation designed to find a weakness in the new design plan. Few problems in the plan could be found. The chief engineer defended his theoretical positions vigorously and continued to demand that schedules be met.

Schedules were met, and the four groups worked simultaneously on related design aspects. Communication with the chief engineer grew in frequency. Communication directly between groups at all levels became common. Design limits were quickly discovered before the effort of other groups was needlessly expended.

The cohesion within technical groups became less pronounced, particularly among lower status engineers and technicians. Several lunch groups comprising members of several technical groups began to appear.

POSTPREDICTION ANALYSIS

Refer to your predictions at the end of Part 3. How closely do they match the information above? Do inaccuracies in your predictions reflect inadequate analysis? If so, explain the analytical failure. If not, what additional information would you have needed in Part 3 to improve your predictive accuracy and how would you have used that information?

CHAPTER 8

Analysis and Action

FINAL CHAPTERS of behavioral science texts are frequently made repositories of the pent-up opinions and feelings which authors have stored while they were being "objective and systematic" in preceding pages. This final chapter will not greatly change that reputation, but it has other goals, as well. Each of these goals relates to the crucial relationship between diagnosis and action in the problem-solving process.

The first goal is to put the diagnostic scheme of the book into perspective by shifting emphasis from the form to the process of systematic analysis. Since the process of analysis is fundamentally personal, a second goal is to examine the potential of functionalism as a basic state of mind. Such a state of mind is critical in integrating analysis and action into a coherent set of behaviors. The third goal is to set forth a concept of the steps which lead from awareness of a problem, through analysis, to decision and action. Finally, some suggestions will be made for the kind of learning situations which might usefully follow upon and reinforce the experience of working with ideas like those in this book.

Systematic Analysis as a Natural Response to Problems

Obviously, the analytic scheme we have been working with here is not the only appropriate one for analyzing human behavior in organizations. It would be foolhardy to pretend otherwise. There are a great many analytical systems whose utility has been validated by someone's productive use of them in helping him to solve some kind of real problem. And, many more such systems will come to light in the future. Some of the schemes we now know about bear little similarity to what you have read here. They differ in emphasis, form, and content. Some, for example, are highly psychoanalytic or psychobiological in character. Others, at the opposite extreme, pivot around certain aspects of the formal organization. There are schemes whose focal categories are overlapping group memberships, psychological stress, power and influence, or field forces of change and resistance. These, rather than our sociotechnical categories, are used to gather and sort data about human behavior in organizations. And, clearly, all of these categories represent important aspects of human behavior.

So, why study our scheme, with its particular set of categories, rather than some of these others? There are two levels of answer to that question. At the first are criteria which any scheme has to satisfy. Is it practical, that is, does it possess internal consistency, and is it simple, yet comprehensive? Is it truly a *system* of analysis, comprehending the complexity and dynamic quality of human behavior? Has its utility been tested by real people on real problems? The answers to these questions in this case are affirmative. Compared to other schemes the author knows about, this one fares well.

There is a more crucial question to be asked at the second level of answer: Is this scheme sufficiently close to the intuitive modes of thought of managers in general so that there is a good chance of it being internalized by those managers? In the process of working with the scheme, is it likely that its use will become natural, or will it remain foreign and mechanical? The reader will have to judge for himself on this score, but from the author's own experience and that of many of his colleagues and students and of managers with whom he has worked, the scheme does possess this crucial quality. It does so not only because its categories are relatively familiar but because its form permits, indeed encourages, practice with the scheme in initial efforts to comprehend it. The framework's potential as a habit of being systematic with familiar variables is more important than its specific components.

It is common to our experience that we are most effective when we feel at home with the methods we are using. This is as true of the analysis of organizations as it is of tennis or skiing. The Introduction commented on the fact that each of us has an intrinsic set of categories and theories. We operate more fruitfully when we are using those familiar ideas than we do with strange ones. Using our own ideas is so automatic that plenty of energy and attention are left over for conducting analysis, for solving the problems which analysis reveals, for being confident enough to act with purpose, and for pre-sensing the next problem before it is quite upon us. So, the familiar and comfortable, aside from whatever inherent qualities they may have as analytic procedures, derive a great deal of their power from the simple fact that they are familiar and comfortable.

The aspiration which the author of a book like this brings to his writing is that the reader will discover from it a way to improve his familiar modes of analysis—through adding greater penetration and coverage to them—without so upsetting his customs that the process of analysis seems awkward and becomes ineffective. While the author hopes that the reader will so involve himself in the new ideas he has been studying that their total pattern and potential become clear, he hopes equally that those ideas will be picked apart and that the most familiar and the most compatible of them will become incorporated into the reader's more familiar, personal pattern of diagnosis. Yet, this process of picking and choosing, if it is to have any lasting effect, cannot be casual.

It has been suggested that any significant learning, instead of being steady and gradual, is a spasmodic process. We seem to stay on plateaus of considerable stability for long periods, following accustomed patterns of behavior and thought. When the time is ripe—when that still somewhat mysterious condition of "readiness for change" arises—we leap up a steep incline of new, formerly untried behavior. This is a perilous time, because unfamiliar terrain makes us unsure of our direction and, often, we try routes which lead nowhere. We feel quite disoriented—sometimes exhilarated by the altitude, sometimes frightened and alone. If we don't slip and fall back, we find our way to a new plateau which, though it has some similarity to the old, displays many new characteristics. In time, we become as familiar with the higher elevation as we had been with the lower. We may stay on the new plateau for a considerable period of time, increasing our familiarity with it, and, in the process, our effectiveness. At the same time, we increase our sense of the limitations of our new patterns of behavior and thought, until we are ready to move on, once again.

This kind of change pattern takes place when we give up smoking or learn to drive a car and when we embark on marriage or enter a profession. Whenever we undergo changes like these, we have to adopt a new state of mind. The same conditions apply when we decide to improve our analytical capacities. For such a decision to have any real meaning, it must include adopting a new way of thinking.

To say that using a set of analytical tools has potential for fundamental cognitive change is not to say that those tools do not have other, more mechanical benefits, too. Such study can give us a kind of checklist, increasing our confidence that we have not overlooked important data. It can serve as a backup, assuring us that, if all else fails, we at least have somebody else's ideas to rely on to bring order into the facts confronting us. It may also serve as a way of getting our analytic search started, although once the situation assumes some familiarity, we may choose to revert to our more intuitive analytic equipment. However, these potential uses of our scheme, important as they may be in themselves, are limited and transitory in comparison to the scheme's potential as a state of mind.

Internalizing Functional Analysis

An eloquent example of the difference between an intellectual and an emotional understanding of our conceptual scheme arose around the meaning and use of the functional analysis set of ideas. After my students completed the course in which they studied this conceptual scheme and applied it to case problems, they moved immediately to a laboratory course in organizational behavior. A basic aspect of this second course involved student participation in organizations of their own. A major goal of the course was to help students internalize what they had been learning by having them observe, analyze, and discuss the behavior taking place in their organizations. Some students were soon preoccupied by the "personalness" of this type of discussion and by the fear that they might do damage to their fellows or be damaged in turn by open exploration of what was causing the behavior in their work group.

As these preoccupations were being expressed in various forms, other students not similarly preoccupied began to question the basis of the anxiety. It became clear that the preoccupation stemmed from a unidimensional view of the relations between students. The troubled students' state of mind led them to feel that if they indicated displeasure with the way their group leader was running the group, for example, such an expression would destroy the group leader. They were led to this feeling by two assumptions: (1) that there were no significant sources of evaluation, self or otherwise, open to the group leader other than that of the preoccupied student; and, (2) that the group leader's behavior was solely a function of his personality, in this case, a function of some personality defect. Under such assumptions, of course, they were right to be hesitant about expressing their feelings about others. Their hesitancy is particularly understandable in light of the fact that their assumptions operated equally well in reverse, that is, if criticism were made of their own behavior, it would indicate some defect in them. Operating under these assumptions, it is no wonder that they balked at exploring their live case of organizational behavior.

The other students, those who were taking a functional point of view about this situation, employed quite different assumptions: (1) Each student had available to him a number of sources of performance evaluation—his own past experience, his present observations of himself, and a wide range of potential feedback from a relatively large number of fellow students. (2) Expressions of criticism, when offered, were not simply a function of the man being criticized but of the criticizer, as well, and this dual functionality was relevant in assessing expressed evalutions. (3) The behavior of criticized students was a function of many forces in addition to those arising from the predispositions of the individual; for example, group leaders were operating in relation to their student superiors, to the faculty, to their assigned task and to a host of other aspects of their school life—and criticism of their behavior could be accepted as a stimulus for finding out more about those many pressures and how to deal with them more effectively.

In all likelihood, as the expression goes, "you had to be there" to appreciate emotionally the impact of these two states of mind. Functional analysis was no longer an abstraction being applied in an analytic exercise. The students involved suddenly realized that their analytic state of mind meant the difference between running away from and jumping into a new learning experience.

The dramatic quality of the difference among students in the degree to which they actually used the analytical tools which they had all been studying gives us some clues about putting new tools to use. No matter how aesthetically attractive a scheme may be, only its utility for each individual can justify its existence. We have said that as important as it is that a scheme objectively reflect reality, that potential is worthless if the individual does not, in fact, use the scheme. We have said, too, that a scheme's use depends on how readily the individual can incorporate it into what is familiar to him. On the other hand, a scheme represents a way of thinking, a mental set toward problems, and to achieve what is intrinsic to that way of thinking, we have to undergo some degree of fundamental change. If a scheme is simply familiar, it provokes no learning. If it represents too abrupt or radical a change in accustomed patterns of thought, the chances are great that it will remain words on a page.

There are hosts of psychological propositions which would help explain why an individual failed to internalize a new way of thinking. Without denying their relevance in any particular case, however, let's look at some common experience with ideas. Frequently we find that what seems an interesting idea gets stored in our heads and remains unused. Once in awhile some new experience calls that idea out of storage and puts a new twist on it. Many parents have had this experience lately as they have been exposed to "the new math." Usually there is a sense of discovery on these occasions, a sensation which somehow makes the idea one's own in a surprisingly personal way. What has been foreign becomes distinctly familiar. These discoveries occur not only when we least expect them but when we are actively seeking to make sense of something, too. It is during our searches for comprehension that we get the "eureka" effect so often quoted of Archimedes when he finally figured a method for determining the purity of gold. If you keep turning an idea upside down and sideways long enough, it will suddenly break through the wall of being someone else's idea to being your own. All it takes is a lot of curiosity, patience, and hard work.

The students who despaired of the new course because they had so limited a view of cause and effect did so for many reasons intrinsic to their own psychological and intellectual histories. Some of them, however, by dint of hard work with the idea of function, by trying it out in their relations with their classmates, finally felt like saying "Eureka". They usually came out with significantly more profound ideas about the relations between things than had been put into the course by design. More important, the frustrating process of forcing strange ideas to come to terms turned the strangeness into an intimate association.

All that can be said, then, about the importance of internalizing new ways of thinking is that it is not an easy process, but it is one that is constantly being achieved. Perhaps the most encouraging aspect of learning something new like an analytic framework is that one needn't start with what is familiar; he only need end up there.

So much for turning analytical tools into analytical intuition. As important as analysis is, it is only part of problem solving. Let's turn now to the activities which must follow diagnosis if it is to turn into effective action.

Selection of Choices in the Analysis-Action Process

It is inevitable that specializing our attention on any part of the problem-solving process gives the impression that each part is somehow discrete, i.e., that one begins and ends each step of the process free from involvement in other steps. We might conceive of problem solving as composed of the following series: (1) awareness of a general issue; (2) gathering information pertinent to the issue; (3) analysis of information; (4) statetment of the problem underlying the issue; (5) establishing possible choices of action relating to the problem; (6) selection of choice(s) against goal criteria; (7) implementation of selected choice(s); and (8) gathering information on outcomes of the implementation (i.e., starting the problem-solving process over at step 2, above). It may seem that, at any stage in the series, we would be free to devote our full attention and energy to the activities appropriate to that stage, but nothing is further from the truth, as practicing administrators know. Furthermore, the appearance of sequential segmentation is illusory not only because real administrators dealing with real problems are simultaneously working on many and variously related problems, each at its own stage of problem-solving development, but because any *one* problem inherently involves simultaneous activity at several of the problem-solving stages at once.

If we think of steps 1–4 and step 8 as analytical in character and 5–7 as action-taking in orientation, the nonsequential nature of the series quickly becomes apparent. How can we gather information without, in some perhaps significant way, influencing the situation, itself? Simply displaying interest in a situation and the people involved in it will have an effect. Such being the case, we need to establish some choices (step 5) and set some goals and select among choices (step 6) before we can do much analysis (step 3). It is equally true, of course, that implementary procedures for our analytic activities be thought through as far as they can be before we get anywhere near step 7 in our series. So, problem solving is not a series of finite steps but a series of approximations which, in reality, has no beginning and no end. It does not even have a middle, since we need to jump about among our stages as well as cycle through them in, hopefully, ever more informative and influential spirals.

There are at least two characteristics of human organization which, in their degree of significance if not in kind, essentially differentiate administrative from other kinds of problem solving. The first is that the problem solver and the problem are intimately related. The problem solver can never really escape the confines of the problem. He is, by definition, part of it. Therefore, the problem solver is forever and constantly enmeshed in analysis while he is acting and in action while he is analyzing. The second characteristic of human organization which confuses our series is the interdependence of problems, their sources and their consequences. In fact, there is no such thing as "a problem," there is only a convenient fiction called "a problem." Any action, whether analytic or implementary in intent, has effects which are not necessarily confined to, or operating in the same direction as, those relating to the problem or aspect of the problem we are focusing our attention on at the moment. In other words, the problems of a human organization are part of a system. We call them problems because we feel a need to do something about them, but they are only facts about an organic whole. The problem with the idea of "problem" is that it seems to separate and make independent of the whole system one set of facts about some part or parts of the system.

One symptom of the problem with "problems," and one close to the experience of the author, has to do with a frequent frustration of his students when they first are exposed to the analysis of business cases. Commonly, after a case discussion is over, students want to know "what happened." "How did the administrator in the case deal with the problem?" Part of their curiosity is in finding out how an experienced man, with more information available to him than is possible to include in a case, thought about the case situation. Even after that curiosity is sated, however, another basis of their questioning emerges, namely, a need to know how the problem was "put to rest," on the assumption that that is what happens to problems. When the instructor, as he often does, responds that knowing what the administrator did would simply be a description of more action, more consequences, more problems worthy of discussion and plans for solution, and that the case arbitrarily has to stop somewhere, students experience some amount of frustration. Only after getting a feel for organizations as systems does this frustration subside.

So, the first aspect of the problem-solving process worthy of note is that it is composed of simultaneous, back-and-forth, spiraling movement on its several dimensions. While, for the sake of cognitive convenience and clarity, we can discern an approximate temporal sequence of activity in the process, we must not allow that perception to lead us to believe that the process is a neat one. In fact, it is quite messy, consistent with the nature of the interdependencies of an organic system.

The fact is, however, and one we have faced before in this book, we can only talk about a very few things at once. So, forewarned that, in reality, our series is really a series of short circuits between various activities, let's look more closely at what is involved in each of steps 5 through 7, the action end of the problem-solving process.

The Selection of Action Choices[1]

The intent of action is to move the organization from one equilibrium whose consequences we are dissatisfied with to another equilibrium whose outputs we expect to find more satisfactory. The intention is also to avoid unintended or unanticipated consequences, particularly as those consequences might arise in related organizations for which we feel some sense of responsibility.

No matter how the above paragraph is stated, somehow a "we," an "I," an "administrator," or some other interested party has to be included to complete the statement. When we are discussing analysis, on the other hand, we take the analyst into account only by warning him to be objective, to stay out of the picture, to keep his values to himself. As soon as we start discussing action, however, we begin using subjective words like "intent," "dissatisfied," "satisfactory," "unintended," "unanticipated," "our responsibility," and so on. As we noted in the very first chapter, whenever we turn from analysis to doing something to affect the situation we are analyzing, we reverse our neutrality and become partisan. The only mood common to these two phases of problem-solving activity is that we be conscious of our own point of view, first, to guard against its biasing effects on our analysis, and second, to be fully aware of where we want our action to take us and why.

Now that we are examining action ideas, we must bring all of our own idiosyncracies into our work, making ourselves, if anything, a more dominant aspect of the situation than facts about it which lie outside ourselves. And we must be prepared, in real life, to switch back

[1]A number of the ideas in this section are based on a working paper prepared by Assistant Professor Jay Lorsch for the basic organizational behavior courses in both the Doctoral and Master's degree programs at the Harvard Business School.

and forth between neutrality and partisanship with each swing from analysis to action—even when the two activities are so interrelated that it is nearly impossible to tell them apart.

To select a course of action, then, the action taker must determine what his goals are vis-à-vis the situation he has been analyzing. What was it about the situation which caused him to want to look into it in the first place? What mix of personally oriented and organizationally oriented aspirations spurred him to want to change the situation? Ideally, how would he like the situation to be? And what expenses, personal and organizational, is he willing to undergo in order to approximate that ideal? Viewing this goal-setting phase of the decision process amorally and dispassionately, the important element in this phase of activity is being aware of one's motivations, whatever they may be, and being clear with oneself about those motivations. Disguising one's personal goals as organizational in character, at least to oneself, is a sure way to reap unintended consequences.

At the same time, this stage of the decision process requires objective mood. What is there to choose from? While whatever we do must take into account our own goals, it must equally make sense within the situation in which we are trying to reach those goals. If we have done our analytic job well, have identified the determinants of behavior and their functional relationship, the possible leverage points for action should be quite evident.

We have cataloged the inputs to behavior as four in number: human, social, technical, and organizational. Examining each input, in turn, will reveal what action possibilities exist. It is quite likely that we shall find combinations of leverage points among the several inputs which, together, represent a unified action plan directed toward one set of goals or another, so we need to look at all of the inputs for clues, not at any one alone. And we need to look for the *several* sets of action combinations and choose that one set which satisfies our goal criteria best.

The first two inputs, human and social, involve determinants of behavior which are somewhat more difficult to work with in a mechanical sense than are the technical and organizational inputs. But they must be examined critically, not only in their own right but as possible adjuncts to change possibilities we may find available among the other inputs.

As we examine human inputs, does it make sense, for example, to consider changing selection criteria or procedures? Do we want to transfer, promote, demote, or fire some of the people involved in the situation? Would training help? Are there some mechanical skills which our people need or is attitudinal or motivational change what is required? Does the action taker have the skills, or do others in the organization, to carry out such changes? What effects from actions such as these would there be in other parts of the organization? What balances now in existence might be upset? Particularly, what concomitant changes in other inputs would have to be made to make these human input changes? As apparently difficult as some of these actions might be in implementation, they require careful consideration, particularly if easier but far less effective changes in other inputs are the only real alternative.

Changing social inputs may be an even more subtle process. If we are dealing with a well-developed social system whose norms run counter to those we feel are consistent with our goals, can those norms be influenced? Are there ways of establishing goals for our people which transcend present parochialisms? If so, we may need to look at technical and organizational inputs for ways to stimulate such superordinate goals. Should we go back to our human inputs and see if selection policies or other devices could change the attitudinal composititon of the social group? Or do we want to try to assault present norms dysfunctional to our goals by special types of group experiences like sensitivity training? Are we willing to undergo the chance of goal change, ourselves, in the process?

Technical inputs are much more visible and, in that sense, more practical leverage points, although their tangibility may give us a false sense of security. After all, what we are interested in is behavior change, and technology by itself does not produce behavior, people do. Technical changes, then, may facilitate social and individual change, but only if social and human inputs are susceptible to such stimulation. Would it help to change the content of specific jobs or the flow of work between jobs? Would the physical arrangement of the work situation free up desirable behavior which is being blocked at present? How, through changes in the physical environment, could we get people into contact who need to be in contact? Is there some way to encourage more of a work orientation among our people through the nature of the jobs they do? Or, do human, social, and organizational input factors make such technical changes hopeless?

The last but most common ground for managerial action is found among the organizational inputs. Would changes in the reward-punishment system alter behavior, perhaps directly or through attraction of different people into the organization? Do our control and information systems need modification? What about the division of labor among organizational subunits—is it consistent with the technical and social realities which exist now or which will exist under changes we may have in mind making? What about leadership styles—are they consistent with our people and the jobs they are doing? Do we need new human inputs at the supervisory level, or some kind of training? Do we have the capacity to make such changes? How will they affect other input necessities and other parts of the organization?

Often, the search for possibilities for action among inputs is a laborious, complex process. The inputs are so interrelated that almost infinite combinations are possible, each requiring careful analysis of potential functions. One happy aspect of the search, however, is that in the process of analysis, itself, possibilities begin to emerge almost automatically. Sometimes their emergence is provoked more by the analyst's subjective goals than by objective possibilities, but so long as that likelihood is taken into account, the search becomes simpler than its outward appearance would indicate. All that is really left to do is the sometimes unpleasant task of ferreting out the choices which one's subjectivity has suppressed or which one's human limits for commanding a complex set of facts have concealed.

Assuming, now, that the possible combinations of action choices have been arrayed, all that is left before implementation is choice or decision. Though less laborious than any other stage of the entire problem-solving process, the decision stage may well turn out to be the most difficult. It involves three activities: (1) measuring available choices against the goals which have been established; (2) assessing the administrator's and the organization's capacity to implement the decision; and (3) actually making the decision by committing oneself to it.

The first stage is somewhat complex in that it requires prediction of the consequences of a complex interrelation of changes. What is the probability that a certain combination of changes in inputs will come closer to desired goals than another combination? The activity required by this stage is plotting several decision trees or networks of initial, secondary, tertiary, and so on, consequences of the several changes contemplated in any one combination. Theoretically, at least, a probability could be assigned to each branch path representing consequential behavior in the desired direction. It should be possible, therefore, that the probabilities of all combinations could be compared.

Except for the simplest of human behavior problems, however, mechanically carrying out such network analysis would not be worth the time spent on it. What is essential is a careful assessment of major probabilities and a "network frame of mind" which operates in terms of rough probabilities, including both intended *and* unintended consequences. It is entirely conceivable that an administrator would choose a course of action which had only a slightly greater probability of success than of failure—either because of a dearth of choices or due to personal preference—but hardly conceivable that he would do so without preparing himself to deal with the consequences if his estimate of probabilities failed to materialize.

The second step in the decision stage of activity—assessing the individual's and organization's capacity to carry out the planned action—will, in practice, probably be included in the calculation of probabilities discussed above. But it is worthy of special mention, particularly in regard to the action taker's capabilities. Was the most likely contender for an action combination chosen despite some of the administrator's important values? Unless he were completely self-oriented in the choice he has made, it would be surprising if some conflicts were not evident. If so, is he emotionally capable of going against his own grain in trying to carry out his plan? It is possible to be too organization- or too other-oriented, just as possible and just as disastrous, perhaps, as being overly self-oriented. Furthermore, is the administrator in the appropriate organizational position to influence or control the inputs he plans to change? Not infrequently, action plans clearly involve power beyond the command of the potential action taker. If this is the case, it may be due to inadequate examination of one's own position. It may also be due to a desire to escape essential responsibility, since failure of the plan can then easily be ascribed to obdurate superiors or subordinates. Such escape is a function of the difficult commitment process involved in decision making which we shall discuss shortly. Finally, does the administrator possess the personal skill and expertise to carry out the plan? If the execution of the plan requires considerable interaction between himself and others, is this his forte? Conversely, if it requires elaborate structural or technical change, does he have the capacity required for this type of work? Assessing not only what one *wants* but what one *is* is an essential precursor to effective implementation.

But the most difficult hurdle of all is one's commitment to the decisions one's analysis and selection of choices turn up. Can the administrator personally get behind his plan and make it work? It sounds easy, but the will to make decisions, say those who have it, is the quality most difficult to inculcate in others. The difficulty is attested to by the criticism of some business schools, that they turn out excellent staff men but few who wish, or have the capacity, to take responsibility. If a plan is to work, with all the inefficiencies built into it by the limits of analysis and the complexity of organizational behavior, it must have the wholehearted support and commitment of its designer and implementer.

Perhaps what makes decisional commitment such a scarce commodity is its corollary, a capacity and desire to measure the consequences (step 8) and to revise the action plan whenever feedback shows such revision to be necessary, then to proceed with the revised plan with as much commitment as one gave to the original, knowing full well that further revision is inevitable. At bottom, what is necessary is a commitment to the process of change.

Implementing the Plan of Action[2]

Action taking in human organizations is essentially a process of social interaction. Even though some of the input changes which have been suggested seem impersonal in impact (for example, a change in job design or work flow) gaining acceptance of the proposal involves human interaction of an influential character. Our analyses help point out what the sensitive aspects of any particular influence attempt will probably be. But in many cases our knowledge of the situation is imperfect indeed, especially when we are just beginning to gather information about the situation. We know, however, that we will communicate messages through our behavior, whether we want to or not. The only way to survive under such uncertainty is to be open to what others tell us we have been communicating to them and to adjust our methods of communication when we find inaccuracies. Basically, this is what the problem-solving process is—an ever-widening knowledge of what is causing behavior and an effort to take that knowledge into account in the process of trying to change behavior in desired directions.

The influence process brings us back to the idea of equilibrium again. Our goal is to help the organization attain a new balance of forces. The present equilibrium may be thought of as being kept steady by

[2]A number of ideas in this section are based on a working paper prepared by Assistant Professor Larry E. Greiner for the basic organizational behavior courses in both the Doctoral and Master's degree progams at the Harvard Business School.

individual forces each pressuring for change. Since each of these interests are, to some degree, in conflict, equilibrium is attained by an equalization of pressures from the various points of interest. If we consider level of productivity as a focus around which a balance of forces has been achieved, some of those forces will pressure for higher productivity, for example, disciplinary measures, training devices, incentive pay systems, and so on, and some will pressure for lower productivity, such as, a sense of craftsmanship, alternate uses of energy, and social pressures. In attempting to change the level of productivity, we must change the strength of one or more of these forces, either increasing or decreasing it or them. Since we are working with a system, however, we know that changing the magnitude of a force may simply engender a comparable increase in opposing forces. How can we so alter the equilibrated situation that the individuals whose behavior we wish to change see a greater value in the new balance than in the old? A review of research on the influence process has turned up several ideas worthy of note.[3]

The content of a change is a far less important cause of resistance than might initially be imagined. What turns out to be more important than the objective facts about the change is the method by which the change is introduced. What this really seems to mean is that resistance to change[4] arises when those affected perceive the method of change introduction to be inconsistent with the way in which they expect to be treated. For example, when people feel their ideas about work have value, they will tend to resist changes whose introduction ignores their ideas. On the other hand, people who feel extremely dependent and insecure might display resistance to a change introduction which attempted to involve them actively in designing and carrying out the change.

In laboratory research into various aspects of what determines the effectiveness of communication about change, three elements of the message have been explored. One[5] involves the choice of communicat-

---

[3]For a focussed discussion of the relationship between the concept of equilibrium and various theories of influence, see Roger Brown, "Models of Attitude Change," in *New Directions in Psychology* (New York: Holt, Rinehart & Winston, Inc., 1962).

[4]See "How to Deal with Resistance to Change," by Paul R. Lawrence, *Harvard Business Review,* Vol. XXXII, No. 3 (May-June, 1954).

[5]C. I. Hovland, A. A. Lumsdaine, and F. D. Sheffield (1949); *Experiments on Mass Communication* (Princeton, N.J.; Princeton University Press); C. I. Hovland, I. L. Janis, and H. H. Kelley, *Communication and Persuasion* (New Haven, Conn.; Yale University Press, 1953).

ing either positive information or both positive and negative sides of the story. The latter is preferable, although the former works to some degree if people are unopposed to the idea anyway or if they have had relatively little education. Another element is the ordering of ideas, the first heard being the most powerful, particularly if it is positive and relates to the personal needs of listeners.[6] A final element in the effectiveness of influence messages concerns the degree to which listeners are upset about the change in general. Those who are upset tend to be influenced more by punitive appeals, while those who are not upset are more persuaded by lenient appeals.[7]

But the message or content of the change is only one aspect of the influence process. Another important determinant of the effectiveness of attempts to influence resides in the characteristics of the influencer. If he is perceived to be trustworthy, expert, and impartial, he stands a good chance of influencing others.[8] In fact, such an influencer tends to create more change the more change he advocates. Such an influencer, however, easily becomes dissociated from his message, people remembering what he said but not that he said it. Such, it appears, is the price of trustworthiness.

A third element in the influence process is the predisposition of the person whose behavior is the focus of the attempted influence. People with strong senses of identity, laboratory studies show, are more easily

---

[6]A. R. Cohen (1957), "Need for Cognition and Order of Communication as Determinants of Opinion Change," in C. I. Hovland (ed.), *The Order of Presentation in Persuasion* (New Haven, Conn., Yale University Press), pp. 79–97; W. J. McGuire (1961), "Resistance to Persuasion Conferred by Active and Passive Prior Refutation of the Same and Alternative Counterarguments," *Journal of Abnormal and Social Psychology,* Vol. LXIII, pp. 326–32; I. L. Janis (1957), "Motivational Effects of Different Sequential Arrangements of Conflicting Arguments: A Theoretical Analysis," in Hovland, *op. cit.,* pp. 170–86.

[7]Walten Weiss and B. J. Fine (1956), "The Effect of Induced Aggressiveness on Opinion Change," *Journal of Abnormal and Social Psychology,* Vol. LII; I. L. Janis and Seymour Feshbach (1953), "Effects of Fear-Arousing Communications," *Journal of Abnormal and Social Psychology,* Vol. XLVIII, pp. 78–92; I. L. Janis and R. F. Terwilliger (1962), "An Experimental Study of Psychological Resistances to Fear-Arousing Communications, *Journal of Abnormal and Social Psychology,* Vol. LXV, 403–10.

[8]C. I. Hovland and Walter Weiss (1951), "The Influence of Source Credibility on Communication Effectiveness," *Public Opinion Quarterly,* Vol. XV, pp. 635–50; H. C. Kelman and C. I. Hovland (1953), "'Reinstatement' of the Communicator in Delayed Measurement of Opinion Change," *Journal of Abnormal and Social Psychology,* Vol. XLVIII, pp. 327–35; Elliot Aronson, Judith A. Turner, and J. M. Carlsmith (1963), "Communicator Credibility and Communication Discrepancy as Determinants of Opinion Change," *Journal of Abnormal and Social Psychology,* Vol. LXVII, pp. 31–36; A. E. Bergin (1962), "The Effect of Dissonant Persuasive Communications upon Changes in a Self-Referring Attitude," *Journal of Personality,* Vol. XXX, pp. 423–38.

influenced than those who fear psychological disorganization.[9] Those with a high need for affiliation will resist influence attempts if their group does so, but they will accede to persuasion if their group goes along or if they are not pressured by messages other than those presented by the influencer.[10] Authoritarians are susceptible to influence from superiors, though not from subordinates. In fact, they are so susceptible to authoritative messages that they tend as easily to adopt attitudes of a liberal as of a conservative character when pressured to do so.[11] Self-esteem is another important element among predispositions toward change. Persons high in self-esteem are more susceptible to influences of an optimistic, self-enhancing nature, while those low in self-esteem respond more readily to pessimism and self-deprecating influences.[12]

A fourth determinant of influence effectiveness, one already alluded to above, is social pressure. Influences which attempt to involve groups in decision making tend to be more effective than those which do not.[13] Where the source of influence is ambiguous, individuals tend to rely on the norms of their group for definition of the situation.[14] An interesting adjunct to these findings, one involving formal rather than informal social groups, supports the practical notion that influence should follow formal channels of authority. The finding is that trying to influence a subordinate without first obtaining his supervisor's support tends to be ineffective.[15]

As interesting as some of these research findings on the nature of the influence process may be, it is their general rather than specific

---

[9]D. Katz, I. Sarnoff, and C. McClintock, "Ego Defense and Attitude Change," *Human Relations,* Vol. IX (1956).

[10]S. E. Asch (1951), "Effects of Group Pressure upon the Modification and Distortion of Judgments," in Harold Guetzkow (ed.), *Groups, Leadership, and Men* (Pittsburgh; Carnegie Press), pp. 177–90.

[11]M. Wagman, "An Investigation of the Effectiveness of Authoritarian Suggestion and Non-Authoritarian Information as Methods of Changing the Prejudiced Attitudes of Relatively Authoritarian and Non-Authoritarian Perosnalities" (Ph.D. Dissertation, University of Michigan, 1953).

[12]Howard Leventhal and S. I. Perloe (1962), "A relationship between Self-Esteem and Persuasibility," *Journal of Abnormal and Social Psychology,* Vol. LXIV, pp. 385–88.

[13]Edith B. Bennett (1955), Discussion, Decision, Commitment and Consensus in Group Decision Vol. VIII, *Human Relations,* 251–73.

Kurt Lewin (1943). "Forces behind Food Habits and Methods of Changes," *Bulletin of the National Research Council,* No. 108 pp. 35–65.

[14]Muzafer Sherif (1935), "A Study of Some Social Factors in Perception," *Archives of Psychology,* Vol. XXVII, No. 187.

[15]E. A. Fleishman, "Leadership Climate, Human Relations Training, and Supervisory Behavior," *Personnel Psychology,* Vol. VI (1953), pp. 205–22.

import which has the most enduring meaning. Being the products of laboratory studies, they will undoubtedly be subject to refinement and even reversal by subsequent research. But their specificity may belie their potential as guidelines for action. We might summarize their generality as follows: (1) The character of a change is less important than its method of introduction. (2) The expectations of those to be influenced must be taken into account in designing and gauging the impact of an attempted change. (3) Other things being equal, the form or organization of an influence presentation makes a great difference to the degree of its acceptance. (4) How the administrator is perceived by those he is trying to influence will be an important determinant of his effectiveness in creating change. (5) The configuration and content of social pressures will have a significant impact on the susceptibility of people to change.

If we turn from the laboratory to the realities of administrative situations, it seems clear that attempting to create change is a far more complex process than a controlled experiment would imply. A statement reflecting the realities of administrative life seems more like the following:[16]

> The administrator must constantly strive to maintain a consistency in his own behavior while accepting the fact that his behavior will always appear inconsistent from any simple, one-dimensional frame of reference.
>
> The administrator must constantly seek for solutions that resolve conflicts between the interests of the several dimensions, but accept the fact that such conflicts are inevitable and never ending.
>
> The administrator must constantly seek to change behavior in the social system he is part of but never break up or destroy the system as a viable entity.
>
> The administrator must seek a perfection of balanced development but accept the inevitability of imperfection. Or to state it the other way around, he must be pleased with signs of progress but never be satisfied with them.
>
> The administrator must, by the very nature of his job, put a heavy emphasis on achieving organizational purpose, but he must also seek balanced progress along other dimensions and not expect all others in the organization to give primacy to the achievement of purpose.
>
> The administrator must maintain the perspective of an outside observer on the organization he leads but not lose his impassioned involvement with the results of the system. Or in the words of F. J. Roethlisberger, he must maintain a "disinvolved-involvement."

[16]Paul R. Lawrence, *The Changing of Organizational Behavior Patterns* (Boston: Harvard Graduate School of Business Administration, Division of Research, 1958, pp. 225–26).

No matter how brilliant the analysis or how thorough the search for and selection of action choices, or how carefully the introduction of change is planned and executed, perfection is not possible. Conflict will arise. Conflict is an inevitability not because of administrative oversight, necessarily, but because points of view differ and must differ if the organization is to prosper. So how do we deal with the certainty of conflict?

The evidence from field research says that facing conflict is more effective than avoiding it. But there are many gradations, from outright withdrawal to direct confrontation. Blake and Mouton[17] have identified five modes of handling conflict. They are listed below from least to most preferred by a large sample of executives. This ordering also coincides with the relative effectiveness of each mode in dealing with conflict:

1. *Withdrawing:* Although least preferred, this mode is often practiced by managers. While defended by "time heals all wounds," the contrary is usually true.
2. *Smoothing:* Playing down the conflict or giving in to keep everyone happy thwarts, in the long run, its own motivation, since the real sources of conflict continue uncorrected.
3. *Forcing:* Use of power, as has been pointed out, often results in compliance, only to produce disguised resistance in subtle forms and at other places.
4. *Compromising:* The parties to conflict get approximately half of what each wanted but neither is fully committed to the compromise outcome.
5. *Confronting:* Most preferred but least practiced, this mode seems the most difficult to accomplish. The characteristic of this mode is to explore the underlying reasons for conflict in viewpoint in an effort to redefine the problem and find productive solutions for both parties. It involves that anomaly we mentioned before in discussing commitment to a decision, i.e., taking a strong but not fixed position, then working through to new understanding.

Our attention in this final chapter has been focused on what one does with his analysis once he has completed it, or, perhaps, why one begins analysis in the first place. We began by looking at the analytic framework, not as an external device to be applied to information, but as a way of thinking. Our subsequent focus has been on the activities which are associated with action, with putting analysis to work. As was

---

[17]Robert R. Blake, and Jane S. Mouton, *The Managerial Grid* (Houston: Gulf Publishing Co., 1964).

true of analysis, our comments about action refer to a state of mind rather than to a protocol. The state of mind involves a capacity to shift rapidly from objective to subjective moods, awareness of one's values and how they influence one's goals and preferences, a willingness to commit oneself to a course of action, a readiness to change one's course according to feedback information, and an appetite for confronting unresolved conflict and for working through to a more substantial understanding of how differences can be productive.

Where Do We Go from Here?

Aside from reading about states of mind in books like this, and, perhaps, getting some feel for a new state of mind by practicing the kind of analysis which has been presented in the preceding chapters, how does one go about exploring and experimenting with this crucial piece of personal equipment?

A great deal of work has been done over the past 10 or 15 years to find the conditions which encourage state-of-mind experimentation and reformulation. Some of the most encouraging of this work has involved organizational behavior in one form or another. The Menninger Clinic, the National Training Laboratories, and, in Britain, the Tavistock Institute deal in their own ways with helping managers to get outside their habits, the better to form new and, hopefully, more productive ones. Lately, David McClelland and his colleagues' results in achievement motivation training have been similarly dramatic. These individuals and organizations, and others like them, continue to present opportunities for the individual manager to move beyond intellectual appreciation of the basic issues in organizational behavior to an emotional comprehension of those issues.[18]

But what some of these people and many others who follow them are now engaged in presents an even more exciting prospect for those interested in the practice of management. They are bent upon the simultaneous development of the individual manager, his working unit, and the organization of which it is a part. These efforts involve modifications in the whole range of our four inputs to behavior, from working with individual predispositions to restructuring the division of labor

[18]For some provocative reading about this movement, see L. P. Bradford, J. D. Gibb, and K. R. Benne, *T-Group Theory and Laboratory Method* (New York: John Wiley & Sons, Inc., 1964); Edgar H. Schein and Warren G. Bennis, *Personal and Organizational Change through Group Methods* (New York: John Wiley & Sons, Inc., 1965); and Chris Argyris, *Integrating the Individual and the Organization* (New York: John Wiley & Sons, Inc., 1964).

among functional units of the organization. The excitement these efforts arouse is due to the reinforcement which changes in one area of input give to changes in the others.[19]

In one company with which the author has had first-hand experience, several top executives engaged in sensitivity training individually outside the company, then they and other senior colleagues began meeting as a group to confront the difficulties they encountered in working productively together. As a result of their work, corporate and divisional goals were clarified and so were interdivisional and staff-line relationships. As each manager began to work more easily at the top level of the company, he saw ways of bringing the developmental framework employed at the executive level into his own area of responsibility. A new cycle of confronting and clarifying discussions are now taking place down through the corporate hierarchy, supported by managers who, though still searching for elusive answers to their own problems, have undergone an experience which has proven to them that states of mind are not only changeable but that the process is a significantly productive one.

Students of management have an increasingly varied array of opportunities to engage in in the involving process of reexamining accustomed ways of thinking and behaving. Several references have been made in this book to a course called "Human Behavior in Organizations, II"[20] which students at the Harvard Business School are required to take. The Sloan School of Management at M.I.T., Case Institute of Technology, U.C.L.A.'s School of Business, and many others are offering courses which provide an organizational context for experimenting with new behavior.

But, inevitably, we return to where we began in the Introduction, to the realization that intellectual achievement must, through whatever medium is available, be married to social skills. Experience seems to indicate that learning is facilitated by only brief separation of efforts on both the intellectual and emotional dimensions of learning. This book is one way of providing the intellectual component of the learning process. No book can provide the conditions for the emotional component, no matter how essential as a follow-up those conditions may be. The environment we all live in, however, *can* provide those conditions, if we make it do so.

---

[19]For accounts of some of these developments, see Blake and Mouton, *op. cit.,* and A. H. Kuriloff, "Management by Integration and Self-Control," in the report of the 15th Annual Industrial Engineering Proceedings, University of California, 1963.

[20]Recently retitled, "Laboratory in Organizational Behavior."

Index

This book has been set in 12 and 11 point Garamond Light, leaded 1 point. Chapter numbers and titles are 24 point Deepdene. The size of the type page is 27 × 45 picas.

HOWARD UNIVERSITY LIBRARIES
3 5969 023 728 350